PARTICIPATORY
BUDGETING

Introduction to the Public Sector Governance and Accountability Series

Anwar Shah, Series Editor

A well-functioning public sector that delivers quality public services consistent with citizen preferences and that fosters private market-led growth while managing fiscal resources prudently is considered critical to the World Bank's mission of poverty alleviation and the achievement of the Millennium Development Goals. This important new series aims to advance those objectives by disseminating conceptual guidance and lessons from practices and by facilitating learning from each others' experiences on ideas and practices that promote *responsive* (by matching public services with citizens' preferences), *responsible* (through efficiency and equity in service provision without undue fiscal and social risk), and *accountable* (to citizens for all actions) public governance in developing countries.

This series represents a response to several independent evaluations in recent years that have argued that development practitioners and policy makers dealing with public sector reforms in developing countries and, indeed, anyone with a concern for effective public governance could benefit from a synthesis of newer perspectives on public sector reforms. This series distills current wisdom and presents tools of analysis for improving the efficiency, equity, and efficacy of the public sector. Leading public policy experts and practitioners have contributed to this series.

The first 14 volumes in this series, listed below, are concerned with public sector accountability for prudent fiscal management; efficiency, equity, and integrity in public service provision; safeguards for the protection of the poor, women, minorities, and other disadvantaged groups; ways of strengthening institutional arrangements for voice, choice, and exit; means of ensuring public financial accountability for integrity and results; methods of evaluating public sector programs, fiscal federalism, and local finances; international practices in local governance; and a framework for responsive and accountable governance.

Fiscal Management

Public Services Delivery

Public Expenditure Analysis

Local Governance in Industrial Countries

Local Governance in Developing Countries

Intergovernmental Fiscal Transfers: Principles and Practice

Participatory Budgeting

Budgeting and Budgetary Institutions

Local Budgeting

Local Public Financial Management

Performance Accountability and Combating Corruption

Tools for Public Sector Evaluations

Macrofederalism and Local Finances

Citizen-Centered Governance

PUBLIC SECTOR
GOVERNANCE AND
ACCOUNTABILITY SERIES

PARTICIPATORY BUDGETING

Edited by ANWAR SHAH

THE WORLD BANK
Washington, D.C.

ISBN-10: 0-8213-6923-7
ISBN-13: 978-0-8213-6923-4
eISBN-10: 0-8213-6924-5
eISBN-13: 978-0-8213-6924-1
DOI: 10.1596/978-0-8213-6923-4

Library of Congress Cataloging-in-Publication Data
Participatory budgeting / edited by Anwar Shah.
    p. cm.
Includes bibliographical references and index.
ISBN-13: 978-0-8213-6923-4
ISBN-10: 0-8213-6923-7
ISBN-10: 0-8213-6924-5 (electronic)
    1. Local budgets–Citizen participation–Case studies. 2. Local finance–Case studies.
I. Shah, Anwar.

HJ9111.P37 2007
352.4'8214–dc22
                                                        2006032525

Contents

Foreword   xiii

Preface   xv

Acknowledgments   xvii

Contributors   xix

Abbreviations and Acronyms   xxiii

Overview   1
Anwar Shah

Part I Introduction to Participatory Budgeting

CHAPTER

A Guide to Participatory Budgeting   21
Brian Wampler
History of Participatory Budgeting   23
How and Where Does Participatory Budgeting Work?   24
State of the Debate   32
Types of Participatory Budgeting Programs   36

Actors and Motivations for Embracing
   Participatory Budgeting   39
Administrative Reform   44
Limitations of Participatory Budgeting   45
How and Where Can Participatory Budgeting
   Be Implemented?   47
Policy Implications   49
References   53

**2 Citizen Participation in Budgeting: Prospects for
Developing Countries   55**

Donald P. Moynihan
Why Is Participation Important?   55
Fostering Broad and Meaningful Participation in
   Developing Countries   62
The Government's Perspective on Public Participation   78
Conclusions   83
Notes   83
References   83

Part II Regional Surveys

**3 Lessons from Latin America's Experience with
Participatory Budgeting   91**

Benjamin Goldfrank
History of Participatory Budgeting   92
Normative and Analytical Approaches to Participatory
   Budgeting   94
National Case Studies   101
Conclusions   116
Notes   119
References   121

**4 Participatory Budgeting in Central and
Eastern Europe   127**

Alta Fölscher
The Central and Eastern European Context   128
Case Studies of Participatory Budgeting   134

Conclusions and Lessons Learned   143
Annex: Achievements, Challenges, and Lessons from
    Participatory Budgeting Processes in Case Study
    Countries   148
Note   155
References   155

5   **Participatory Budgeting in Asia**   157
Alta Fölscher
How Can Citizen Participation Enhance
    Development?   158
The Asian Context   159
Types of Participatory Budgeting Initiatives   164
Lessons from the Asian Experience   179
Conclusions   187
Notes   188
References   188

6   **Sub-Saharan Africa's Experience with
Participatory Budgeting**   191
Adrienne Shall
Legal Framework, Mechanisms for Participation, and
    Impact of Participatory Budgeting   192
Challenges and Lessons Learned   216
Conclusions   221
Notes   222
References   222

7   **Participatory Budgeting in the Middle East and
North Africa**   225
Alta Fölscher
Potential for Participatory Budgeting   225
Democracy and Islamic Rules and Values   237
Notes   240
References   240

Appendix: A Primer on Effective Participation   243
Alta Fölscher
Citizen Participation and State Effectiveness   243
Types of Participation   246
Preconditions and Enabling Factors for Citizen Engagement with
    Public Decisions   247
References   255

Index   257

On CD ROM

Part III Country Case Studies on Civic Participation in Subnational Budgeting

Bangladesh: Civic Participation in Subnational
    Budgeting   1
Atiur Rahman, Mahfuz Kabir, and Mohammad A. Razzaque
Civic Participation in Subnational Budgeting   3
Capacity Building to Support Civic Participation   18
Conclusion   22
Annex 1: I-PRSP's Medium-Term Agenda to Enhance Civic
    Participation in Local Governance   23
Annex 2: Internal Sources of Revenue of LGIs   24
References   27
Abbreviations   29

India: Civic Participation in Subnational Budgeting   31
Samuel Paul
The Three Levels of Government in India   32
Case Study 1: DISHA, Participation in State-Level
    Budgeting   33
Case Study 2: PROOF, a Citizen's Forum for Monitoring
    City Budgets   38
Lessons Learned   43
Capacity Building for Civic Participation   45

Annex: DISHA Budget Briefs Provided to Legislators,
        1997–98   47
References   48

The Philippines: Civic Participation in Local
        Governance—Focus on Subnational Budgeting
        and Planning   49
Alex B. Brillantes, Jr.
Context of Civil Society Participation in Local Governance   50
Civil Society Participation in Subnational Planning   53
Participatory Budgeting Framework   58
References   65

Russia: Civic Participation in Subnational Budgeting   67
Elena Krylova
National Framework: Local Government and
        Budgeting   67
Civil Participation Experiences in Budgeting Process   72

South Africa: Civic Participation in Local Government
        Policy Making and Budget Processes   91
Adrienne Shall
Participation Approaches   93
Mangaung Case Study   101
Ekurhuleni Case Study   109
National Framework   114
Conclusion   122
References   125

Thailand: Civic Participation in Subnational
        Budgeting   127
Charas Suwanmala
Local Service Responsibilities   128
Local Revenues   128
Local Budgeting   129
Summary of Case Studies   130
Building Knowledge   143
Recommendations   151
Abbreviations and Acronyms   154

Ukraine: Civic Participation in Subnational
   Budgeting   155
Elena Krylova
General Framework   155
Citizen Participation in Local Budget Process in Ukraine   163
Capacity Building to Support Civic Participation   170
Annex 1: Government System Levels   176
Annex 2: Local Self-Governance System   177
References   178

BOXES
4.1   The Bulgarian Legal Framework for Citizen Participation
      in Local Self-Government   131
7.1   Think Tanks in the Arab World   230

FIGURES
1.1   Annual Participatory Budgeting Cycle   29
2.1   Participatory Budgeting Process in Porto Alegre, Brazil   67
2.2   Citizen Satisfaction with Government Services in Bangalore,
      1994–2003   78
2.3   Administrative Costs and Instrumental Benefits
      of Participation   81
A.1   State Attitude toward Citizen Voice and
      Effective Participation   250

TABLES
1.1   Desired Outcomes and Unintended Consequences of
      Participatory Budgeting   27
1.2   Roles of Government and Participants during the First Round of
      the Participatory Budgeting Process (March–June)   29
1.3   Roles of Government and Participants during the Second Round
      of the Participatory Budgeting Process (July–November)   30
1.4   Roles of Government and Participants during Project
      Implementation   31
1.5   Number of Participants in Participatory Budgeting Processes
      in Selected Cities in Brazil, 1990–2003   33
1.6   Frequency of Participation in Participatory Budgeting
      in Belo Horizonte and Betim, Brazil   34
2.1   Typology of Citizen Participation   62

3.1   Characteristics of Case Study Municipalities in Bolivia,
        Guatemala, Nicaragua, and Peru   113
3.2   Key Aspects of Institutional Design and Measures of Success of
        Participatory Budgeting in Case Study Municipalities   115
4A.1   Achievements of and Lessons from Citizen Participation in
        Central and Eastern Europe   148
5.1   Constitutional and Legal Provisions for Decentralization and
        Participation in Bangladesh, India, Indonesia, the Philippines,
        and Thailand   160
6.1   Budget Cycle for Subnational Governments in Kenya   206
6.2   Budget Process in Mangaung, South Africa   208
6.3   Budget Process for Subnational Governments in Tanzania   209
6.4   Budget Process for Subnational Governments in Uganda   210
6.5   Budget Process in Kabwe, Zambia   211
6.6   Budget Process in Gweru, Zimbabwe   212

Foreword

In Western democracies, systems of checks and balances built into government structures have formed the core of good governance and have helped empower citizens for more than two hundred years. The incentives that motivate public servants and policy makers— the rewards and sanctions linked to results that help shape public sector performance—are rooted in a country's accountability frameworks. Sound public sector management and government spending help determine the course of economic development and social equity, especially for the poor and other disadvantaged groups, such as women and the elderly.

Many developing countries, however, continue to suffer from unsatisfactory and often dysfunctional governance systems that include rent seeking and malfeasance, inappropriate allocation of resources, inefficient revenue systems, and weak delivery of vital public services. Such poor governance leads to unwelcome outcomes for access to public services by the poor and other disadvantaged members of society, such as women, children, and minorities. In dealing with these concerns, the development assistance community in general and the World Bank in particular are continuously striving to learn lessons from practices around the world to achieve a better understanding of what works and what does not work in improving public sector governance, especially with respect to combating corruption and making services work for poor people.

The Public Sector Governance and Accountability Series advances our knowledge by providing tools and lessons from practices in improving the efficiency and equity of public services provision and strengthening institutions of accountability in governance. The series highlights frameworks to create incentive environments and pressures for good governance from within and beyond governments. It outlines institutional mechanisms to empower citizens to demand accountability for results from their governments. It provides practical guidance on managing for results and prudent fiscal management. It outlines approaches to dealing with corruption and malfeasance. It provides conceptual and practical guidance on alternative service delivery frameworks for extending the reach and access of public services. The series also covers safeguards for the protection of the poor, women, minorities, and other disadvantaged groups; ways of strengthening institutional arrangements for voice and exit; methods of evaluating public sector programs; frameworks for responsive and accountable governance; and fiscal federalism and local governance.

This series will be of interest to public officials, development practitioners, students of development, and those interested in public governance in developing countries.

Frannie A. Léautier
Vice President
World Bank Institute

Preface

Participatory budgeting has been advanced by budget practitioners and academics as an important tool for inclusive and accountable governance and has been implemented in various forms in many developing countries around the globe. Through participatory budgeting, citizens have the opportunity to gain firsthand knowledge of government operations, influence government policies, and hold government to account. However, participatory processes also run the risk of capture by interest groups. Captured processes may continue to promote elitism in government decision making.

This book provides an overview of the principles underlying participatory budgeting. It analyzes the merits and demerits of participatory budgeting practices around the world with a view to guiding policy makers and practitioners on improving such practices in the interest of inclusive governance. This publication includes five regional surveys, and seven country case studies can be found on the accompanying CD ROM.

Participatory Budgeting advances the World Bank Institute agenda on knowledge sharing and learning from cross-country experiences in reforming public governance. It is intended to assist policy makers and practitioners in developing countries in making more-informed choices.

Roumeen Islam
Manager, Poverty Reduction and Economic Management
World Bank Institute

Acknowledgments

This book brings together learning modules on participatory budgeting prepared for the World Bank Institute learning programs directed by the editor over the past three years. These learning modules were primarily financed by the government of the Netherlands under the Bank-Netherlands Partnership Program. The government of Sweden, through its Public Expenditure Management and Financial Accountability Partnership Program with the World Bank, directed by the editor, provided financial support for the publication of this book.

The volume has benefited from contributions to World Bank Institute learning events by senior policy makers from Africa, Asia, Central Asia, and the Middle East. The editor is grateful to the leading scholars who contributed chapters and to the distinguished reviewers who provided comments. Sandra Gain, Mike Lombardo, Chunli Shen, and Theresa Thompson helped during various stages of the preparation of this book and provided comments and contributed summaries of individual chapters. Kaitlin Tierney provided excellent administrative support for this project.

I am grateful to Stephen McGroarty for ensuring a fast-track process for publication of the manuscript. The quality of this book was enhanced by excellent editorial inputs provided by Barbara Karni. Production—including editing, typesetting, proofreading, indexing, and design—was managed by Janet Sasser. Stuart Tucker is to be thanked for the excellent print quality of the book.

Contributors

ALEX B. BRILLANTES, JR., is dean and professor of public administration at the National College of Public Administration and Governance, the University of the Philippines; secretary-general of the Association of Schools of Public Administration of the Philippines; and deputy secretary general of the Eastern Regional Organization for Public Administration. He is the author of *Innovations and Excellence in Local Governance* (2004), *The Philippine Presidency* (1992), and *Dictatorship and Martial Law* (1988), as well as many scholarly articles on local government, development administration, and civil society.

ALTA FÖLSCHER is a principal consultant with Mokoro Ltd., Oxford, United Kingdom. She has worked with development institutions, civil society organizations, ministries of finance, and legislatures on governance, budget and financial management, and pro-poor public policy issues.

BENJAMIN GOLDFRANK is assistant professor of political science at the University of New Mexico. His teaching and research interests focus on Latin American politics, subnational governments, processes of democratization, and social movements. He is the coeditor of *The Left in the City: Participatory Local Governments in Latin America* (2004) and the author of several book chapters and scholarly articles.

MAHFUZ KABIR is a research fellow at the Bangladesh Institute of International and Strategic Studies in Dhaka. He has published extensively on participation and participatory budgeting in scholarly books and journals.

ELENA KRYLOVA is the managing director of Development Partnership International, a Switzerland-based development consultancy company specializing in governance issues in Eastern Europe and the former Soviet Union. She is an expert on citizen participation in governance, democratic decentralization, public sector transparency and accountability, and participatory development management.

She has served as a consultant to international development agencies, including the European Commission, One World Action (a nongovernmental organization), the Organisation for Security and Cooperation in Europe, the Swiss Agency for Development and Cooperation, the Swiss Red Cross, the United Nations Development Programme, and the World Bank.

DONALD P. MOYNIHAN is assistant professor at La Follette School of Public Affairs at the University of Wisconsin—Madison. His research and teaching interests include performance management, homeland security, citizen participation, public budgeting, and the selection and implementation of public management reforms. He is the author of numerous scholarly articles and a forthcoming book, *Rethinking Performance Management.*

SAMUEL PAUL is founder and chairman of the board of the Public Affairs Centre in Bangalore, India. He spearheaded the development of citizen report cards as a public accountability tool. A former director and professor of economics at the Indian Institute of Management in Ahmedabad, he has served as an adviser to the Indian government, the United Nations, and the World Bank. His latest book, which he coauthored, is *Who Benefits from India's Public Services? A People's Audit of Five Basic Services* (2006).

ATIUR RAHMAN is professor of development studies at the University of Dhaka; honorary chairman of Unnayan Shamannay, a Bangladeshi think tank; and chairman of Credit Development Forum, the largest networking organization of multinational financial institutions in Bangladesh. He is the author or coauthor of many scholarly articles and books, including *Budget and the Poor* (2002), *People's Budget: An Illustrative Exercise Using Participatory Tools* (2002), and *Peasants and Classes: A Study in Differentiation in Bangladesh* (1986).

MOHAMMAD A. RAZZAQUE is an assistant professor in the Department of Economics at the University of Dhaka, and is currently serving in London as an economic adviser in the Economic Affairs Division of the Commonwealth Secretariat of the United Kingdom. He has been involved in research projects sponsored by various multilateral organizations and national governments, including the Asian Development Bank, the European Commission, the International Development Research Centre, the International Labour Organization, the United Nations Development Programme, the United Nations Conference on Trade and Development, the World Institute for Development Economics Research, and the governments of Bangladesh and Japan.

ANWAR SHAH is the lead economist and program leader in public sector governance at the World Bank Institute. He is also a fellow of the Institute for Public Economics in Edmonton, Alberta, Canada, and a board member of the International Institute of Public Finance in Munich, Germany.

ADRIENNE SHALL is an economist specializing in public sector budgeting and financial management. Her consulting company has worked extensively with national, provincial, and local governments as well as with the national parliament, provincial legislatures, and civil society groups in South Africa. She has served as a consultant to the World Bank Institute and worked on intervention projects in Lesotho, Malawi, Nigeria, Swaziland, and Zambia.

CHARAS SUWANMALA is professor of political science at Chulalongkorn University in Bangkok. He has been deeply involved in decentralization processes in Thailand for more than two decades. He has served as a consultant to the United Nations Development Programme, the World Bank, and other international agencies. He recently created a knowledge and learning network on local government initiatives in Thailand.

BRIAN WAMPLER is assistant professor of political science at Boise State University in Idaho. He has published scholarly articles on participatory politics, some of which have been translated into Chinese, Portuguese, and Spanish. He is writing a book entitled *Delegation, Cooperation, and Contestation: Participatory Democracy in Eight Brazilian Cities.*

Abbreviations and Acronyms

CBO	community-based organization
CCAGG	Concerned Citizens of Abra for Good Governance (the Philippines)
CSO	civil society organization
DISHA	Development Initiatives for Social and Human Action (India)
ESCWA	United Nations Economic and Social Commission for Western Asia
FSLN	Sandinista National Liberation Front (Nicaragua) (Frente Sandinista de Liberación Nacional)
HIPC	Heavily Indebted Poor Countries (Initiative)
IDASA	Institute for Democracy in South Africa
KDP	Kecamatan Development Program (Indonesia)
LASDAP	Local Authority Service Delivery Action Plan (Kenya)
MKSS	Mazdoor Kisan Shakti Sangathan (India)
NGO	nongovernmental organization
PAC	Public Affairs Centre (India)
PROOF	Public Record of Operations and Finance (India)
PRSP	Poverty Reduction Strategy Paper
TAO	Tambon (subdistrict) Administrative Organization (Thailand)
UNDP	United Nations Development Programme
UNICEF	United Nations Children's Fund
USAID	United States Agency for International Development

Overview

ANWAR SHAH

Participatory budgeting represents a direct-democracy approach to budgeting. It offers citizens at large an opportunity to learn about government operations and to deliberate, debate, and influence the allocation of public resources. It is a tool for educating, engaging, and empowering citizens and strengthening demand for good governance. The enhanced transparency and accountability that participatory budgeting creates can help reduce government inefficiency and curb clientelism, patronage, and corruption.

Participatory budgeting also strengthens inclusive governance by giving marginalized and excluded groups the opportunity to have their voices heard and to influence public decision making vital to their interests. Done right, it has the potential to make governments more responsive to citizens' needs and preferences and more accountable to them for performance in resource allocation and service delivery. In doing so, participatory budgeting can improve government performance and enhance the quality of democratic participation.

Participatory budgeting comes with significant risks. Participatory processes can be captured by interest groups. Such processes can mask the undemocratic, exclusive, or elite nature of public decision making, giving the appearance of broader participation and inclusive governance while using public funds to advance the interests of powerful elites. Participatory processes can conceal and reinforce existing injustices. Participatory budgeting can be abused to facilitate the illegitimate and unjust exercise of power. It can be used to deprive marginalized and excluded groups of having a say in public affairs. It can do so by unleashing the "tyranny of decision making and control" by overriding existing legitimate decision-making processes—by limiting the role of elected local councils in budgetary decisions, for example. The "tyranny of group dynamics" can allow manipulative facilitators to preserve and protect the interests of the governing elites. The "tyranny of method" can be used to exclude more inclusive methods of democratic voice and exit, such as parental choice in school finance, under which both government and nongovernment schools are publicly financed based on enrollments (Cooke and Kothari 2001). To prevent these abuses, participatory process must fully recognize local politics and formal and informal power relations, so that the processes yield outcomes desired by the median voter.

This book examines the potential and perils of participatory budgeting, as observed from practices around the globe. It is divided into three parts. Part I presents the nuts and bolts of participatory budgeting. Part II surveys experiences with participatory budgeting in various regions of the world. Part III is on the CD ROM accompanying this book, and it examines case studies of practices in seven countries.

Part I: Introduction to Participatory Budgeting

Two chapters introduce the concept and the processes of participatory budgeting and assess the feasibility of implementing them in developing countries. In chapter 1 Brian Wampler provides a guide to the practice of participatory budgeting. He stresses that a combination of four factors makes it more likely that participatory budgeting programs will be adopted: strong mayoral support, a civil society willing and able to contribute to ongoing policy debates, a generally supportive political environment that insulates participatory budgeting from legislators' attacks, and the financial resources to fund the projects selected by citizens.

While the rules of the game in a representative participatory budgeting program vary from city to city and from state to state, Wampler identifies the guiding tenets of participatory budgeting programs:

■ The municipality is divided into regions to facilitate meetings and the distribution of resources.
■ Government-sponsored meetings are held throughout the year, covering different aspects of the budgeting and policy-making cycles: distribution

of information, policy proposals, debates on proposals, selection of policies, election of delegates, and oversight.

- A "Quality of Life Index" is created by the government to serve as the basis for the distribution of resources. Regions with higher poverty rates, denser populations, and less infrastructure or government services receive a higher proportion of resources than better-off and wealthier neighborhoods. Each municipality devises its own formula to guarantee the equitable distribution of resources.
- Public deliberation and negotiation over resources and policies take place among participants and between participants and the government.
- A "bus caravan of priorities" is conducted, in which elected representatives visit all preapproved project sites before the final vote. The visits allow delegates to evaluate the social needs of proposed projects.
- Elected representatives vote on all final projects. Voting can be done by secret ballot or through a public showing of hands. The results become part of the public record.
- A municipalwide council is elected. All regions elect two representatives to this council, which oversees participatory budgeting and makes final budget recommendations. The council meets regularly with the municipal government to monitor the program.
- After final approval of the annual budget by participatory budgeting delegates, the mayor sends it to the municipal legislative chambers to be approved. The legislative branch can block specific projects.
- A year-end report is published detailing implementation of public works and programs.
- Regional or neighborhood committees are established that monitor the implementation of projects.

Wampler argues that political and social actors have different motivations for promoting and participating in participatory budgeting. Local governments implement participatory budgeting programs in order to build a base of political support, achieve a more equitable distribution of scarce resources, foster public learning, and promote transparency in government. Citizens participate in participatory budgeting programs in order to increase access to public decision-making activities, gain access to information, and improve the quality of services provided under a participatory budgeting system. Civil society organizations (CSOs) participate in order to build broader networks of supporters and enhance their ability to influence policies.

Several factors limit the impact of participatory budgeting programs on social justice, public learning, and administrative reform. These include the primary focus on specific public works, the dependence of the participants on the mayor's office, the role of long-term planning within participatory budgeting, the emphasis on local issues and local public policies, and the danger that participatory budgeting programs may be manipulated due to the central role played by the mayor's office. Participatory budgeting programs are, in Wampler's words, "an important step toward political inclusion and greater social justice, but they are by no means a magic bullet."

In chapter 2 Donald Moynihan examines the prospects for citizen participation in developing countries, with a focus on participation in the budget process. Citizen participation refers to citizens or citizen representatives (who are not elected officials) interacting with and providing feedback to government at the policy formulation or implementation stages of governance. Four interrelated arguments support the rise of public participation: postmodern discourse theory, disillusionment with bureaucracy, the search for a democratic ideal, and the particular need for participation in a developing-country context. From these arguments, Moynihan gleans two basic criteria for participation forums: participation should be broadly representative of the population, and it should involve meaningful dialogue that affects public decision making. Based on a review of participation in Poverty Reduction Strategy Processes, he concludes that participation in developing countries often fails to meet these criteria.

The cases reviewed in chapter 2 demonstrate a variety of ways in which participation can shape resource allocation, budget execution, and performance evaluation. One of the lessons is the importance of civil society in developing-country settings. In most of the cases, a nongovernmental organization (NGO) or group of NGOs undertook analysis of the budget. These NGOs seek to represent the poor and disseminate their views to the government. They do not offer direct citizen participation, but without their involvement, the prospects for any type of participation would be reduced. Even in Porto Alegre, Brazil, where citizen involvement is most direct, an active civil society aided the process of citizen involvement. Organizing citizen involvement, or simply analyzing public budgets, depends a good deal on NGOs and their capacity.

Another major lesson is the importance of government attitudes toward participation. If the goal of participation is to have an impact on public sector decisions, then pro-participation arguments must understand the perspective of government and how it influences whether they are supportive of participation and willing to listen to public feedback. Understanding the administrative perspective raises the question of how participation can be fostered when the government is hostile to it. The cases discussed in chapter 2 suggest that certain types of participation can influence government actions even if government has not embraced direct citizen involvement in decision making. Much depends on the ability of NGOs to communicate their analyses of spending choices, budget execution, and the performance of public services to the media, the public, and elected officials, who can then use the information to affect public policy.

Part II: Regional Surveys

Chapters 3–7 survey the practice of participatory budgeting in each of the five regions of the developing world. In chapter 3 Benjamin Goldfrank notes that within a relatively short period, from 1990 to 2005, participatory budgeting expanded from about a dozen cities, most of them in Brazil, to hundreds or perhaps thousands of locales (depending on how strictly participatory budgeting is defined) in Latin America alone. Through a broad comparison of national experiences in Bolivia, Brazil, Guatemala, Nicaragua, and Peru and an analysis of case studies in 14 non-Brazilian municipalities, he tests the hypothesis that the design and results of participatory budgeting depend on both the designers' intentions and preexisting local conditions. He asserts that introducing participatory budgeting is never a neutral political act but always a form of "competitive institution building."

Several lessons can be drawn from the Latin American case studies. First, national legal mandates for participatory budgeting have not created widespread local success in encouraging citizen participation, fiscal transparency, or effective municipal government. This is partly because designers of national laws had other goals in mind and partly because of local obstacles, including reluctant mayors or opposition parties, the weak fiscal and administrative capacity of municipal governments, and fragmented, conflict-ridden civic associations.

Second, despite these problems, participatory budgeting has succeeded in some remarkably diverse locales, from small, poverty-stricken, indigenous rural villages to large, ethnically diverse cities. While carefully identifying necessary and sufficient conditions will require further study, success seems correlated with several factors:

- The mayor is indigenous, from a party on the left, or both.
- Opposition from local political elites is weak or nonexistent.
- Project funding, technical assistance, or both are provided by national or international aid organizations.

- The municipality has sufficient revenues to make significant investments in public works or programs.
- There is a tradition of participation and cooperation within and among local civic associations, indigenous customary organizations, or both that has not been destroyed by guerrilla warfare or clientelist politics.

Third, even where participatory budgeting succeeds on some dimensions, it does not dramatically reduce poverty (especially in terms of income) on its own. For this to occur in the future, fundamental principles of participatory budgeting as originally conceived—transparency and direct participation—need to be applied to all public spending.

Chapter 3 highlights four main points regarding the future direction of participatory budgeting in Latin America. First, none of the normative approaches to participatory budgeting accurately describes its results, which vary extensively across cases. Participatory budgeting does not always strengthen the state with respect to the market or insulate pro-market reforms.

Second, the ideological contests surrounding participatory budgeting continue and are likely to persist. Development agencies are advocating and local governments are adopting participatory budgeting from Albania to Zambia. Participatory budgeting also has old and new champions in the recently ascendant Latin American left.

Third, within the struggle to define, propose, and implement participatory budgeting, the formal approaches are gaining currency. The open, informal, deliberative design pioneered by Porto Alegre seems to be out of fashion. In its place are more regulated, formal, consultative designs focused on preexisting CSOs, such as those implemented in Bolivia, Nicaragua, and Peru.

Fourth, to strengthen the future chances of successful participatory budgeting at the local level, its original principles should be applied to higher levels of national and international governance. Even in the relatively small number of municipalities that succeeded in improving local service provision with participatory budgeting, low incomes and joblessness remain serious problems. Applying participatory budgeting principles of transparency, participation, and redistribution to decision-making spheres where larger sums of money are at stake may have two positive effects on encouraging local participatory budgeting efforts. First, it may produce more universal, egalitarian social policies, strengthening local social capital and allowing citizens in desperately poor countries to think beyond their next meal. Second, it may convince mayors and citizens that participatory budgeting is indeed about these principles—and not a politically motivated subterfuge—and perhaps worth trying.

Chapter 4, by Alta Fölscher, discusses selected examples of citizen participation in resource decisions in local, municipal, and submunicipal areas in Central and Eastern Europe. She examines experiences in Albania, Armenia, Bulgaria, Moldova, Poland, Romania, the Russian Federation, and Ukraine, countries with very different dynamics despite a shared history as communist states.

Participatory budgeting techniques have been introduced at the local level in several localities in this region within enabling legal frameworks. Many countries in the region have introduced additional legislation that makes provisions—albeit usually at a fairly high level—for direct citizen engagement with public resource decisions. However, legislation, while perhaps necessary, is not sufficient to increase participation. Participation in the region remains weak for a variety of reasons:

- Historically, citizens in this region have been detached from decisions that affect them. They are mistrustful of collective action and passive receivers of public services.
- Collective forms of political and social organization, such as political parties and CSOs, are relatively new, as is an elected, independent, and autonomous local government.
- Intergovernmental fiscal systems are still in development; roles and responsibilities are weakly and ambiguously assigned to local levels.
- Local governments' expenditure responsibilities do not match their revenue capacity, and transfers from upper levels are nontransparent and unreliable.
- Local governments have insufficient authority to make decisions and often are still developing the practical capacity to use resources effectively and efficiently to solve local problems.
- Citizens are dissatisfied with local services, but they do not believe they can affect them or that local governments can do anything about the problems they face.

With few exceptions, development agencies or international NGOs were the initiators of participatory budgeting mechanisms in this region. Even where initiatives resulted from local action, international organizations fund key organizations, and contact with networks of CSOs worldwide preceded local action. Although this does not necessarily detract from the value of the initiatives, it may have implications for sustainability.

Local government autonomy, local resource availability, citizen organization and interest, and developed political party systems are often seen as prerequisites for successful participatory budgeting. In Central and Eastern Europe, these mechanisms are proposed as an entry point to overcome governance weaknesses: participatory budgeting initiatives are often introduced precisely to help establish the kinds of institutions and arrangements that are often seen as a prerequisite for them to function. In other regions of the world, successful engagement by citizens with local resource decisions has catalyzed or occurred in a virtuous circle of governance: good governance demands good local capacity, which in turn supports and is supported by participation.

Several conclusions on the potential value of participatory budgeting initiatives emerge from the case studies in this chapter:

■ Participatory budgeting increases opportunities for participation. Questions remain regarding whether the quality of participation is sufficient to ensure lasting interest in participating and whether it is sufficiently broad based.
■ Participatory budgeting can break down barriers between citizens and government, improving mutual understanding and communication.
■ Participatory budgeting strengthens local CSOs, which may improve local governance in the long term. However, the organizations that gain access to decision making and partnership with local government may themselves become arms of local government.
■ Participatory budgeting can help make infrastructure and services more relevant to the communities they serve.
■ Participatory budgeting can result in additional revenue for local development.

The case studies suggest that certain conditions facilitate effective participation. Initiatives may need to establish these conditions before introducing participatory budgeting. They also identify certain factors that may improve results:

■ Better information produces better results.
■ Single participation mechanisms are less effective than combinations of mechanisms.
■ Awareness raising and education of stakeholders are necessary.
■ Incentive structures count.
■ Clear rules for participation and decision making are required.
■ Partnerships contribute to more effective arrangements.
■ Localities learn by doing.

■ Ownership by local leadership is critical.
■ CSOs and local government officials need specific skills.
■ Public relations campaigns and media involvement are needed.
■ Coalition building among local NGOs strengthens initiatives.
■ External catalysts play a key role in initiating and developing participatory practices in the region.

Alta Fölscher surveys the Asian experience in chapter 5, where she examines participatory budgeting mechanisms in Bangladesh, India, Indonesia, the Philippines, and Thailand. The case studies offer evidence that civic participation mechanisms can improve development outcomes while improving the quality of the citizen/state relationship, particularly in terms of local-level responsiveness to citizen preferences, improved accountability of public officials and elected representatives, better democracy, and more trust in government.

From the Asian experience, the author draws useful conclusions about necessary and supporting factors for successful replication elsewhere. Whether initiatives are successful depends on both factors in the environment in which an initiative develops and the design and implementation of the initiative itself. Initiatives in which public actors are willing to listen to citizen voice (supported by a local political culture that is driven by issues of public policy) and where well-designed mechanisms allow civil society direct access and participation to public decision making have the greatest impact on policy decisiveness, accountability, democratic practice, and trust in government. Implementation details of projects remain important in determining how successful they are.

The greatest risk facing initiatives is that they draw citizens into the state action space when the political culture is not policy based and local officials and office holders have no real interest in aligning policy and spending with citizen preferences. In such cases, participation can be counterproductive. Although risks can be managed by providing external funding and bypassing state structures, doing so may yield short-term benefits at the expense of the sustainability of such initiatives. Long-term engagement can be effective only if sufficient local taste and capacity for participation are built to create an environment in which state actors engage substantively.

Citizens' own initiatives to improve public transparency and the accountability of state actors can yield successful results even in environments where their voice may not have an immediate effect. Three case studies in this chapter illustrate how citizens who are thoroughly prepared and work through coalitions can push their way into space and demand a hearing.

Such initiatives can transform the participatory environment from one in which state actors are unwilling to engage with citizens into one in which they have little choice but to do so. Success depends largely on selecting the correct entry point and designing and implementing projects that maximize citizen participation.

In chapter 6 Adrienne Shall reviews the experience of participatory budgeting by subnational governments in Kenya, Mozambique, South Africa, Tanzania, Uganda, Zambia, and Zimbabwe, where local governments manage their own fiscal revenues and expenditures. Although participation is not legislated in all of these countries, all recognize that participation is an important tool for improving service delivery to communities. To allow for more inclusiveness in the planning and budgetary processes at the local level, countries have therefore put in place a variety of mechanisms, including ward committee structures, participatory planning processes, public meetings, budget conferences, consultative sessions, budget campaigns, monthly newsletters, a participatory poverty assessment project, and various forms of media intervention.

In each country the budget preparation process includes a stage that allows for civic participation in identifying needs and priorities. In some cases participation occurs only at the beginning of the process; in other cases once the draft budget is finalized, citizens are given another opportunity to provide input regarding the allocation of resources. In many instances citizen input is limited and the allocation of resources is still determined largely by officials and councillors within the local authorities. Moreover, citizens are usually allowed to provide input only with regard to the capital budget, which represents a small proportion of the total budget. In some cases citizens are not given adequate time to analyze and discuss their input into the process.

Despite these impediments, most countries believe that civic participation has increased the number and range of local projects that have a direct impact on communities that are involved in the participation process. Participation has also improved relations between citizens and local authorities, as citizens feel that local authorities have become more transparent and trustworthy.

Local authorities face challenges in implementing participatory budgeting. These challenges include lack of capacity, limited understanding of the roles and responsibilities of all actors, limited scope of participation, legislative constraints, inadequate monitoring and evaluation systems, lack of transparency and trust, breakdown in communication, insufficient resources, and political and social differences.

In overcoming these challenges, some local authorities have learned valuable lessons:

- Enabling legislation and commitment by leadership with strong political will are critical.
- Extensive and continuous capacity building of councillors, officials, and citizens is necessary.
- The process must be initiated well in advance of the budget presentation to enable serious discussion and evaluation of priorities and resource allocation.
- All key stakeholders need to be identified, in order to ensure broad-based representation of all sections of society.
- Joint commitment by both elected and appointed local officials is necessary.

In chapter 7 Alta Fölscher considers participatory budgeting in the Middle East and North Africa. She shows that many of the factors that facilitate citizen initiatives are absent in this region. These include the openness and democratic depth of political and governance systems; the existence of enabling legal frameworks, including guarantees of basic freedoms; the capacity for participation both inside and outside of government; the existence of functional and free media institutions; and the willingness and capacity of the state to make available budget information. Political contestability in this region is very low. Power is based on traditional networks; elections are often within the control of the ruling elite; and freedom of opinion, speech, association, and the media is not guaranteed. Although many countries in the region have committed themselves to decentralizing and empowering local authorities, real decision-making power has not been devolved nor resources decentralized. Given the political and sociocultural systems in the region and its weak decentralization frameworks and practice, citizen budgeting initiatives are unlikely to succeed, unless local leadership is interested in participation, efforts are supported by external development partner funding, or both.

One of the hopes for participatory budgeting initiatives is that with careful design and targeted support they can initiate positive change in the political and governance environment, particularly by whetting citizens' appetite for positive, empowered engagement with the state and contestable government. This notion is borne out by some examples of successful initiatives in the region. The question remains, however, whether even successful initiatives will be able to overcome the systemic barriers identified and support a regional shift toward better governance. Fölscher argues that this is possible only if the underlying social, cultural, and religious norms in the region are not incompatible with notions of representivity, consultation, and democracy. This suggests that the design of participatory budgeting initiatives must take account of the local political, cultural, and social environment.

In an appendix, Fölscher provides an overview of basic concepts and approaches to participatory budgeting.

Part III (on CD ROM): Country Case Studies on Civic Participation in Subnational Budgeting

Part III presents seven country case studies on participatory budgeting on the accompanying CD ROM. The countries include Bangladesh, India, the Philippines, Russia, South Africa, Thailand, and Ukraine.

First, Atiur Rahman, Mahfuz Kabir, and Mohammad A. Razzaque examine Bangladesh, where no formal government regulations promote civic participation in subnational budgeting and planning processes, and local government institutions possess little autonomy. As a result, some locally elected governments have created informal mechanisms to engage civic participation, primarily with the assistance of international organizations and local NGOs. There is little evidence indicating significant change. Local government institutions in Bangladesh are organized at several levels. In rural areas these include the *zila parishad* (district), *upazila parishad* (subdistrict), and union *parishad* (the lowest tier). In urban areas they include the *paurasabha* (town) and the city corporation. The authors examine subnational budgeting and planning processes at the level of the union parishad.

An example of an informal mechanism designed to engage civic participation is the Sarajganj project, the product of a joint effort by the United Nations Development Programme, the United Nations Capital Development Fund, and the government of Bangladesh. The project first divided the union *parishad* into smaller communities, called wards, and established four committees to gather citizen input. The ward development committees, which coordinate citizen participation, are the most significant players in this process. They are responsible for holding participatory planning sessions through public forums, the last step before budget approval at the union *parishad* level. A separate committee is responsible for monitoring the implementation of the budget at the local level.

Despite this project, the level of civic participation in local budgeting and planning processes in Sarajganj is minimal at best. Certain institutional factors continue to hamper participation. At the municipal and union parishad levels, only selected individuals are invited to discuss the proposed budgets before they are approved. These individuals often include supporters and members of the ruling political party. Low levels of citizen education and the lack of transportation to and from the final budget meeting also inhibit greater civic participation. Bangladesh's male-dominated culture minimizes the active role of women in the budgetary process. The Sarajganj project attempts to counter this cultural norm by ensuring female participation in the ward development committees.

The authors argue in favor of widespread capacity-building reforms to strengthen the role of civil society in subnational budgeting and planning processes. Local government institutions lack training and training manuals designed to teach civic participation strategies, especially the targeting of marginalized groups. Local government institutions also need to be provided with tools with which to effectively monitor the implementation of local programs following budget approval.

Second, Samuel Paul describes two case studies on the role of CSOs in India's subnational budgetary process. The first describes the role of the Development Initiative for Social and Human Action (DISHA), a local CSO in the state of Gujarat, that conducts budget analyses and advocacy campaigns on behalf of the poor at the state level. The second examines the Public Record of Operations and Finance (PROOF) consortium, which conducts budget analyses and facilitates public discussion at the local level.

DISHA developed a program to promote citizen participation in the state budgetary process. Pathey, the unit responsible for this program, conducts budget analysis, dialogue with policy makers, and education of and advocacy on behalf of the public. It examines overall estimated revenue and expenditures across departments, sectors, and programs targeting the poor. It also verifies expenditures through field research. It disseminates "briefs" to legislators and members of the media and holds training sessions with coalitions of volunteer groups. These sessions serve as a conduit to reach the targeted population—the poor—and encourage local leaders and organizations to meet with district-level authorities. Pathey also interacts with senior public officials on behalf of all the groups and individuals it represents. According to Pathey's own reports, legislators welcome their briefs and public awareness has improved. The impact of its work on policy making is difficult to assess.

PROOF is a campaign for citizens to participate in the budgetary process in the city of Bangalore. Unlike DISHA, PROOF focuses on the entire budget. Its strategy is based on creating a public forum to review the city budget, its performance, and its problems and to educate citizens about the budget process. PROOF comprises four primary civic organizations, each of which plays a separate and integral role in its citizen campaign. Although this program has improved citizen participation in Bangalore and increased dissemination of financial statements to the public, it continues to face a variety of challenges.

Given the diversity of country contexts and political systems, case-specific strategies are needed. Strengthening the capacity for citizen participation in the budget process requires the development of a close working relationship with policy makers, budget analysts, civic organizations, and citizens at large.

Third, Alex Brillantes, Jr., discusses civil society's role in subnational planning and budgeting process in the Philippines. In 1991 the government approved the Local Government Code, a constitutional amendment that decentralized power to local governments. While civil society participation in subnational planning is effective, challenges remain.

Traditionally, the notion of governance in the Philippines was limited to government as the only institution involved in the budgetary process. Once the Local Government Code became law, the concept of governance included alternative mechanisms and institutions. This legitimized the role of NGOs in this process and increased citizen involvement in subnational budgeting. After the Local Government Code was implemented, NGOs were allocated a minimum of one-fourth of the seats on the local development council—the primary policy-making and budgetary planning body at the community level. Before adoption of the new code, NGOs were allocated a maximum of one-fourth of the seats. The change in the code has institutionalized civil society participation in local budgeting and planning processes, supported by law.

Several participatory mechanisms were established in Naga City. These mechanisms included continued accreditation of NGOs, multilevel consultations to identify citizen priorities, citywide referenda on development issues, and the establishment of the Naga City People's Council. This council, which is made up of accredited businesses and NGOs, serves as the peoples' representative. It plays an active role in the legislative budget process.

Despite the success of Naga City and the recent amendments to the constitution, civic participation in subnational budgeting and planning process is not widespread in the Philippines. Brillantes argues that there is a need to implement new strategies to engage the wider public. Local governments need to identify both formal and informal mechanisms for civil society to play a more active role in this process. Whether or not they can do so depends on policy changes, capacity building, formal systems of accountability, and efforts to eliminate resource duplication.

Fourth, Elena Krylova examines the Transparent Budgeting Program implemented by Centre Strategiya, a St. Petersburg–based NGO. The objective of the program was to establish mechanisms for public budget hearings and independent budget analyses. Krylova's analysis focuses on the experiences in Murmanks, Novosibirsk, Petrazavodsk, Pskov, St. Petersburg, Samara, Velikiye Luki, and Yuzno-Sakhalinsk.

Russian budgeting at the regional and local levels operates according to a four-step process: planning and preparation of a draft budget, review and approval of the budget by a regional or local body, implementation of the budget, and review of budget reports by regional or local bodies. At any point in this process, civil society and the general public have the right to influence local decision-making and budgeting processes through a variety of mechanisms, including organizing local referenda, participating in public hearings, conducting public opinion polls, and organizing public debates.

The transparent budgeting program grew out of a civil society initiative in 1998 based on the principles that budget activities should be open to the public and that regular interaction should take place between authorities and civil society. The first objective of the program was to establish local budget analyses by independent experts in order to determine if budgeting policies took the interests of all citizens into account. The second objective was to establish public hearings. These hearings are organized by special committees composed of representatives of groups and organizations that initiate the hearings. The committees are responsible for all preparatory work and for appointing a moderator for the hearing. All hearings are concluded with a vote by all those present and a final recommendation to local authorities. Summaries of the hearings are published and placed on file in public libraries.

Several factors are impeding the success of these programs, according to program officials. Low levels of civic participation in public budget hearings are attributed to the lack of a clear division of responsibilities between regional and local governments, the lack of organizational development among NGOs, widespread illiteracy, weak local media, nontransparent mechanisms of interaction between government and civil society, and the misconception of participation by government officials. The lack of trust between authorities and civil society is also problematic. Independent budget analyses have been hindered by difficulties. In some locations program officials were unable to find local independent experts capable of conducting the analyses. In other locations local experts were apprehensive about criticizing the local authorities.

Krylova offers several recommendations for improving civic participation in subnational budgeting in Russia. Resources must be directed to educating local government officials and legislative representatives about the advantages of budget transparency and the role civic society can play in the budgeting process. Equally important is the need to increase political will among local officials and to build awareness among citizens about the role they can play in the budget process. Strengthening the capacity of local media as well as the academic and NGO communities to serve as independent budget experts is also important.

Fifth, Adrienne Shall describes the impact of the transformation of local governments in South Africa on civic participation in policy-making and budgetary processes by looking at two municipalities, Mangaung and Ekurhuleni. As a result of South Africa's 1993 constitution as well as the adoption of several new laws in the mid-1990s, new participatory laws were created and municipalities formed. Despite these changes, civic participation processes in South Africa's 284 municipalities vary widely.

South Africa's Constitution of 1993, the Municipal Structures Act of 1998, the Municipal Systems Act of 2000, the Municipal Finance Management Act of 2003, and the Municipal Property Rates Act of 2004 all contain provisions promoting two primary forms of participation at the local government level. The first mechanism, the ward committee system, is designed to provide a forum in which communities can play an active role in their municipality. Each ward directly elects a ward councillor, who represents the ward's interests as a member of the municipal council. The second mechanism, the subcouncil, comprises ward councillors as well as other councillors appointed by the council to ensure equal political party representation. Additional participatory mechanisms are available to each municipality.

The municipalities of Ekurhuleni and Mangaung have similar mechanisms for participation. Both have implemented the ward committee system as the primary vehicle for civic participation. The objective is to obtain feedback from the community for the Integrated Development Plan, which establishes the strategic goals of a municipality over a five-year period. Each municipality has also established additional mechanisms for civic participation that cater to the specific needs of its communities. In Ekurhuleni several consultative structures are in place to ensure stakeholder input into policy-making and budget processes from different sectors. The planning approach adopted in Mangaung is called community-based planning. It allows the ward committees to identify different social groups and meet with each group separately to assess its needs.

The South African legal framework establishes mechanisms for public participation in the planning, policy-making, and budgetary processes of municipalities. It is too early to determine the extent to which these mechanisms have been fully implemented with the desired results. In Ekurhuleni and Manguang, government offic ials implemented several consultative processes. Several challenges remain, however, including the low level of capacity, language barriers, the lack of communication between councillors and other officials, and a lack of resources.

Sixth, Charas Suwanmala reviews Thailand's experience with participatory budgeting. Local government in Thailand comprises five units: the provincial administrative organization, the municipality, the subdistrict administrative organization (TAO), and two special forms of local government, which include the Bangkok Metropolitan Administration and Pattaya City. Suwanmala examines civic participation at the municipal and subdistrict administrative levels, referred to as "communal tiers." These levels of government are governed directly by locally elected councils and chief executives.

Suwanmala examines the mechanisms for civic participation in Suan Mon TAO, Huai Kapi TAO, Khon Kan City, and Rayong City. Suan Mon TAO and Huai Kapi TAO have established similar mechanisms for civic participation in the local government budgeting process. In both locales, civic forums have been adopted at the village and subdistrict levels. At the village level, civic forums are composed of the village leader and other community representatives. The members of the village civic forum are responsible for discussing and submitting a proposed list of budget priorities to the subdistrict, which is composed of representatives of village civic forums. The members of the subdistrict civic forum then discuss each of the proposed budget priorities and produce a final proposal for the chair of the subdistrict administration. Huai Kapi TAO has also implemented household surveys to assess public opinion of local services and to increase civic participation.

Khon Kan and Rayong cities have adopted different tools for civic engagement to elicit wider participation. In Khon Kan City, officials use focus groups and town hall meetings as their primary mechanisms. The focus groups help generate visions, policy directions, and strategic actions for local budgeting and planning. Town hall meetings are designed to facilitate dialogue between the public and local officials. Rayong City has created a civic town hall development commission and a civic fiscal policy commission. It also conducts focus groups and has developed a manual for participatory planning.

Focus group consultations, the most widely used mechanism, have proven especially successful in Thailand because of the flexibility to adopt formal and informal approaches. Town hall meetings and civic forums have proven successful in building consensus and increasing trust of local government. Assessing the impact of civic committees and citizen surveys is more difficult. Suwanmala argues for the need to continue strengthening the capacity of civic organizations and training local officials and residents to fully understand their roles.

Seventh, Elena Krylova surveys Ukraine's experience with participatory budgeting. Ukraine's 1996 constitution and the adoption of several subsequent laws created government regulations designed to increase civic engagement in local budgeting and planning. The overall framework for local governance, however, is largely the result of the 1997 Law on Local Self-Government and the 2001 Budget Code. According to the 1997 law, local self-government is established through direct elections of local councils (*radas*) every four years. Local councils are responsible for establishing their own executive committees and assume responsibility for local development programs and budgets. Krylova discusses the impact of these laws on the town of Kamyanets-Podilski and its process of subnational budgeting.

Public budget hearings are the primary vehicle for civic participation in local budgeting processes in Kamyanets-Podilski. The objective of these hearings is to provide a forum in which citizens and officials can engage in dialogue regarding local budget issues. Public budget hearings are initiated by a group of residents, the town council, or the mayor or by an executive committee. They involve the establishment of special hearing committees to conduct public surveys and opinion polls addressing specific budget and planning issues. Actual hearings, which may involve voting, are then held and the results published. Since national laws in Ukraine do not provide clear guidance on procedures for public budget hearings, local authorities may adopt municipal statutes to govern the implementation of civic participation mechanisms.

Krylova concludes that the success of civic participation in budgeting and planning processes in Ukraine is contingent on three factors: the leadership of the mayor, the extent to which local NGOs play active roles in promoting citizen engagement, and public knowledge of budget processes. Other, less significant factors include the presence of a local ombudsman and the adoption of a program performance approach to budgeting in place of line-item budgeting. Poor government capacity to mobilize citizens, the lack of diverse training materials, and the lack of general information available to the public continue to hinder civic participation in subnational budgeting processes.

Reference

Cooke, Bill, and Uma Kothari. 2001. *Participation: The New Tyranny?* London: Zed Books Ltd.

PART One

Introduction to
Participatory Budgeting

1

A Guide to Participatory Budgeting

BRIAN WAMPLER

Participatory budgeting is a decision-making process through which citizens deliberate and negotiate over the distribution of public resources. Participatory budgeting programs are implemented at the behest of governments, citizens, nongovernmental organizations (NGOs), and civil society organizations (CSOs) to allow citizens to play a direct role in deciding how and where resources should be spent. These programs create opportunities for engaging, educating, and empowering citizens, which can foster a more vibrant civil society. Participatory budgeting also helps promote transparency, which has the potential to reduce government inefficiencies and corruption. Because most citizens who participate have low incomes and low levels of formal education, participatory budgeting offers citizens from historically excluded groups the opportunity to make choices that will affect how their government acts. Put simply, participatory budgeting programs provide poor and historically excluded citizens with access to important decision-making venues.

Participatory budgeting is noteworthy because it addresses two distinct but interconnected needs: improving state performance and enhancing the quality of democracy. It helps improve state performance through a series of institutional rules that constrain and check the prerogatives of the municipal government while creating increased opportunities for citizens to engage in public policy debates. It helps enhance the quality of democracy by encouraging the direct participation of citizens in open and public debates, which helps increase their knowledge of public affairs.

Improving state performance and enhancing the quality of democracy are desired goals, but they are not necessarily produced by participatory budgeting programs. Participatory budgeting programs have produced results that run the gamut from highly successful to very weak.

Participatory budgeting was initially implemented in 1990, in 12 Brazilian cities. By 2005 it had been expanded to more than 300 municipalities worldwide (Cabannes n.d.; Wampler 2004a; Wampler and Avritzer 2005).

There is broad variation in how participatory budgeting programs function, which means that the effects of participatory budgeting on accountability, the decentralization of decision-making authority, and empowerment are conditioned by the local social, political, and economic environment. Participatory budgeting opens up obscure budgetary procedures to ordinary citizens and helps create a broader public forum in which citizens and governments discuss spending, taxation, and implementation. It is simultaneously a policy process that focuses on the distribution of resources and a democratic institution that enhances accountability, transfers decision-making authority to citizens, and empowers citizens.

Participatory budgeting programs confront social and political legacies of clientelism, social exclusion, and corruption by making the budgetary process transparent and public. Social and political exclusion are challenged, as low-income and traditionally excluded political actors are given the opportunity to make policy decisions. By moving the locus of decision making from the private offices of politicians and technocrats to public forums, public meetings help foster transparency.

Participatory budgeting programs also serve as "citizenship schools," as engagement empowers citizens to better understand their rights and duties as citizens as well as the responsibilities of government. Citizens learn to negotiate among themselves and with the government over the distribution of scarce resources and public policy priorities.

When participatory budgeting programs function poorly in terms of policy outputs, there is still the potential for participants to enhance their knowledge of governmental responsibilities and citizens' rights, which can enhance their capacity to negotiate with and place demands on state officials. However, when participatory budgeting programs function poorly, increased cynicism about democracy, decentralization, and participation may be generated, as participants become disillusioned with an ill-performing institution.

There is no precise model for participatory budgeting programs. While there are similar tenets and institutional mechanisms, participatory budgeting programs are structured in response to the particular political, social, and economic environment of each city or state. While alluding to the differences, this chapter presents a synthesis of the most representative cases.

The assumption of this chapter is that the tools and institutional means developed to date are, in small or large part, transferable to other locales. Cities, municipalities, states, and regional governments in diverse parts of the world should be able to draw on the experiences described here to develop tools that link budgeting, policy making, and citizen participation. NGOs and local political activists can draw on these experiences to promote formal participatory budgeting programs or informal monitoring programs inspired by the participatory budgeting example.

History of Participatory Budgeting

Participatory budgeting programs are part of a larger effort in Brazil to extend and deepen actual, existing democracy (Abers 2000; Avritzer 2002; Baiocchi 2001; Wampler and Avritzer 2004). Since the reestablishment of democracy in 1985, Brazilian politics has continued to be dominated by traditional patronage practices, social exclusion, and corruption. Numerous governments, NGOs, social movements, and political parties have turned to the ideas, values, and rules associated with participatory budgeting in an effort to improve policy outcomes and enrich Brazil's young democracy. One of the reasons why participatory budgeting is transferable to other locations, especially in developing countries, is that clientelism and social exclusion are everyday realities in many parts of the developing world.

Participatory budgeting began in 1989 in the municipality of Porto Alegre, the capital of Brazil's southernmost state, Rio Grande do Sul. Porto Alegre has more than 1 million inhabitants and is wealthy by Brazilian standards. In 1988 the Workers' Party, a progressive political party founded during the waning years of the 1964–85 military dictatorship, won the mayoral election. Its campaign was based on democratic participation and the "inversion of spending priorities"—that is, the reversal of a decades-long trend in which public resources were spent in middle- and upper-class neighborhoods. Participatory budgeting was intended to help poorer citizens and neighborhoods receive larger shares of public spending.

When the Workers' Party won the mayor's office in Porto Alegre, it inherited a bankrupt municipality and a disorganized bureaucracy. During its first two years in office, the new administration experimented with different mechanisms to tackle financial constraints, provide citizens with a direct role in the government's activities, and invert the social spending priorities of previous administrations. Participatory budgeting was born through this experimental process. In 1989 and 1990, the first two years of participatory budgeting, fewer than 1,000 citizens participated in the participatory budgeting process; by 1992 the number of participants had jumped to nearly 8,000. After the Workers' Party was reelected in 1992, the program took on a life of its own, with participation increasing to more than 20,000 people a year. Participation grew as citizens realized that participatory budgeting was an important decision-making venue.

How and Where Does Participatory Budgeting Work?

What are the basic conditions associated with the establishment of a participatory budgeting program? Why do governments, NGOs, CSOs, and citizens choose to adopt participatory budgeting? What basic financial issues must be considered?

Conditions Conducive to Participatory Budgeting

A combination of four factors makes it more likely that participatory budgeting programs will be adopted: strong mayoral support, a civil society willing and able to contribute to ongoing policy debates, a generally supportive political environment that insulates participatory budgeting from legislators' attacks, and financial resources to fund the projects selected by citizens.

It is generally municipal-level governments that implement participatory budgeting programs, although there are some participatory budgeting programs at the state and provincial levels.

Governments that are willing to implement participatory budgeting generally have a reformist tinge—the political leadership tends to include political entrepreneurs willing to experiment with a new institutional format or political reformists willing to adopt parts of a program that have proven successful elsewhere. Government support is vital, because government officials must make the decision to delegate authority. After they do so, they must build the necessary logistical, informational, and financial support needed for participatory budgeting to function.

Governments that enjoy strong bases of support from social movements, unions, and NGOs are more likely to initiate participatory budgeting, because doing so involves reaching out to a constituency they already know. Participatory budgeting programs have been most successful in municipalities with deep civil society roots. Preexisting networks of social movements, community organizations, and other voluntary associations provide important support for experimental programs. Programs depend on the active participation of citizens not only to select new policies but also to legitimize the government's reform efforts. Higher rates of participation will help legitimize a government's policies.

Although participatory budgeting is implemented at the behest of the mayor, the municipal legislature can be involved in the process. Because participatory budgeting offers the potential to undermine traditional patronage networks, many legislators will resist fully implementing it. If the legislative branch is weak relative to the mayoral administration, legislators may be able to act as spoilers, trying to undermine the process if they feel it threatens their interests. If the mayor and the legislative branch are at odds, it is possible that the mayor will be unable to delegate authority to participatory budgeting because of the need to expend political energy on working with legislators.

While many participatory budgeting programs address the overall financial health of the municipality, the principal focus remains discretionary spending. Having discretionary funding available is important because it increases the likelihood that citizens can directly select policy outcomes. The more financial flexibility a government enjoys, the greater the influence citizens can exercise on the selection of new public works. Governments must have the resources to implement the projects that participants select.

If a financially strapped municipality decides to implement a participatory budgeting program, the focus shifts from the selection of specific public works projects to a more general discussion of debt, taxes, and the efficient use of limited resources. The municipal government must first dedicate considerable time and energy to explaining to participants the dire financial situation of the municipality. Participants must then vote on the general policy priorities of the government. Participants will not select specific public works to be implemented but will indicate in a broad fashion how the government should spend available resources.

The Rules of the Game

What are the rules of the game in a representative participatory budgeting program? What are the specific ways that citizens are incorporated into policy- and budget-making arenas?

The rules of the game are similar but not identical in the majority of participatory budgeting programs. They tend to be designed by the elected government with input from citizens. Participants generally must approve the rules and any subsequent changes to them.

While the rules vary from city to city and from state to state, it is possible to identify the guiding tenets of participatory budgeting programs. For the sake of parsimony, the discussion focuses on the municipal level of government. The basic tenets of participatory budgeting include the following:

- The municipality is divided into regions to facilitate meetings and the distribution of resources.
- Government-sponsored meetings are held throughout the year, covering different aspects of the budgeting and policy-making cycles: distribution of information, policy proposals, debates on proposals, selection of policies, election of delegates, and oversight.
- A "Quality of Life Index" is created by the government to serve as the basis for the distribution of resources. Regions with higher poverty rates, denser populations, and less infrastructure or government services receive a higher proportion of resources than better-off and wealthier neighborhoods. Each municipality devises its own formula to guarantee the equitable distribution of resources.
- Public deliberation and negotiation take place among participants and between participants and the government over resources and policies.
- A "bus caravan of priorities" is conducted, in which elected representatives visit all preapproved project sites before the final vote. The visits allow delegates to evaluate the social needs of proposed projects.
- Elected representatives vote on all final projects. Voting can be done by secret ballot or through a public showing of hands. The results become part of the public record.
- A municipalwide council is elected. All regions elect two representatives to this council, which oversees participatory budgeting and makes final budget recommendations. The council meets regularly with the municipal government to monitor the program.
- After final approval of the annual budget by participatory budgeting delegates, the mayor sends it to the municipal legislative chambers to be approved. The legislative branch can block specific projects.
- A year-end report is published detailing implementation of public works and programs.
- Regional or neighborhood committees are established to monitor the design and implementation of policy projects.

The rules of participatory budgeting were designed to produce specific outcomes, such as engaged deliberation, social justice, and active citizens.

New institutions and policies often produce unintended consequences that have the potential to pervert the institution's original intent, however, as the political science and public administration literature documents (table 1.1).

The participatory budgeting defines the division of responsibilities between government and citizens (figure 1.1). It also includes lists of tasks that need to be accomplished at each phase of the process.

TABLE 1.1 Desired Outcomes and Unintended Consequences of Participatory Budgeting

Rule	Desired outcome	Undesirable potential consequence
Establish district boundaries.	Improved efficiency, accountability, and decentralization; intradistrict competition over resources	Meetings at the district level may limit the formation of citywide CSO networks. Small groups within the district may be unable to mobilize sufficient numbers to secure projects.
Conduct year-long series of meetings.	Higher level of participation, which produces greater deliberation and potential for empowering citizens	Mobilization becomes an end in itself to secure resources; participation becomes inattentive, as people attend meetings with the sole purpose of voting for specific policy proposals.
Create Quality of Life Index.	Increased allocation of resources to low-income districts; increased participation as citizens compete within each region	Poor neighborhoods are not uniformly distributed, so small, marginalized populations may not receive benefits. Well-organized groups benefit at the expense of poorly organized and small groups, discouraging participation among citizens unlikely to receive funding.
Conduct "bus caravan of priorities."	Increased solidarity and knowledge about proposed projects	Delegates lack basic skills to evaluate need and may be swayed by passionate appeals.
Have elected representatives vote on final projects.	Smaller number of projects allows qualified participants to directly participate in decision making	Process can become dominated by community leaders rather than citizens.

(continued)

TABLE 1.1 (*continued*)

Rule	Desired outcome	Undesirable potential consequence
Elect municipalwide council.	Direct negotiation between small body of citizens and government officials/legislators, to reduce inefficiencies, enhance quality of debate, and make difficult decisions	Small group of community leaders may use their access to government officials to promote their own interests, creating a new type of political actor who may not be accountable to base of support.
Have government provide participants with detailed financial information.	Education of public on financial information	Participants are dependent on government for information.
Form neighborhood committees to monitor participatory budgeting.	Transparency, accountability	Participants are dependent on government for information.

Source: Author.

Selecting projects

The first round of participatory budgeting, which typically runs from March to June, involves the distribution of information, the initial discussion of policies, and the determination of the number of elected representatives (table 1.2). Mobilization in neighborhood meetings is high, because turnout determines the number of elected representatives from each neighborhood to the regional meetings. Because final votes are taken at the regional level, a larger number of elected representatives (citizen-delegates) from a neighborhood increases its likelihood of having a project selected.

Meetings at the regional and neighborhood levels tend to be about two hours long. The first part of the meeting provides an opportunity for participants to inform their colleagues of upcoming events and issues of concern. The second part of the meeting is a formal presentation of participatory budgeting–related information by government officials. The last part of the meeting is dedicated to a question and answer session, in which participants ask government representatives to clarify their concerns. Participants are generally limited to three minutes to speak or ask questions. The three-minute

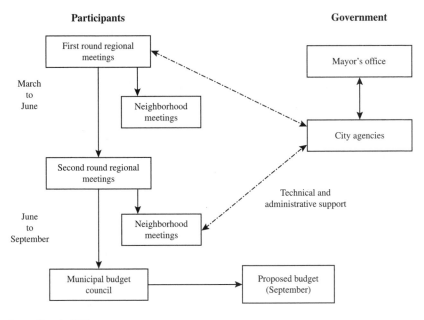

Source: Wampler 2000.

FIGURE 1.1 Annual Participatory Budgeting Cycle

TABLE 1.2 Roles of Government and Participants during the First Round of the Participatory Budgeting Process (March–June)

Government's role	Participants' role
Regional meetings	
Draw district and subdistrict boundaries.	Mobilize citizens.
Prepare Quality of Life Index.	Hold capacity-building meetings.
Distribute financial information.	Analyze financial information.
Present projects it wants participants to approve.	Hold preliminary discussions of available resources.
Neighborhood meetings	
Provide detailed technical information.	Discuss priorities for municipality.
Provide administrative support to participants (access to telephones, photocopiers).	Discuss specific public works.
Establish meeting places and times.	Preselect public works.

Source: Author.

time limits help to keep the meeting moving along. Deliberation over priorities and projects occurs informally, as participants analyze the probable level of resources for their region and begin negotiating with one another over proposed projects. Citizen delegates are not paid for their participation, although some municipalities provide bus fare to offset the transportation costs.

The second round of the process defines the policies and projects that the government will implement in the coming fiscal year (or even two years) (table 1.3). By this stage, participants should have acquired sufficient information to promote the priorities of their communities and to make decisions at the regional meetings. Final decisions on specific public works projects or the definition of general social priorities are made at the regional meetings.

Distribution of resources is based on two criteria. The first is the Quality of Life Index. Each region receives a specific percentage of the budget depending on its overall need. Wealthier regions with more advanced infrastructure receive a smaller percentage than poorer regions with less formal infrastructure. The goal is to ensure that the limited resources available are spent in the poorest neighborhoods and on the most vulnerable sections of the population. Democracies tend to favor organized groups, with middle- and upper-income groups having the greatest advantages. Participatory

TABLE 1.3 Roles of Government and Participants during the Second Round of the Participatory Budgeting Process (July–November)

Government's role	Participants' role
Regional meetings	
Draft initial cost estimates for proposed projects.	Debate proposed policies or public works.
Distribute information and arrange a "bus caravan of priorities" in each district.	Visit proposed public works projects.
Monitor vote.	Vote on policies or public works to be implemented.
Oversee Municipal Budget Council.	Elect two representatives from each region to Municipal Budget Council.
Neighborhood meetings	
Have technical staff work closely with oversight committees.	Continue to mobilize citizens on behalf of projects and policies.
Draft technical plans.	Elect oversight committees; approve technical plans.

Source: Author.

budgeting allows individuals and groups to compete against other groups that have similar means.

The mobilization and deliberation processes within the region represent the second criterion for the distribution of resources. Organized groups compete, mobilize, negotiate, and deliberate within their own regions over available resources. Because all projects cannot be supported, groups form alliances to promote particular projects. The "bus caravan of priorities" is a key part of this process, as participants must visit the sites of proposed projects in order to personally evaluate the level of need.

Implementing projects

While most attention focuses on the selection of policies, an important aspect of participatory budgeting is the implementation of the selected projects. Implementation is an ongoing process. Some projects can be implemented during the subsequent year; larger projects may take several years to implement.

One of the important reforms associated with successful participatory budgeting programs is that participatory budgeting projects are implemented through a regularized, bureaucratic process. Administrative procedures are followed, replacing the direct intervention of politicians into bureaucracies. Participants have a reduced role in this process, although they do take part in oversight meetings to ensure that the policies are being implemented according to previously established criteria (table 1.4).

In Belo Horizonte, for example, regional committees must approve all technical plans. These committees also oversee that the public works are implemented according to the approved technical plans. Neighborhood

TABLE 1.4 Roles of Government and Participants during Project Implementation

Government's role	Participants' role
Prepare technical plans, contracts, and so forth.	Approve technical plans.
Integrate administrative agencies.	Monitor order of project implementation.
Have technical staff work closely with oversight committees.	Monitor project implementation (on site).
Oversee Municipal Budget Council.	Have delegates attend weekly meeting of Municipal Budget Council.

Source: Author.

committees monitor on-site construction projects, helping to ensure that public works are implemented according to the established criteria. This is a crucial part of the process, as it diminishes the likelihood of overt corruption. It is telling that in the city of Recife, where participatory budgeting has had moderate successes, the oversight committees are weak. Effective and independent monitoring committees have not been supported by the government, restricting the ability of citizens to monitor the quality of the work.

State of the Debate

The attention of scholars on participatory budgeting programs has been associated largely with two broad areas of analysis: the factors that lead to the initiation of participatory budgeting programs and the effects participatory budgeting has generated. The debate on initiation of participatory budgeting programs has focused on the innovation (1989–96) and diffusion (1997–2004) phases.

The innovation phase has been studied most intensely in Porto Alegre, Brazil. Abers (1998, 2000) argues that synergy between government officials and civil society leaders in Porto Alegre allowed them to create an institution that served both of their interests (see also Baierle 1998; Torres and Grazia 2003). Baiocchi (2003a, 2003b) places greater emphasis on the role of the leftist Workers' Party as the "instigator" of the program, but he recognizes that CSOs played a fundamental role. A third line of analysis suggests that the formation of a broader civil society during the 1980s led to the formation of new strategies and tactics by CSOs (Wampler and Avritzer 2004). Through the formation of "participatory publics," citizens learned to deliberate and press for new institutional formats, which were most likely to be implemented when the CSOs aligned themselves with elected governments (Baierle 1998; Wampler and Avritzer 2004). The differences among scholars relate largely to the weight and importance they place on CSOs and government actors.

While there is broad consensus on the reasons for adoption during the first phase of participatory budgeting programs, the debate on the diffusion of participatory budgeting programs is at a preliminary stage, due to the paucity of data and the relatively recent need for this type of analysis. The 2003 study by Torres and Grazia represents the first effort to collect similar sets of data on cases in Brazil. The evidence demonstrates that the basic social and political characteristics of municipalities that implement participatory budgeting have changed since the original set of 12 cases in 1990. Centrist and conservative political parties now implement more than 40 percent of participatory budgeting cases in Brazil, up from less than

10 percent in 1990. Participatory budgeting is now implemented in all five of Brazil's regions, although it is still concentrated in the south and southeast. While the original cases of participatory budgeting were in municipalities with above-average Human Development Index (HDI) scores, municipalities that had participatory budgeting in 2004 had HDI scores similar to the majority of large Brazilian municipalities.

The second major line of analysis has been to establish the effects of participatory budgeting on participation rates, citizens' and governments' attitudes and behaviors, policy-making outcomes, and social justice. Participation in participatory budgeting meetings gradually increased over time in Belo Horizonte, Ipatinga, Porto Alegre, Recife, and São Paulo, although just 1–4 percent of the population participates (www.ibge.gov.br). Over time, programs have drawn larger numbers of citizens into formalized policy-making venues (table 1.5).

There are several reasonable explanations for the increase in participation rates. One is that citizens affiliated with the governing party participate in higher numbers to support their party. There is some evidence in support of this explanation. In two small Brazilian municipalities, Betim and João de Monlevade, many of the most active leaders were affiliated with or at least sympathetic to the Workers' Party, the party that implemented participatory

TABLE 1.5 Number of Participants in Participatory Budgeting Processes in Selected Cities in Brazil, 1990–2003

Year	Belo Horizonte	Ipatinga	Recife	Porto Alegre	São Paulo
1990	n.a.	630	n.a.	976	n.a.
1991	n.a.	470	n.a.	3,694	n.a.
1992	n.a.	483	n.a.	7,610	n.a.
1993	n.a.	563	n.a.	10,735	n.a.
1994	15,216	572	n.a.	9,638	n.a.
1995	26,823	681	n.a.	11,821	n.a.
1996	36,508	604	30,000	10,148	n.a.
1997	31,795	683	n.a.	11,908	n.a.
1998	19,418	1,533	30,000	13,687	n.a.
1999	21,175	2,136	n.a.	14,776	n.a.
2000	31,369	2,018	30,000	14,408	n.a.
2001	n.a.	5,015	42,800	16,612	34,000
2002	28,124	981	67,100	28,549	55,000
2003	n.a.	2,374	69,500	26,807	80,000

Source: Wampler 2007b; Wampler and Avritzer 2004.
n.a. Not applicable.

budgeting in both municipalities (Nylen 2003b). However, this evidence tells us little about the larger numbers of ordinary participants who do not assume leadership roles. Evidence from Belo Horizonte, Ipatinga, Porto Alegre, Recife, and São Paulo suggests that most participatory budgeting delegates were supportive of leftist political parties (Wampler 2007a).

A second explanation is that participatory budgeting provides new opportunities for the already politically active (Nylen 2002). About half of participants in Belo Horizonte and Betim are single-time participants (table 1.6). If these data are representative of other participatory budgeting programs, the empowerment capacity of the process may be dampened.

Nearly 75 percent of respondents participated only one or two times. This finding is troublesome, because little public learning is likely to occur where few participants remain involved in the process. Wampler's survey of eight participatory budgeting programs indicates that first-time participation rates are higher in more recently established programs (Wampler 2007b). In municipalities in which participatory budgeting has been used since the 1990s, such as Ipatinga or Porto Alegre, participation is high, but a core group of activists participates every year. In places where participatory budgeting has been in place for many years, restrictions are placed on participation by activists, who are allowed to run for office only every second or third year, in order to allow a broader number of people to hold elected office. However, it may be that a small group of activists rotates the positions among themselves.

TABLE 1.6 Frequency of Participation in Participatory Budgeting in Belo Horizonte and Betim, Brazil

Number of times respondent participated	Belo Horizonte		Betim	
	Number of respondents	Percentage of respondents	Number of respondents	Percentage of respondents
Once	526	54.5	92	49.5
Twice	168	17.4	32	17.2
Three times	78	8.1	19	10.2
Four times	70	7.2	13	7.0
More than four times	64	6.6	14	7.5
No response	60	6.2	16	8.6
Total	966	100.0	186	100.0

Source: Nylen 2002.

Demonstration effects, based on deliberation, negotiation, and implementation, may also account for the rise in participation (Wampler and Avritzer 2004). If individual citizens have positive experiences (because their demands are heard or their proposals selected for implementation), they will have incentives to participate again. These incentives are short term, immediate (policy changes), and long term (deliberation and accountability), but they depend, in large part, on the ability of the government to implement projects selected by participants.

Very few eligible citizens participate in participatory budgeting processes. Getting citizens to attend meetings remains difficult, for reasons that plague participation in any public setting. These include the time and financial cost of attending meetings, general apathy, the lack of awareness of participatory budgeting, and the perception of partisanship within the participatory budgeting process. Participatory budgeting has been successful at encouraging participation when municipalities have been able to produce outputs that reflect the decisions made through the process. Citizens are willing to give their time to this process if they believe that the outcomes will benefit them.

Most participatory budgeting programs allow citizens to have a say only on new capital investment expenditures. (Many participatory budgeting programs claim that participants make decisions on the entire budget, but there is little evidence that participants make meaningful decisions outside of discretionary funding.) When analyzing participatory budgeting, it is important to distinguish between proposed spending and actual spending.

Porto Alegre had the lowest annual budget but allocated the largest amount to participatory budgeting—$201 per capita in 1996–98. This figure far exceeded per capita spending in Belo Horizonte ($42) or Recife ($11). Differences in spending are attributable to the financial health of the municipalities, especially debt commitments and personnel expenditures. Porto Alegre cleaned up its finances, allowing more resources to be dedicated to investment spending. Belo Horizonte and Recife spent more on debt and personnel and on investment projects selected outside the participatory budgeting framework.

Spending outcomes are important indicators of the success or failure of a program, because they link the demands of participants to the municipal government's commitment to implementation. Governments that are able to follow through on spending decisions send clear signals to participatory budgeting participants and the larger community that they value the choices made within the participatory budgeting process. Porto Alegre's government was able to meet nearly 100 percent of its commitments (projects are often backlogged, but they are generally completed). In contrast, Recife completed few projects and spent less than 10 percent of the proposed resources. Thus, there are positive demonstration effects in Porto Alegre but few in Recife.

Since participatory budgeting programs are geared toward redistributing public resources, evaluations of participatory budgeting should include an analysis of where resources are spent within the municipality. Such an analysis requires that similar data be produced over a number of years to allow plausible inferences to be made about spending patterns.

Only one study, of Porte Alegre, has measured the distribution of resources within a municipality (Marquetti 2002). This study combines 10 years of participatory budgeting data and 1991 census data to determine if there is a relationship between participatory budgeting investments and lower social indicators.

The results show that participatory budgeting spending in Porto Alegre has indeed been concentrated in the poorer regions of the municipality. Poor regions receive more spending per capita than wealthier regions. This is the most compelling evidence that participatory budgeting is promoting social justice by increasing the investment of municipal resources in lower-income neighborhoods. Marquetti (2002) claims participatory budgeting has had a distributive effect, because Porto Alegre's municipality spent the majority of its investment resources during the 1970s and 1980s in middle-class neighborhoods. He thus infers that participatory budgeting has had a significant redistributive effect.

Types of Participatory Budgeting Programs

Participatory budgeting programs have two main tracks. One track, "participatory budgeting public works," focuses on specific public works projects, which range from the paving of specific streets to the building of day care centers. This track garners the lion's share of citizens' interest, because it involves the distribution of resources to specific projects.

The second track, "participatory budgeting thematics," focuses on general spending policies. These policies focus on more general trends, such as allocating increased spending to a particular type of health care program. These meetings tend to draw better-informed activists, who are more likely to be part of an issue-oriented social movement.

Public Works Programs

Most participatory budgeting programs initially focus on public works; over time discussions broaden to include general social policies. There are several pragmatic reasons why governments initially dedicate their time and energy to specific projects.

First, the focus on specific public works establishes a direct connection between participation and outcomes. When participants select a specific project, an expectation is created that the government will implement it. When the government successfully implements selected projects, it reinforces the notion that participation in participatory budgeting is a valuable tool for promoting change (Wampler 2004b; Wampler and Avritzer 2004). The government of Porto Alegre, for example, has established a track record of implementing participatory budgeting projects within two to three years. Participants know that decisions they make will result in government action. The government's efforts have helped stimulate accountability in Porto Alegre because participants believe the government will fulfill its promises.

Second, the focus on specific public works represents an effort to allow communities to define their own development. The underlying assumption is that citizens understand their own problems better than government officials and will therefore be able to match proposed public works to their needs. By giving citizens the power to select public works, participatory budgeting programs contribute to the decentralization of the decision-making process. Many neighborhood groups first propose small projects and then expand the range and size of their demands over time. For example, a neighborhood association might initially work for street paving but later make demands for housing projects or the establishment of health centers. Public learning occurs, especially when the government successfully implements participatory budgeting projects, as delegates begin to strategize about how to receive additional (and often larger) projects.

Third, local governments are often responsible for small infrastructure projects (in wealthier cities, governments can sometimes also tackle major infrastructure projects, such as housing). In countries where state or provincial governments provide these services, it may be more appropriate to adopt participatory budgeting at these higher levels of government. Public works have long been a key source of patronage between governments and community leaders. By placing public works at the center of participatory budgeting, it is hoped that the cycle of patronage politics can be broken. Breaking the cycle of patronage entails public discussions of public works, access to technical information, and the eventual implementation of projects. By removing public works from the clientelistic exchange, governments and community leaders hope to generate a new type of politics.

Fourth, focusing on specific public works allows participants to gain a better understanding of what authority and responsibility the municipal level of government actually has. Participants learn to understand the division of authority, which should aid them in directing their demands to the appropriate level of government. This educates the population and benefits the government, as community leaders gain a better understanding of the government's limited powers. In the municipality of Santo Andre, Brazil, many participants initially raised concerns about violence and police corruption. The government, however, did not have jurisdiction over the police. As participants grew to understand this, they shifted their focus to issues on which the municipal government had the authority and resources to act.

Thematic Programs

The purpose of participatory budgeting thematics is to further democratize the policy-making process by letting citizens establish the general priorities of the municipal government. This encourages participants to analyze and understand the city as a whole rather than concentrate on problems specific to their neighborhood. This process is part of the larger empowerment or "citizenship school" component of participatory budgeting, in which citizens are encouraged to envision and work for broader social change.

Participatory budgeting thematic meetings allow participants to set broad priorities for public policies. The first stage of this process requires that the government provide detailed information on current policies and spending priorities. The second stage is a series of discussions in which participants evaluate the government's priorities. The last stage is the ordering of priorities by participants. To date, participants do not propose and debate their own policies but focus on the government's preexisting policies. For example, participants prioritize the level of spending that should be dedicated to prenatal care or to the eradication of infectious diseases. They do not, for the most part, independently propose new policies. This suggests that citizens work closely with government officials to determine the best ways to spend resources. Governments bring their expertise, and participants signal their policy preferences. When government officials believe strongly in a policy program, they strongly argue its merits to convince participants to support it. There is a fine line between providing information and coercing participants, which governments must tread carefully. Often they cross this line. If there is complicity between government officials and citizens (especially leaders), participatory budgeting runs the risk that participants simply rubberstamp the government's policy positions.

The quality of the meetings and debates varies. Some participants are longtime advocates of particular issues. Their knowledge of other policy issues may be limited. One of the most complicated parts of participatory budgeting as a policy-making process is that citizen participants have low levels of information and knowledge about most policy arenas. Broad policy decisions may be largely acts of rubberstamping, as most participants follow the lead of the most experienced policy advocates or adopt the positions of the government. The fact that citizens with low levels of information and expertise are involved in making important public policy decisions is a clear drawback of participatory budgeting programs.

The key tension within participatory budgeting thematics concerns whether the best-informed political activists try to lead or dominate political discussions. This tension is most acute during the initial years. As a program is consolidated, the average participant's political knowledge should expand.

Is public learning actually occurring? This question lies at the heart of the controversies over participatory budgeting programs. It is not clear whether participants are gaining the information and knowledge necessary to become full-fledged policy advocates or whether their participation is being used to legitimize the policy choices of the government.

Another problem with participatory budgeting is that uninformed citizens may select policies that do not conform to the constraints placed on the government (that is, they may vote to spend more resources than are available). There is a danger that uninformed citizens will make decisions that derail a program (by demanding spending far beyond the capacity of the government, for example). However, most participants seem to be aware that the overall impact of participatory budgeting programs is limited by the revenue and authority constraints the government faces.

Actors and Motivations for Embracing Participatory Budgeting

Political and social actors have different motivations for promoting and participating in participatory budgeting. Motivations range from wanting to have one's own street paved to wanting to create a deliberative public sphere. Both self-interested behavior and community-building behavior (behavior that creates solidarity) can find rewards in participatory budgeting.

Local Governments

Local governments implement participatory budgeting programs to accomplish a variety of aims. These include building a base of political support, achieving a more equitable distribution of scarce resources, fostering public learning, and promoting transparency in government.

By its nature, participatory budgeting is a collaborative effort between citizen participants and government. This makes a strengthened base of popular political support a natural consequence of effective participatory budgeting programs. A reformist government is the most likely to successfully implement participatory budgeting, because of the high level of government support needed. Participatory budgeting programs subvert clientelism by providing open, transparent policy-making processes. Reformist governments gamble that by delegating decision making to citizen participants, they will weaken old clientelistic politics and strengthen their own positions. As participatory budgeting takes place outside government itself, its activities largely bypass the legislature and the multiple patronage networks embedded therein. This is one of the most controversial aspects of participatory budgeting programs: legislators have virtually no role in the policy-making processes.

A second reason why governments adopt participatory budgeting is to try to increase the distribution of resources to low-income neighborhoods. The rules of participatory budgeting promote social justice; the emphasis on participation helps the government build support for redistributing resources among low-income and middle-class groups. Low-income citizens have access to greater levels of resources in participatory budgeting, which allows the government to provide a specific forum to address their needs. Low-income citizens are not competing against middle- and upper-income citizens and groups in their efforts to secure desperately needed services and public works.

A third reason why governments adopt participatory budgeting is that mobilizing citizens provides opportunities to change their political and social consciousness. The lack of political knowledge about government, policy making, and rights among most low-income Brazilians is an obstacle that reformist governments believe limits social change. Governments will implement participatory budgeting if they believe that improving the quality of citizens' political knowledge is an integral part of a more expansive effort to reform political, social, and economic structures. Many citizens in the developing world lack basic information on the responsibilities and authority of different levels of government; governments use participatory budgeting as a means to provide them with these basic tools.

A fourth reason why governments adopt participatory budgeting is to promote transparency, in the hope of reducing corruption and bureaucratic inefficiencies. Participatory budgeting may reduce corruption by increasing the number of citizens that monitor the distribution of resources. Where corruption is rampant, reformist governments use multiple public meetings and oversight committees to reduce the likelihood of corruption. In Ipatinga and Porto Alegre, all participatory budgeting projects are assigned tracking numbers. Any interested citizen can use a computer terminal at a municipal government office to check the status of a project and verify if resources have been spent as promised.

Individual Citizens

Citizens have many incentives to participate in participatory budgeting programs. First, participatory budgeting increases their access to public decision-making activities. Public meetings and decision-making processes reduce the likelihood that overt, clientelistic means will be used to distribute goods. This is an obvious benefit to citizens who did not gain from clientelism under previous government regimes. The public nature of meetings empowers some citizens to speak out for the first time. This general sense of empowerment is strengthened even further if citizens can draw a direct connection between their participation efforts and policy outcomes.

A second important incentive for citizens is that they gain access to information. Informational meetings provide citizens with a broader understanding of government, governmental responsibility, policy, and policy making. Budgets and policy making are often viewed as "black boxes" in which inputs and outputs are unknown to all but a handful of government officials. Participatory budgeting programs provide a structure for citizens to gain the necessary information to develop a better understanding of their political and administrative environments. In addition to budgetary information, citizens gain access to technical information about subjects such as zoning and land-use laws. The complex sets of rules involved in these issues are often beyond the reach of the average citizen. Participatory budgeting programs offer the opportunity for citizens to work with officials in the bureaucracy to resolve legal and technical problems.

A third benefit of participatory budgeting for citizens is the direct relationship between participation and the quality of services provided. Citizens select public works, directly shaping their neighborhoods. They approve technical plans, for the installation of sewer systems or the construction of new housing units, as well as oversee project implementation. In Belo Horizonte all technical plans must be presented to neighborhood forums. After discussion and clarifications, which may require the plan to be redrawn, the neighborhood forum must approve the plan. This helps ensure that contractors provide the goods and services they promised. This process is widely believed to improve the quality of services, because it reduces the likelihood that contractors will try to cheat on their contracts.

Civil Society Organizations

The primary incentive for CSOs, such as social movements or neighborhood groups, to participate in participatory budgeting is indirect. Since one of the criteria for the distribution of goods is the number of citizens who attend meetings, the more citizens CSOs are able to mobilize, the more goods and resources their neighborhood is likely to receive. A relationship between mobilization and outcomes is established, strengthening the importance of CSOs.

A second reason why CSOs participate is that participatory budgeting programs provide them with the opportunity to build broader networks of supporters. Participation provides CSOs with contact with potential allies, increasing opportunities to build broader social and political coalitions. Since many of the specific demands negotiated within participatory budgeting originated from associations around basic issues (housing or sewage problems), it is incumbent upon the associations to negotiate with other associations. One of the drawbacks of participatory budgeting, discussed below, is that there is an increased potential for competition among CSOs. Rather than create bonds of solidarity, contact can heighten conflict.

A third reason why CSOs participate is to influence policies. Neighborhood associations shape the neighborhood's infrastructure. Associations work with government technocrats and NGO specialists to design development plans. Issue-oriented social movements participate in participatory budgeting to shape broader public policy. The process gives them the opportunity to work with government officials to influence short-term funding as well as long-term planning. The close working relationship provides issue-based social movements with many opportunities to influence policy outcomes. Of course, this relationship may not be wholly positive for the CSOs. Closer ties to the state have the potential to drastically alter the character and goals of the social movements. This is a tension that government officials and CSOs are continually forced to address.

Nongovernmental Organizations

Participatory budgeting programs provide a mechanism for NGOs to work with citizens and government to tackle pressing social problems. In some municipalities, NGOs play a direct role, sitting on a governing or oversight board or acting as mediator between the government and participants. When NGOs play a direct role in the process, they tend to promote citizen empowerment and transparency in government.

In other municipalities, NGOs act in an advisory role, providing support to participants. Many NGOs have staffs of professionals with strong technical and administrative skills. Architects, accountants, social workers, and other specialists are able to understand policy proposals and their implications more easily that the average citizen. The NGOs' distance from government gives them the opportunity to promote the general values of participatory budgeting while keeping an eye on government to guarantee that it is working for the citizens. One NGO in Porto Alegre, Cidade, publishes a monthly report on participatory budgeting for citizen-delegates and citizens in general. It monitors spending and policy decisions, acting as a watchdog as well as an advocate of the participatory budgeting program.

NGOs also play a prominent role in the initial empowerment or learning meeting. Because of their skill and experience in public education, NGOs are often contracted by government to provide this service. This can create a certain tension between NGOs and participants, because it blurs the role of the NGO.

Business Community

The business community may support participatory budgeting programs because these programs promote transparency, reduce corruption, and increase efficiency. While participatory budgeting programs do not inherently or necessarily involve fiscal reform, the increased attention on the budget often leads the government to take better care of the city's financial health. Better financial health is an indirect consequence of participatory budgeting programs.

Within the business community, some contractors and builders benefit directly. The selection of projects and the systematic ordering of the projects' implementation allow contractors to bid in an open and fair system. Small contractors benefit, because many of the projects selected through the participatory budgeting process tend to be small. Contractors no longer pay kickbacks and bribes to ensure that their projects will actually be funded and implemented. Instead, the timing and ordering of the projects become part of the public record. Of course, businesses that benefited from closed and corrupt practices are not enthusiastic about participatory budgeting.

When participatory budgeting programs are consolidated as the principal policy-making method, business associations must participate in order to secure funding for projects. A neighborhood business association that wants to have streets paved or lighting installed, for example, would have to organize its members to attend meetings to press their demands.

Administrative Reform

While the reform of bureaucracy was not initially considered to be a vital element of participatory budgeting programs, it has emerged as an unintended consequence that strongly influences the success of the process. Participatory budgeting contributes to administrative reform in three ways.

The first is by decentralizing the administration. This tends to start with the physical decentralization of the municipal administration, as branch or regional offices are established. Branch offices provide citizens direct and easy access to government and administrative officials. This is especially important in outlying neighborhoods, where the poorest residents tend to live. Meetings are held at the neighborhood level rather than in the city center, which makes it easier for citizens to overcome time and financial costs long identified as barriers to participation.

The decentralization of decision-making venues is also an important step. Decisions are no longer made by a small group of political and technical elites located within the confines of the city government but in public forums at the local level. This provides citizens with unprecedented access to professional and technocratic bureaucrats. Citizens are able to work with these bureaucrats to navigate the complex world of policy making.

Decentralization allows for targeted information to be provided to relevant groups. Through the branch offices, technocrats develop better ideas of the types of information participants need to make informed choices. For example, citizens who live in a mountainous region may need information about drainage and water flows; citizens in the urban center may require information about the costs and complexities of overhauling decaying infrastructure.

The second way in which participatory budgeting contributes to administrative reform is by integrating different bureaucratic units into the policy-making and implementation processes. Administrative agencies, such as the departments of health or education, cannot operate as isolated units within the participatory budgeting process. They must work closely with the planning agency and with participatory budgeting participants to define their policy agendas. New investments cannot generally be undertaken without the explicit approval of participatory budgeting participants. This requires different departments to work with community leaders to design projects. City agencies must work together to coordinate the timing of projects to ensure that they are completed in the most efficient method possible. This requires coordination over a number of years to ensure that drainage, paving, housing, and other projects are implemented according to the plans designed by urban planners and participatory budgeting participants.

Within the government there must be a concerted effort by politicians and bureaucrats to implement the selected projects. Government officials must gain control of the bureaucracy to ensure, for example, that technical plans are drafted, contracts are prepared, and implementation occurs according to established schedules. This intensive, hands-on process was not anticipated by participatory budgeting's founders, but it has helped revitalize and reform existing bureaucratic structures.

The third important component of administrative reform is the creation of a more transparent relationship between the business community and the government. Participatory budgeting establishes projects that will be implemented over a two- or three-year period. Contractors and builders know which projects will be implemented and are able to plan more efficiently. The fact that bribes no longer have to be paid to have a project implemented reduces the cost of business, increases profit margins, and fosters governmental credibility.

Limitations of Participatory Budgeting

Several limitations to participatory budgeting programs reduce its overall impact on social justice, public learning, and administrative reform. While there are important differences in how participatory budgeting programs function in different municipalities and states, the limitations discussed below appear to be present in most cases. These limitations suggest that participatory budgeting programs have a moderate capacity to challenge social and political exclusion while promoting social justice. Participatory budgeting programs are an important step toward political inclusion and greater social justice, but they are by no means a magic bullet.

The first limitation stems from the focus on specific public works, which diminishes the impact of the public learning or empowerment sessions. Many participants are less interested in learning about rights, the fiscal responsibility of the government, or broader social policies than they are in obtaining a small infrastructure project.

This is the principal Catch-22 of participatory budgeting. Participatory budgeting programs flourish when citizens discover that the specific decisions they make in regional meetings will be implemented. The message is clear: the government values your time and energy. While this seems to be a necessary first step to encourage participation, it associates participatory budgeting programs with the distribution of specific goods. After improvements are made, the community organization stops participating. The community receives the desired public good, which was the reason they originally organized. Participants immediately exit the program and demonstrate little interest in working with it. In such a case, public learning is low and participation is geared toward short-term and instrumental ends; participants are not engaged in public learning processes but focused on how they can secure specific resources for their community.

A second limitation is the dependence of participants on the mayor's office. While participatory budgeting programs directly incorporate civil society actors in the policy-making process, the government remains the principal actor. It organizes meetings, provides information, ensures that bureaucrats meet with citizens, and guarantees that selected policies will be implemented. The influence of the mayor and the governing coalition is substantial.

The lack of a strong commitment to participatory budgeting by government leaders makes it difficult for participatory budgeting programs to succeed. In Recife, for example, the mayor began to use participatory budgeting as a means to distribute public monies for the yearly carnival. Instead of holding open, transparent meetings, he manipulated the release of funds so that "friendly" participants would benefit. Nonparticipating citizens and "unfriendly" citizen-delegates did not have access to the public resources. Participatory budgeting participants expressed concern that if they did not act a certain way they would be "boycotted" by the government. This does little to empower citizens and may just be a new form of clientelism.

A third limitation concerns the role of long-term planning. Many participatory budgeting participants are interested in securing short- to medium-term public works projects. The focus on specific public works makes it more difficult to generate discussions on planning for the future of the city. Several municipal governments have tried to stimulate discussions and develop long-term plans, but the results have been limited. The complexity of the issues involved requires that citizens have substantial technical and analytical skills to weigh different arguments. Participatory budgeting programs slowly build these skills, but it may take years for participants to develop a grasp of the complexities of the proposed solutions.

A fourth limitation is the emphasis on local issues and local public policies. Many participants, including experienced political and social activists, spend their time and energy on the intricacies of local public policies. This reduces the amount of time they are able to dedicate to regional, national, or global problems. While participants dedicate their efforts to securing changes in local public policies, the principal problems their communities face are often related to unemployment, violence, or the lack of educational opportunities. Participatory budgeting does not provide the opportunity for participants to challenge the underlying reasons for their social and economic exclusion. In Recife many active participatory budgeting participants devoted 5–10 hours a week to participatory budgeting. But when asked what the major problem in their neighborhood was, they responded "unemployment." The participants, mainly women, worked in participatory budgeting in the hope that they could improve the day-to-day conditions of their neighborhoods, but their greatest concerns focused on broader socioeconomic change that was far beyond the scope of participatory budgeting.

Citizens and governments hope that a participatory budgeting program will increase awareness of the broader, global social problems that affect Brazil's urban poor. There are, however, no guarantees that participants will make the leap from addressing their communities' lack of basic infrastructure to understanding and challenging the broader socioeconomic forces that shape their lives. While this is obviously much to ask of participatory budgeting participants, it is clearly the goal of the governments and the most active participants.

Finally, there is the danger that participatory budgeting programs may be manipulated due to the central role played by the mayor's office. If city agencies, bureaucrats, or elected officials wish, they may try to use participatory budgeting programs to advance their own agendas. Nondisclosure of key information, the lack of implementation of selected public policies, or the weakening of citizen oversight committees are all potential ways that the program can be manipulated. Some participatory budgeting programs in Brazil at the municipal and state levels have been rejected by social movements and NGOs due to the government's interference.

How and Where Can Participatory Budgeting Be Implemented?

Can participatory budgeting programs be implemented by governments in other countries? Can the idea be adopted in other regions of the world? Government officials contemplating adopting participatory budgeting should ask themselves a few questions:

- Is there sufficient discretionary funding to allow citizens to select specific public works?
- Can participatory budgeting programs be used to increase tax collection?
- Is the government prepared to delegate authority to citizens?

- Will participatory budgeting programs subvert traditional patronage networks? Does the government want to do so?
- Can participatory budgeting help the government establish new bases of political support?
- Is the government willing to try to reform the local bureaucracy?
- How viable is delegating decision-making authority along political and administrative lines?

At the heart of any consideration must be the viability of the delegation of decision-making authority along political and administrative lines. Participatory budgeting is a cumbersome process that often takes several years to run relatively smoothly. If a government faces intense political pressures from other political parties or the media, the cumbersome and public nature of participatory budgeting may exacerbate governability problems. Governments must have sufficient political flexibility to engage citizens in an innovative policy-making process. Furthermore, the government must have the resources and capacity to reform the bureaucracy so that the program will actually be implemented according to the established rules.

Financial flexibility and independence is a second issue to be considered. For example, do Mexican municipalities or Indian states have enough independent financial resources to incorporate citizens directly into the policy-making process? If a government has few financial resources or little flexibility, it should consider how a focus on financial and budgetary issues will affect its overall political agenda. If the government lacks financial autonomy, can it use a type of participatory budgeting to have citizens help prioritize some types of social spending? In this case, a participatory budgeting program could be used as an educational tool rather than as a means to allocate scarce resources.

When governments are unable or unwilling to implement participatory budgeting programs, NGOs can play a vital role, by disseminating information and monitoring government spending. NGOs have played an important role in promoting participatory budgeting programs throughout Brazil. They can work with governments to implement participatory budgeting programs, or they can set up parallel monitoring programs.

One initial challenge is to engage social movements and NGOs on seemingly arcane issues of taxation, representation, and more efficient policy making. Before the implementation of a participatory budgeting program, it would be helpful if civil society activists begin to question how public resources are being used and how they could be used. The first step would be to focus on the budget and social spending.

While there is no set or minimum level of civil society activism neces-sary to establish a participatory budgeting program, the program is more likely to flourish if there are networks of citizens and CSOs that will strongly support it. During the founding phase, many of the initial participants tend to be political activists. Higher levels of participation help legitimize a government's reform efforts. Preexisting networks often lay the foundations for progressive governments and citizens to support innovative policy-making forums.

Previous experiences with decentralization may make bureaucrats more amenable to accepting administrative reforms. Governments must be able to reform the bureaucracy so that it will be open, transparent, and oriented toward citizens. When citizens participate in the policy-making process, bureaucrats lose some of their power. If local government has discretionary resources available, it is more likely that it can embark on a participatory budgeting program. Local governments need to have control over their own finances in order to implement a reform policy of this type.

Policy Implications

The results of participatory budgeting programs vary widely. While many participatory budgeting programs, especially those in initial stages of devel-opment, have had mixed results, programs that have endured for more than five years have spawned important changes. To examine the most significant policy implications, it is necessary to return to the three central tenets of participatory budgeting: public learning and active citizenship, social justice, and administrative reform.

Participatory Budgeting Increases Public Learning and Promotes Active Citizenship

Participation in participatory budgeting programs tends to increase over time. Citizen participation steadily rises, with significant jumps often occur-ring after the third year. Participation rises more quickly when the govern-ment commits significant support and resources to participatory budgeting. Participation appears to rise because citizens realize that there is a direct con-nection between the time they dedicate to participatory budgeting and changes in policy outcomes. Citizens who did not initially participate are drawn into the process as it becomes clear that the principal way to secure public works or changes in broader social policies is through participatory budgeting. In Belo Horizonte and Porto Alegre, participatory budgeting was expanded to include projects and programs that would attract the middle class. In Belo Horizonte political activists who had long favored clientelism had to retool their political strategies to provide resources for their neighborhoods. Traditional political organizers could no longer rely on clientelism but had to mobilize and deliberate in new ways.

Participatory budgeting programs act as "citizenship schools." The first stage of the participatory budgeting process, at the beginning of the yearly budgetary cycle, consists mainly of information meetings. These meetings provide governments, NGOs, and the most well-informed activists the opportunity to discuss matters pertaining to the budget, government authority and responsibility, taxation, and citizenship rights (social, political, and civil). New citizens are inundated with information, while longtime participants sharpen their own understandings. This is where NGOs play a large role, working with longtime participants to improve their political strategies while providing help to new participants.

Citizenship rights play an important role because participatory budgeting participants address issues of government authority and citizens' duties. Participants, especially citizens with a long history of political activism, draw on the rights guaranteed by the 1988 Brazilian Constitution to support their arguments during the negotiation stages. During the initial "empowerment" meetings, participants are taught about their rights, their duties as citizens, and the responsibility of the government. The extension of citizenship rights, governments and participants assert, depends on the strengthening of community ties and the dismantling of the entrenched social, political, and economic positions that separate individuals in many developing countries. Participatory budgeting programs provide an opportunity for citizens to forge solidarity bonds based on the similarity of their demands. Community ties, between groups and individuals, may be strengthened as the programs enable them to address their problems and look for collective solutions. If citizen demands for rights are one of the bedrocks of democracy, then participatory budgeting is helping strengthen the consolidation of democracy.

The "bus caravan trip" is one of the best examples of this effort. Representatives from each neighborhood visit all proposed public works within their region so that they can personally evaluate the social need for a proposed project. Participatory budgeting delegates are known to change their positions when they visit a project site where social needs appear much greater than at sites of other proposed projects. When the bonds of solidarity are emphasized and promoted, the participatory budgeting program fosters a stronger sense of community.

Participatory budgeting gives traditionally excluded citizens the opportunity to voice their demands in a formal public sphere. The legitimization of their demands and the ability (right) to raise contentious issues in a public arena are important steps forward in breaking down rigid social hierarchies.

Participatory Budgeting Promotes Social Justice

The resources allocated through the participatory budgeting program tend to be implemented in low-income areas. Neighborhoods or subregions with lower levels of infrastructure and higher poverty rates receive more resources than better-off subregions. The Quality of Life Index, based on income, education, physical infrastructure, and social services provided, forms the basis for the distribution of resources. It guarantees that the poorer regions of a city receive more resources than better-off neighborhoods. The division of resources along regional and subregional lines is an effective instrument for redistributing resources to low-income and underserviced neighborhoods. Participatory budgeting helps distribute wealth to poorer areas of a municipality, and it allows the poorest members of the community to decide how to spend resources in their community.

Between 1996 and 2003, the participatory budgeting program in Porto Alegre spent $400 million on projects selected by participants (Wampler 2007b). The vast majority of these resources went to underserviced and poorer districts. While it is impossible to establish precisely the volume of resources allocated to low-income areas, it is possible to document that the poorest regions of Porto Alegre received funding that had not been previously available. It is also possible to confirm that low-income neighborhoods in Belo Horizonte received more resources than did middle- and upper-income neighborhoods. Low-income neighborhoods also received more than they had traditionally received. The policy implication is clear: when participatory budgeting programs function well, they affect the lives of lower-income individuals and communities.

A second way in which participatory budgeting programs promote social justice is through the development of thematic decision-making bodies. Citizens concerned with the lack of health care services or poor quality education can express their demands in participatory budgeting forums. The debates may lead the government to allocate more resources to the underserviced areas.

Evidence suggests that governments that are already dedicated to spending more resources in poorer neighborhoods implement participatory budgeting programs. It is not clear whether the increase in social spending stems from the participatory budgeting program or the political ideology of the progressive government. While it is impossible to separate the political agenda of a reformist government from the workings of participatory budgeting, participatory budgeting programs tend to co-exist with significant changes in social spending. Participatory budgeting helps the government make better allocation decisions in substantive policy areas.

Social justice is also achieved by means of more efficient and community-oriented policies. Less corruption, fostered by transparent processes, helps ensure that public resources will be used more effectively. More efficient use of public resources most directly affects poor and low-income citizens, as a greater number of projects can be implemented. These projects often have an immediate impact on the quality of life for a neighborhood or an underserviced policy arena. The policy implication is clear: participatory budgeting helps promote transparent processes that reduce government corruption and waste. Highlighting budgetary issues within participatory budgeting creates a spillover effect, as parts of the budget that fall outside the purview of participatory budgeting also come under increased scrutiny.

Finally, social justice is advanced through the entrance of traditionally excluded groups and citizens into vital decision-making venues. While this is not a material benefit directly linked to social justice, the creation of this institutional sphere provides low-income citizens with the opportunity to address their political and social demands in a formal environment. Traditionally excluded citizens have the opportunity and right to participate in new decision-making venues. Their decisions and their votes result in specific changes in their communities. Being granted the opportunity to make decisions that shape their lives and the lives of their fellow citizens is an extraordinarily empowering process for low-income and previously excluded citizens.

Participatory Budgeting Spurs Administrative Reform

Implementing new decision-making processes requires changes to the bureaucracy so that implementation conforms to the new criteria. In successful participatory budgeting programs, considerable time and effort are dedicated to decentralizing the government. Officials are appointed to aid the administration of each district. The reorganization of local administrative processes facilitates contact between the government and the population. These officials act as intermediaries between citizens and the technical staff.

In all successful participatory budgeting programs, a substantial effort has been made to develop close contacts between participants and bureaucrats.

Technical information, vital to the implementation of any public works projects, becomes part of the public debate. Citizens need to understand the specific requirements for building a road or installing drainage. This information, traditionally available only to bureaucrats, is provided to citizens so that they can make informed decisions. Clear, rational, and systematic rules for the implementation of projects are also established. This reduces the power of the most powerful or well-entrenched bureaucrats, who are no longer able to manipulate the allocation of public monies. The establishment of a clear set of rules provides all interested parties—citizens, government officials, bureaucrats, businesspeople—with the knowledge that policy decisions made in participatory budgeting's public forums will be translated into actual policy outputs. The implementation process, while not 100 percent transparent, is generally open to any interested citizen. Any citizen can check on the status of a project (planning, bidding, and implementation).

Participatory budgeting encourages government officials to reform local government. Government officials have a vested interest in doing so when they gain positive responses from the voting public, members of their political parties, or national politicians. Instituting a successful participatory budgeting program requires that bureaucrats work with citizens in new ways. There is an incentive to reduce waste and corruption so that additional resources are available for participatory budgeting projects. Governments that are heavily invested in participatory budgeting will also reform their administrative units.

References

Abers, Rebecca. 1998. "From Clientelism to Cooperation: Local Government, Participatory Policy, and Civic Organizing in Porto Alegre, Brazil." *Politics and Society* 26 (4): 511–37.

———. 2000. *Inventing Local Democracy: Grassroots Politics in Brazil.* Boulder, CO: Lynne Rienner.

Avritzer, Leonardo. 2002. *Democracy and the Public Space in Latin America.* Princeton, NJ: Princeton University Press.

Baierle, Sergio. 1998. "The Explosion of Citizenship: The Emergence of a New Ethical-Political Principle in Popular Movements in Porto Alegre, Brazil." In *Cultures of Politics/Politics of Cultures: Re-visioning Latin American Social Movements,* ed. Sonia E. Alvarez, Evelina Dagnino, and Arturo Escobar. Boulder, CO: Westview Press.

Baiocchi, Gianpaolo. 2001. "Participation, Activism, and Politics: The Porto Alegre Experiment and Deliberative Democratic Theory." *Politics and Society* 29 (1): 43–72.

————. 2003a. "Participation, Activism, and Politics: The Porto Alegre Experiment." In *Deepening Democracy: Institutional Innovations in Empowered Participatory Governance*, ed. Archon Fung and Erik Olin Wright. London: Verso.

————. 2003b. *Radicals in Power: The Workers' Party and Experiments in Urban Democracy in Brazil*. London: Zed Books.

Cabannes, Yves. n.d. *Municipal Finance and Participatory Budgeting: Base Document*. Harvard University, Graduate School of Design, Department of Urban Planning and Design, Cambridge, MA.

Marquetti, Adelmir. 2002. "Democracia, equidade e effciencia, o caso do orçamento participativo em Porto Alegre." In *A inovação democratica no Brasil*, ed. Leonardo Avritzer and Zander Navarro. São Paulo: Cortez.

Nylen, William. 2002. "Testing the Empowerment Thesis: The Participatory Budget in Belo Horizonte and Betim, Brazil." *Comparative Politics* 34 (2): 127–45.

————. 2003a. *Participatory Democracy versus Elitist Democracy: Lessons from Brazil*. New York: Palgrave Macmillan.

————. 2003b. "An Enduring Legacy? Popular Participation in the Aftermath of the Participatory Budgets of Joao Monlevade and Betim." In *Radicals in Power: The Workers' Party (PT) and Experiments in Urban Democracy in Brazil*, ed. Gianpaolo Baiocchi. London: Zed Books.

Torres, Ana Clara, and Grazia de Grazia. 2003. *Experiência de orçamento participativo no Brasil: Periodo de 1997 a 2000*. São Paulo: Editora Vozes.

Wampler, Brian. 2000. "A Guide to Participatory Budgeting." Paper presented at the third conference of the International Budget Project, Mumbai, November 4–9. http://www.internationalbudget.org/cdrom/papers/systems/ParticipatoryBudgets/Wampler.pdf.

————. 2002. "Orçamento participativo: Uma explicação para as amplas variações nos resultados." In *A inovação democratica no Brasil*, ed. Leonardo Avritzer and Zander Navarro. São Paulo: Cortez.

————. 2004a. "The Diffusions of Participatory Budgeting across Brazil." Paper presented at the annual meeting of the Latin America Studies Association, Las Vegas, October 7–9.

————. 2004b. "Expanding Accountability through Participatory Institutions: Mayors, Citizens, and Budgeting in Three Brazilian Municipalities." *Latin American Politics and Society* 46 (2): 73–100.

————. 2007a. "Can Participatory Institutions Promote Pluralism? Mobilizing Low-Income Citizens in Brazil." *Studies in Comparative International Development* 41(4): 57–79.

————. 2007b. *Participatory Budgeting in Brazil: Contestation, Cooperation, and Accountability*. University Park, PA: Pennsylvania State University Press.

Wampler, Brian, and Leonardo Avritzer. 2004. "Participatory Publics: Civil Society and New Institutions in Democratic Brazil." *Comparative Politics* 36 (3): 291–312.

————. 2005. "The Spread of Participatory Democracy in Brazil: From Radical Democracy to Participatory Good Government." *Journal of Latin American Urban Studies* 7 (Fall 2005/Winter 2006): 37–52.

2

Citizen Participation in Budgeting: Prospects for Developing Countries

DONALD P. MOYNIHAN

This chapter examines the potential of citizen participation as part of the budgeting process in developing countries. The first section examines why participation is important and assesses the prospects for participation in a developing-country setting. The second section identifies ways of fostering broad and meaningful participation in developing countries, providing examples of participation during different stages of the budget process. The third section examines the perspective that governments have toward participation. The last section summarizes the chapter's main conclusions.

Why Is Participation Important?

To understand the role and importance of participation in budgeting, it is important to understand why participation itself is important. Most arguments in support of participation portray it as a means of improving both the performance and accountability of a bureaucracy that is outdated, unrepresentative, and underperforming (Barber 1986; King, Feltey, and Susel 1998).[1] These arguments appear particularly relevant for developing countries.

Calls for governments to overturn exclusionary bureaucratic conventions rest largely on a normative perspective (Olivo 1998). The democratic ideals celebrated in the normative approach are often vague or implicit, creating "mandates that do not always specify what the participation is intended to achieve" (Kweit and Kweit 1981, p. 8). Such ambiguity prevents the creation of clear standards by which to judge participation efforts and careful reform prescriptions. This section seeks to add some clarity to the normative perspective by presenting a typology of participation goals based on normative values that allow participation efforts to be categorized. This framework is applied to developing countries, using examples of participation during the development of Poverty Reduction Strategy Papers.

Arguments for Participation

The literature on participation catalogues the virtues of civil society and public deliberation of issues (Cooper 1984; Crosby, Kelly, and Schafer 1986; Fox and Miller 1996; Frederickson 1982; Habermas 1989, 1996; Putnam 1993; Stivers 1994). A result is an increased call for direct citizen participation in public decision making (King, Feltey, and Susel 1998). Citizen participation occurs when citizens or their representatives (who are not elected officials) interact with and provide feedback to government at the policy formulation or implementation stage of governance. Four interrelated arguments support the rise of public participation: postmodern discourse theory, disillusionment with bureaucracy, the search for a democratic ideal, and the need for participation in developing countries.

The postmodern argument

Citizen participation is frequently characterized as an inevitable outcome of a logical movement from insulated, bureaucratic modes of governance to more open, transparent, and participatory approaches. Democratic theorists propose that current societal conditions and an understanding of the dynamics of individuals in relation to their governments in liberal democracies make it ever more likely that citizens will seek to involve themselves in public decisions through discourse (Fox and Miller 1996; Maier 1994; Wamsley and Wolf 1996).

One broad rationale underlying such a movement is a shift in citizen values in a "postmodern" age. Cross-time and cross-country surveys provide evidence of a worldwide shift to "postmodern values," including a distrust of formal institutions such as government and political parties and a desire for more participatory democracies (Inglehart 1997). Proposed reasons for the value shift include the increased mobility of individuals, the weakening of the traditional family structure, and the erosion of values that structure produced, including a benevolent view of authority (Kweit and Kweit 1981). Societal change, particularly increased education, leads to greater demand for involvement and access to information (Thomas 1995). Access to information is facilitated by new technologies. Citizens therefore enjoy both the will and the means to break the monopoly and centralized control over public information enjoyed by the government (Cleveland 1985). Given these changes, the isolated hierarchical structures of the traditional bureaucratic form appear increasingly out of step with the societies they serve. Many of these societal changes are more clearly apparent in richer countries, but there are additional rationales for looking to participation in the developing setting as well.

Disillusionment with bureaucracy

Disillusionment with the traditional governance model of hierarchical bureaucracies and insulated public servants and a belief that participation checks administrative power have spurred interest in participatory processes. For many years the Weberian hierarchical-bureaucratic model has been attacked from various sides as lacking responsiveness. Bureaucratic organizations have proved unable to create an inclusive relationship with the citizenry (Zajac and Bruhn 1999). The value of bureaucracy stems from its expertise, which puts it in conflict with the democratic or representative values that underpin the idea of participation.

Popular unease with the perceived growth in government and acknowledgment of the discretionary authority of bureaucracies gave rise to a search for alternative modes of democratic accountability and bureaucratic control. One of the main alternative models of governance is the participatory model, which involves the "search for more political, democratic, and collective mechanisms for sending signals to government" (Peters 1996, p. 47).

Public participation operates as an external check on bureaucracies, whose power grew in the twentieth century. Recent proposals for participation appear equally distrustful of bureaucrats and elected officials, both of which are part of the "representative bureaucracy" (Barber 1986). According to this view, "representative bureaucracy" undermines individual responsibility for beliefs, values, and actions and is incompatible with freedom, because it delegates and alienates political will. In place of "representative bureaucracy," advocates of participation support the development of "strong democracy," characterized by increased citizen participation (Barber 1986). Local governments are particularly suited to this model. As Peters (1996, p. 58) notes, "Local governments, by their very size, make participation more meaningful. Moreover, local governments tend to use more mechanisms that permit direct citizen involvement than do national or regional governments . . . in ways that would probably be impractical for national governments."

The search for the democratic ideal

The idealistic nature of the goals of participation, particularly the yearning for the democratic ideal, explains much of its appeal. Minimalist treatments of participation (for example, Easton 1990) emphasize the importance of participation in preventing popular alienation from government and maintaining the stability of the political system. A more active approach, typical of normative theory, shows greater concern for participation that produces benefits to citizens and offers them the chance to fulfill the "democratic wish" to exert real influence on the governing process (Morone 1998). These ideals are closely associated with the fulfillment of citizen rights in a democratic society.

Support for democratic ideals appears to have grown with the rise of postmodern values. Such ideals are often considered in abstract terms and tend to evoke affective rather than cognitive responses from individuals. Any form of citizenship beyond simple legal status requires active citizen involvement in public matters and the community (Cooper 1984). Participation serves to establish the worth of individual citizens, allowing them to feel a sense of ownership and take an active part in controlling their surroundings and developing their capacity to act as citizens (King and Stivers 1998; Kweit and Kweit 1981). The process of public deliberation is expected to generate benefits not only to individuals but also to society, in terms of democratic legitimacy and a deliberative political culture (Habermas 1996).

The needs of developing countries

Many of the arguments presented so far are abstract. But in developing countries the need for participation is very real. Participation is particularly important because it fosters good governance, promotes transparency, increases social justice by involving the poor and excluded, and helps individuals become better citizens.

PARTICIPATION FOSTERS GOOD GOVERNANCE. Poorer countries desperately need accountability and competent performance; participation is one way to achieve these goals. Proponents of participation in richer countries share a disappointment with representative government. In poorer countries criticism of the status quo is more pertinent. Proponents of participation in poorer countries point to corruption, opaque resource allocation, the failure to deliver basic services, and a power structure that offers nonelites little opportunity to have their views heard. The criticism of representative government in many poor countries is not so much that it has failed to promote citizen involvement but that it has failed to meet its basic responsibilities. A failure to govern in an open, competent, and predictable fashion has also stymied economic development.

Some scholars (such as Lynn 2002) argue that participation undermines institutions of representative government. Such claims are less convincing in the developing-country context, where citizen involvement can force comparison between clientelist or corrupt representatives and participatory forums (Heimans 2002). Political systems that have a record of poor governance may decide to foster participatory forums in order to increase the government's legitimacy (Moynihan 2003; Olivo 1998). The more representative the budget process appears to be, the more credible it will be in the eyes of citizens and external stakeholders.

In addition, some forms of participation can strengthen the ability of the legislative branch and external parties, such as the media and interest groups, to check the centralization of power in the executive branch. Where legislators have little experience, little understanding of the budget process, or inadequate information upon which to make judgments, NGOs that provide budget analysis can strengthen the ability of one branch of government to require accountability of the other.

Another argument for participation in a developing-country context is that it is a desired and natural outgrowth of trends toward fiscal decentralization (Robinson 2004). Fiscal decentralization is intended to reduce central control in favor of local preferences that foster allocative efficiency. The promise of fiscal decentralization is therefore also a promise of participation, and the success of one depends on the other. The good governance argument also links directly to overarching economic development concerns. Top-down investment strategies and public policies that fail to incorporate the preferences and oversight of those they serve will struggle.

PARTICIPATION PROMOTES TRANSPARENCY. Related to the good governance argument is the view that participation provides additional sources of information not available through traditional political institutions. Participation is particularly useful in developing countries because it not only provides information to the government on citizen preferences but can also provide an alternative guide to external stakeholders who normally deal directly with government.

Participation and transparency may go hand in hand in developing-country governments. Fölscher, Krafchik, and Shapiro (2000, p. 43) note that in South Africa "a closed budget drafting process and lack of legislature amendment powers severely restrict legislature and civil society participation in the budget process. Whereas some legislatures have carved a space for themselves in monitoring the implementation of the budget, they are also largely unable to effectively scrutinize budget plans before passing the budget. In turn this restricts civil society input into the budget."

PARTICIPATION INCREASES SOCIAL JUSTICE. Many of the arguments for participation rest on the normative claim that citizens have a right to a say in decisions that affect their future in any democratic system. The exclusion of the poor has been so extreme in developing countries that some deliberate form of empowerment is needed.

PARTICIPATION HELPS INDIVIDUALS BECOME BETTER CITIZENS. Participation can benefit citizens and society more broadly by providing "citizenship schools" for people who have had limited involvement in civic life (Wampler 2000). Participation helps citizens learn about their rights, express their views to representatives, and see these views affect policy and action. Through participation citizens learn the basic language and practices of governance. NGOs and governments can play a vital role in offering advice to citizens on how to understand what government policies mean for them, how to present their views, and how to assess government services. As citizens become skilled in the art of democracy and social capital builds, their ability to hold their governments accountable and to foster high performance should increase (Putnam 1993).

The Need for Real Participation

The arguments for participation overlap and complement one another to some degree. The literature on participation also suggests that not all modes of participation are created equal. Some are better able to foster accountability and represent the views of the public than others. A typology of the goals of participation must be developed to evaluate its different forms.

Pro-participation arguments portray participation as a channel for direct democratic voice in decision making. These arguments call for direct and open involvement of citizens in decisions that affect them. A primary goal of this approach is to increase the direct representation of all citizens. All citizens, not just those who are qualified by election, position, expertise, influence, or money, should be able to provide input.

According to Habermas (1989), participation processes must include all affected by a decision and disregard the social status of the partici-pants. The first element of the typology, therefore, is the range of citizen involvement (the extent of representative participation). The range of involvement is narrow when only a handful of citizens or a particular socioeconomic group dominates decision making. The range becomes broader with the involvement of interest groups. It is broadest when large numbers of citizens representing different socioeconomic groups are directly involved. The involvement of more citizens helps reduce the uncertainty inherent in any effort to make decisions about the future (Hellström 1997).

A second primary goal of participation is that government provides for genuine discourse with its citizens and takes their input seriously, which Pateman (1989) labels full participation. Participation should be authentic and have a genuine impact on public decisions (Fox and Miller 1996); the use of participatory budgeting forums is of little benefit if the government does not listen. Such forums may be attractive to government for the symbolic value they provide. As Wampler (2000, p. 3) notes, among local governments in Brazil that have adopted Porto Alegre's model of participatory budgeting, "there is wide variation in the success, as some administrations only play lip service to the programs."

Under full participation each member of a decision-making body has an equal say in the outcome of decisions. The second aspect of the typology is, therefore, the level of citizen involvement, measuring the extent to which full participation occurs (Arnstein 1969; Pateman 1989). Three levels of partici-pation can be distinguished (table 2.1). Pseudo participation suggests a token effort at fostering public involvement. Partial participation suggests that citizens are consulted but have limited impact on public policy. Full partici-pation indicates that citizens have an authentic discourse with government, and their views are taken into account.

TABLE 2.1 Typology of Citizen Participation

	Representativeness	
Level	Broad	Narrow
Full		
Decisions	Public officials make decisions, but citizens have strong influence.	Public officials and selected interest groups make decisions.
Participation	Large, diverse groups of citizens engage in meaningful discourse with government.	Interest groups exert significant influence; most citizens lack opportunities to participate.
Partial		
Decisions	Public officials make decisions; citizens have limited influence.	Government elite make decisions; interest groups have limited influence.
Participation	Large, diverse groups of citizens engage in limited discourse with government.	Interest groups exert influence; most citizens lack opportunities to participate.
Pseudo		
Decisions	Public officials make decisions.	Public officials make decisions in nontransparent manner.
Participation	Participation is symbolic but involves large, diverse groups of citizens.	Participation is symbolic, involving only a small number of citizens.

Source: Adapted from Moynihan 2003.

Fostering Broad and Meaningful Participation in Developing Countries

Fostering broad and meaningful participation in developing countries is particularly difficult because governments are not inclined to share decision-making power with the public. The limited capacity of many of the actors also limits participation. The poor generally have limited education, a low level of literacy, and little familiarity with the policy process. Governments often cite this lack of capacity as the reason why they resist participation by the poor.

These concerns may be overstated. The quality of participation depends a great deal on how participation is organized, how citizens are asked to express their views, and how they are presented with information about topics such as resource limits and tradeoffs. Even in developed countries, where participants' education and their knowledge of government are presumably higher, there is wide variation in the quality of participation.

This variation can be explained chiefly by how the participation forum is organized (Moynihan 2003). Organizers of participation processes need to consider the capacity of citizens and design a system that maximizes the quality of involvement (as they did in the case studies discussed in the next section).

If low citizen capacity is indeed a problem, it must be addressed before the participation process gets started. If capacity cannot be improved, another solution must be found. One capacity-improving task is to provide citizens with basic information: what participation hopes to achieve, what is at stake, and how participation contributes to the decision-making process. An alternative to capacity building of citizens is for NGOs to provide technical analysis of budgets and policy proposals. NGO staff tend to be among the best educated among the population and therefore may be classified as elite. Without their help, however, citizen views may go unrepresented or be represented in a very limited fashion. Given the capacity limitations of the public, it is reasonable to expect that NGOs will play an important role and that it may not always be possible to achieve the goal of broad participation. Donors can help by investing in the capacity of local NGOs (Heimans 2002).

Even where participation is fostered, citizens may focus only on narrow issues that affect them directly. They may be unwilling to make tradeoffs and determined to exclude some groups. (Higher-income individuals, for example, were more likely to participate in Porto Alegre's participatory budget processes [Navarro 1998].) A basic function of organizing participation is fostering a process that discourages these tendencies. This involves encouraging citizens to think about their interests broadly, to make tradeoffs, to recognize the limits on resources, and to avoid sectionalism.

While participation forums rest on the assumption of civic duty, they are more likely to succeed if they can tap into motivations of self-interest. At the same time, such forums must limit the downsides of self-interest. The traditional budget process also faces this danger, as agencies compete for scarce resources. Some of the lessons from the traditional budget process may be helpful. Hard and explicit budget constraints can help identify the limits on resources available and prompt citizens to make tradeoffs.

Another danger is unrealistic expectations. Citizens may assume that once they have a voice in making decisions, dramatic changes will occur immediately—unemployment will disappear, poverty and inequality will be reduced. Such expectations are unrealistic, especially if participation is occurring chiefly at the local level. Part of the challenge to organizers is communicating the limits on available resources.

Participation in Poverty Reduction Strategy Papers

One way of assessing participation in developing countries is to assess participation in the development of Poverty Reduction Strategy Papers (PRSPs). As the World Bank sought to establish a program of debt forgiveness for heavily indebted poor countries, it asked governments to develop PRSPs based on an open and participatory process (McGee and Norton 2000). The initiative created something of a natural experiment in participation, testing the willingness and ability of governments to engage in broad and meaningful participation when tangible rewards are at stake. The studies that have examined these efforts suggest that fostering participation in developing countries is difficult.

In their analysis of PRSP participation in 10 African countries, McGee, Levene, and Hughes (2000) suggest that governments conceived of participation as requiring consultations rather than broad citizen involvement. Among the weaknesses they observed were "poorly conceived, rushed, exclusive, and badly organized consultation procedures, failure to provide essential information to participants, inadequate time allowed for participants to analyze drafts before commenting on them, and lack of transparency in selecting participants" (p. 7).

Andrews (2004) finds that officials in Mozambique claimed that participation efforts were consistent with a tradition of public consultation but were actually characterized by a bias toward including groups with technical or financial backgrounds and strong connections to government. Broader civil society, NGOs, local governments, and citizens were poorly represented. Government departments defended their approach by pointing to the difficulty of interacting with civil society within a limited time line. NGOs that were consulted complained that they were included only to rubberstamp decisions that had already been made. This suggests that the involvement of some participants was for symbolic purposes only. Another indicator of the symbolic approach was the very limited time for consultation, which provided little room for actual dialogue.

Andrews also notes a bias in favor of the national capital. The government was more likely to involve citizens who could easily reach the capital. Local leaders had little sense of the purpose of the planning and little possibility to access resources. They were therefore not motivated to hold the government accountable for the way resources were allocated. "Citizens have no idea that these funds even exist, or that a plan to improve their lives is in place, and thus they have no expectations or demands of government. Their relationship with the authorities can best be described as a 'hope and pray' approach" (Andrews 2004, p. 27). "There is a distinct lack of any kind of meaningful participation in the ongoing development or implementation of PARPA [the Action Plan for the Reduction of Absolute Poverty] or in the monitoring and evaluation of the strategy" (p. 29).

A similar pattern is evident in Honduras. "The major obstacle for civil society participation in the PRSP process is that the central government will not enter into a dialogue with NGOs," writes Forner (2002, p. 117). "Without the direct input from the municipalities and localities, governments lack the capacity to develop a realistic poverty-reduction plan, and their current PRSPs reflect the absence of input." An analysis of PRSP participation in Bolivia, Malawi, and Rwanda concludes that the process was rushed, poorly organized, and dominated by elite groups (Painter 2002).

These reviews suggest that participation has fallen well short of its goals. Participation appears relatively narrow, excluding large sections of society based on geography or income. It also appears to be consultative at best, characterized by rushed processes that allow little prospect for meaningful dialogue.

Participation in Budgeting

There is no agreement on what *participatory budgeting* means or how to go about it: the study and dissemination of the idea of participatory budgeting are following practice rather than the other way around. In developing countries around the world, innovative ways are being found to increase public involvement in the budgeting process. As these examples and others become better known, their influence can be expected to grow.

Participatory budgeting aims to infuse the values of citizen involvement into the most basic and frequently the most formal procedure of governance—the distribution of resources through the budgeting process. Citizen involvement can foster accountability, transparency, and more effective distribution of resources. Proponents of participatory budgeting also see it as a way of challenging the exclusion of nonelite groups from the process. Wampler (2000, p. 1) describes the ambitious and multiple goals of participatory budgeting:

> These programs are designed to incorporate citizens into the policy-making process, spur administrative reform, and distribute public resources to low-income neighborhoods. Social and political exclusion is challenged, as low-income and traditionally excluded political actors are given the opportunity to make policy decisions. Governments and citizens initiate these programs to

promote public learning and active citizenship, achieve social justice through improved policies and resources allocation, and reform the administrative apparatus.

This section examines the potential for participation at each of the four different stages of the budget process: budget preparation and budget approval (or resource allocation), budget execution, and audit and performance evaluation. The approach provides lessons from a series of case studies on how participation might be organized at each stage of the budget process.

Participation in resource allocation

The preparation and approval stages of the budget process are traditionally bottom up in nature, driven by agencies with some basic guidance on budget constraints and priorities from elected officials. Agencies tend to budget based on previous allocations. This maintains rigidity in the distribution of resources. Agencies usually submit their proposed budget to a central budget office, which amends the budget before forwarding it to the legislature. Once the budget reaches the legislature, the budget approval process begins. It is still possible for participation to occur at this stage, but the basic procedures of approval are centralized in legislative committees. The modes of participation that can have an effect at this stage (committee hearings, lobbying of members, providing analysis of the executive budget proposal) do not lend themselves to direct citizen involvement. In political systems in which the executive branch is dominant, it is unlikely that the legislature will radically change the proposed budget. For these reasons there is greater opportunity for the active participation of citizens during the budget preparation stage than during the budget approval stage.

PARTICIPATORY BUDGETING IN PORTO ALEGRE. An example of participation in setting priorities and proposing allocations can be seen in the participatory budgeting processes in more than 100 municipalities in Brazil. The prototype is Porto Alegre, the capital of the Brazilian state Rio Grande do Sul, which began using participatory budgeting in 1989. Before the introduction of participatory budgeting, the city government was dominated by a clientelistic approach, in which public resources were used to maintain a political machine (Fung and Wright 2001).

A key event leading to the use of participatory budgeting was the election of the Worker's Party candidate as mayor. The party had campaigned on the issue of democratic participation and redistribution of public spending toward the poor. When it assumed power, it faced a bankrupt municipality and a disorganized bureaucracy (Wampler 2000).

In Porto Alegre the mayor's office is responsible for initiating the budget bill (figure 2.1). The municipal government then organizes a series of public meetings by region. The schedule of meetings is made publicly available. Additional information is distributed to the public, often in the form of a Quality of Life Index, which provides measures of basic indicators of well-being.

Two meetings a year occur in each of 16 regions. The meetings include broad representation. "City executives, administrators, representatives of community entities such as neighborhood associations, youth and health clubs, and any interested inhabitant of the city attend these assemblies, but only residents of the region can vote in them. They are jointly coordinated by members of municipal government and by community delegates" (Fung and Wright 2001, p. 13).

The first meeting includes a discussion of how the previous budget was spent. Meeting attendees choose citizen-delegates, who are responsible for articulating regional priorities. The number of delegates chosen by each region in the municipality is determined by turnout at the meetings. This motivates

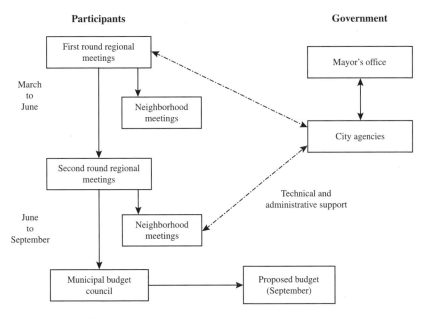

Source: Adapted from Wampler 2000.

FIGURE 2.1 Participatory Budgeting Process in Porto Alegre, Brazil

mobilization and turnout at the regional level. Citizen-delegates hold neighborhood meetings, usually weekly, to assess the region's spending priorities.

At the second set of regional meetings, citizen-delegates report their findings from neighborhood meetings. Two delegates and a substitute are selected to represent each region at the municipal budget council, called the Participatory Budgeting Council. This council also includes 10 delegates elected to represent the city as a whole on specific thematic issues, a union representative, a representative from the union of neighborhood associations, and two representatives of central municipal agencies. The council, which meets at least once a week from July to September, develops a set of proposals that it delivers to the mayor on September 30.

The mayor can accept the budget or ask the council for revisions (a request that the council can override with a two-thirds majority). The mayor's office incorporates the proposals (which usually deal with public works) in its proposed budget. The mayor presents the budget to the local legislature, which usually approves it.

Throughout the process the municipal government works as a partner with the Budgeting Council. Bureaucrats offer logistical and technical support, and the municipal government sets and publicizes meeting times. City agencies provide seminars on budgeting to Budgeting Council members and other interested delegates.

The multiple steps in the process allow for very broad participation. The municipality estimates that more than 100,000 people—8 percent of the population—were involved in the 1996 budget process (Fung and Wright 2001). Citizen participation appears to have had measurable benefits, including the expansion of access to basic public services such as sewerage systems, water, and paved roads. Wagle and Shah (2002) argue that the increased transparency of the budget process has reduced the motivation to avoid taxes, increasing municipal revenues.

CITIZEN SUMMITS IN WASHINGTON, D.C. Governance problems in Washington, D.C., were so severe in the 1990s that the city was dubbed "America's worst-run city" (Elliott 1995). Nearly three-quarters of residents viewed their municipal government as corrupt (Riley 1989).

The use of citizen summits in Washington, D.C., illustrates the potential for citizen participation in the context of strategic planning and budgeting. The case also offers insight into the use of technology to facilitate participation. Technological innovations may not be feasible in poorer regions in developing countries, but they are becoming more affordable and are a useful example of a way to foster dialogue.

In 1999 the city's mayor, Anthony Williams, established a series of citizen summits to involve the public in the strategic planning and budget process. The Office of Neighborhood Action was created to organize citizen participation that would link to district strategic planning. It initiated a goal-setting process with the mayor's office and developed a four-page tabloid version of the strategic plan, which it presented to citizens before and during the summit. The document informed citizens of the basic issues in order to improve the quality of the dialogue.

The citizen summit lasted more than seven hours and included the development of city-level and neighborhood vision statements, discussion of city-wide priorities and the draft strategic plan, and identification of action items for each neighborhood.[2] Efforts were made to ensure that all elements of Washington's diverse citizenry were reached. The summit was open to all comers, and summit literature and translations of the proceedings were available in Chinese, Korean, Spanish, and Vietnamese. Demographic surveys found the summit to be racially representative of the city's population.

The nearly 3,000 people who attended the summit were divided into tables of 10. Trained facilitators sat with each group to facilitate meaningful dialogue. The messages developed at each table were recorded using networked laptop computers, which fostered discussion among the individuals in each group and consensus about those messages. The computers also allowed the mayor to receive and respond to the messages during the forum, thus providing greater interaction. Polling keypads allowed the mayor to ask citizens to vote on any question at any time during the summit. The instantaneous results were displayed on large screens at the front of the room. Citizens prioritized citywide goals and ranked them according to level of support. The data collected from the keypads were cross-referenced with demographic data collected at the beginning of the program, when participants completed a short survey.

Input from the meeting helped shape the format of the budget and the allocation of resources. In preparing budget requests, each department asked for resources to pursue the strategic issues raised at the summit and codified in the strategic plan. The meeting also pushed for suggestions on how to solve problems at a more local level. Residents from different wards were encouraged to express their opinions on neighborhood issues. The summit became the first step for more localized district and citizen planning and action efforts through a series of Strategic Neighborhood Action Plans. These plans were designed to link to actual resource provision and operations at the micro level. Management teams made up of agency officials were appointed for each ward and tasked with addressing persistent neighborhood problems raised in these local plans. Goals from the district plan were linked to performance standards for senior officials. Each department head was given a performance contract and a public performance scorecard, consisting of a one-page list of key performance targets and measurements of success or failure in achieving those targets. Targets incorporated goals that had been raised at the summit and were of relevance to the particular department.

Following the summit, a revised strategic plan was presented to citizens at a second summit. About 1,500 citizens (60 percent of whom had participated in the first summit) attended. They had the opportunity to hold the mayor accountable for the revisions and offer comments before the plan was completed. The final version of the strategic plan bore the clear imprint of the meetings. The front section of each issue-driven chapter identified specific citizen concerns and priorities and the resulting strategic goals. Each goal was tied to a specific action item that described what implementation steps were taking place to achieve the goal. A performance target accompanied each action item. The plan identified the agency responsible for the target and the date by which the target would be achieved.

BUDGET MONITORING BY AN NGO IN SOUTH AFRICA. By analyzing allocations in a budget, stakeholders can see where government spends money. They can also determine if allocations match stated goals and how specific groups are affected.

Such an approach is exemplified by the Institute for Democracy in South Africa (IDASA), an NGO that combines advocacy, training, and research. IDASA specializes in budget analysis, providing detailed policy analyses of proposed resource allocation choices. In a country where legislative institutions are poorly staffed, such expertise ensures that policy capacity is not the monopoly of the executive branch of government. IDASA recognized that "one of the fundamental obstacles to democratic consolidation was the flow of critical, timely and accessible information from citizens to the legislature and back again" (Krafchik 1999). To meet this need, it took upon itself the task of providing this information.

IDASA started by helping train the wave of inexperienced legislators who came to power in the first post-apartheid elections of 1994. In 1995 IDASA began analyzing the budget from the perspective of women (the Women's Budget) and children (the Children's Budget), an idea inspired by the United Nations conventions on the rights of women and children. The purpose is to assess whether expenditure and taxation policies are in line with the goals of these conventions. IDASA uses researchers from other NGOs who specialize in women's and children's issues. It gives them budget training and puts them in contact with a source (usually from the government or legislature) who can provide access to information and advice on how to use expert analysis effectively (Budlender 1999). For the Women's Budget, IDASA partnered with the Community Agency for Social Enquiry and other groups.

IDASA strengthens its advocacy efforts through research and training on gender-sensitive budgeting. Its research looks at the extent to which budgets and associated policies are gender sensitive. Its training builds the capacity of organizations, legislatures, and government agencies to conduct gender-sensitive budget analysis. Training fosters the sharing of research information and empowers others to undertake research themselves. Knowledge of advocacy is passed along through training sessions.

Research conducted by IDASA generates a range of products. The Women's Budget analyzes how allocations affect gender issues. It suggests how reorganizing spending priorities could improve gender equity and general welfare. IDASA has also examined the relationship between gender and revenues, finding that despite progress toward removing discriminatory aspects in the tax code "there are still significant elements of discrimination against women in South Africa's taxation policy" (Smith 2000, p. 1). IDASA has published a series of working papers that examine how different national government departments use resources in ways that affect women (see, for example, Sadan 2005).

IDASA makes frequent use of the media. It responds to every budget with a press release. IDASA members make themselves available for interviews with the media, targeting newspapers with broad circulation and those likely to be read by policy makers (Krafchik 1999). They record a radio program to reach a still wider audience. IDASA also actively uses the Internet (http://www.idasa.org.za/) to disseminate its analyses. In all public relations efforts, IDASA attempts to tailor its message to the audience. It prepares the Women's Budget and Children's Budget in two forms (a longer, more complex version and a simpler version) so that information is accessible to a broad range of the public.

Participation in budget execution

Budget execution involves the disbursement and spending of resources. In theory, the intent of the budget approved by the legislative branch is carried out. In practice, this does not always occur, for two main reasons.

First, governments tend to provide bureaucrats with some measure of discretion in the allocation of resources. The degree of discretion depends very much on the nature of the budgeting system. One extreme is a pure line-item budget system, in which the legislature identifies spending items in great detail, specifying every machine to be purchased, every employee to be hired, every well to be dug. At the opposite end of the spectrum is a program budget, in which legislatures specify general goals but let bureaucrats decide how to spend the resources allocated to reach those goals. Most governments fall somewhere in between, specifying major items to be purchased but leaving the details to bureaucrats.

Regardless of the approach, participation matters. Where bureaucrats face a strict line-item approach, citizens can track exactly what should be provided and assess whether resources were actually spent as promised. Where bureaucrats have a high measure of discretion, citizens become more important players. They may undertake lobbying activities and form partnerships to influence the shape of disbursement decisions.

Second, actual spending is often at odds with the stated intent of the government. Sometimes this may be due to spending cuts as a result of declines in revenue. In this case, money previously allocated is simply not available (World Bank 1998). In other cases, money allocated to service providers is siphoned off as it goes through various administrative levels.

TRACKING SPENDING IN UGANDA. Despite a doubling of spending on primary education between 1992 and 1995 (mostly on salaries), student enrollment appeared to remain stagnant in Uganda (Reinikka and Svensson 2001). One explanation was that the schools were not actually receiving the money allocated.

To determine where spending on education was going, the World Bank, in collaboration with the Ugandan government, the local Economic Policy Research Centre, and an independent Ugandan consulting firm, MSE Consultants, surveyed 250 government schools, randomly selected from 19 of Uganda's 39 districts. The survey compared allocations to schools by the central government with the individual schools' records of funding received.

The results showed that between 1991 and 1995, only 13 percent of non-salary spending on education reached the schools that the funds were intended to help (Reinikka and Svensson 2004). Most schools received no capitation grants at all. Education offices at the district level had been keeping most of the nonsalary funding—as well as the bulk of the tuition fees paid by parents.

Although the problem was widespread, some schools were more likely than others to suffer the effects of leakage. Smaller schools, schools serving children from poorer families, and schools with less qualified teachers received less capitation funding (Reinikka and Svensson 2001). This suggested that leakage was less likely to affect schools that actively mobilized and used their political resources.

As a result of the survey findings, changes were made. The government reported amounts of school transfers to local media. Schools and districts were required to make public the amount of government money they received. The expectation was that the provision of this information to local parents would discourage the leakage of funds for noneducation purposes. With this information, parents and teachers were more likely to mobilize and demand the full funding that government had allocated.

Schools were also given more direct control over resources. Allocations were deposited directly into individual school accounts, and schools became responsible for buying their own goods rather than relying on central purchasing at the district level. A 1998 survey by the government found that these measures were effective in increasing the flow of funding to schools. By 2001, 80 percent of budgeted funds were reaching the schools, as intended (Reinikka and Svensson 2001).

DEMYSTIFYING THE BUDGET AND TRACKING SPENDING IN INDIA. In the western state of Gujarat, India, the NGO Development Initiative for Social and Human Action (DISHA) created a relatively simple yet effective way to monitor implementation of budgeted allocations. The state budget provides very specific line-item detail on where public resources will be spent and what resources will be spent on. For DISHA this provided an opportunity to hold the government accountable and to demystify what appeared to be an arcane budget process to all but a few government officials.

DISHA is an NGO with very broad membership. Its more than 80,000 members include tribespeople, miners, and forest, agricultural, and construction workers. Tribal and other indigenous groups, who live in the hilly regions in Gujarat, make up about 15 percent of the state's population (Mistry 2000).

Since the early 1980s, India's national government has sought to target spending toward tribal regions through a Tribal Area Sub-Plan. While spending increased, the level of economic development and infrastructure spending remained low. DISHA sought to understand where the resources were going.

DISHA examined the budget for allocations to specific projects, such as the construction of roads and the digging of village wells. (The state budget details allocations for all sectors, schemes, and programs to the village level.) It then surveyed village authorities and asked them whether and to what extent the project had actually been implemented. M. D. Mistry of DISHA (1999) summed up the approach as follows:

> One can really find out, which we do in our office, that the money that was put in was spent. We write to the village saying that this money, the 10,000 rupees, was spent in constructing a road from your village to the main road linking your village to the main road. Please let us know whether this road is built or not. And you get an answer from them. . . . So it is easy to find out whether the money is spent or not, and if not, then raise it a) in assembly b) you write and c) give it to the press and raise it, thereby holding them accountable.

By surveying villages, DISHA raises awareness of political promises and provides village authorities with valuable information about what resources they should have received. DISHA is then able to incorporate the village's political support in efforts to lobby for these resources (World Bank 2001).

DISHA has also cultivated the support of local officials by offering budget training to village representatives (*sarpanches*). Some 300 current and former *sarpanches* from about 140 different villages took part in a budget workshop in 2000. They learned skills such as how to read and understand budgets, identify allocations for their villages, recognize and discuss local investment needs, and plan lobbying and protest efforts.

DISHA has complemented budget execution analysis with other types of analyses that contribute to the approval stage. In analyzing a budget, DISHA identifies what spending will benefit the poor, points out any errors in calculations or in fiscal discipline, and looks at the relationship between public statements by the finance minister and proposed allocations. Some of the information DISHA develops is very basic and would be taken for granted in most budget systems. For example, DISHA lists resources allocated for each department and how they compare with previous allocations. It also identifies major areas of new spending or spending cuts. These analyses are converted into short budget briefs that aim to equip legislative members, the media, and civil society with basic facts and questions about resource allocation priorities (World Bank 2001). This information, written in local languages and tailored to local interests, is also disseminated to the public, usually through schools in remote areas.

DISHA disseminated its analysis to members of the state legislature and the media. It found that many legislative members were sympathetic to their claims but had trouble understanding the budget. The information DISHA provided gave legislators facts and figures they could use to assess the efficacy of disbursements. As M. D. Mistry of DISHA notes, "The elected members of the party at various levels felt 'empowered' with handy information and began to participate in the debate on public expenditure. [Provision of this information] shifted the debate on public expenditure from the selected few to a majority of members, thus improving governance through improved/enlightened debates" (Mistry 2000). DISHA's analysis of the execution process in one budget cycle thus influenced the approval process in the next cycle.

DISHA's activities have raised the quality of debate on the budget and grounded it in facts and research. Media coverage is better informed. The finance minister takes greater care to ensure that statements match allocations and that allocations reach intended projects. The demystification process that DISHA fostered has improved basic communication about spending and priorities and enhanced the transparency of the budget process.

Participation in audit and performance evaluation

The final phase of the budget process is its evaluation. Traditionally, this meant that spending was audited to ensure consistency with intended spending. More recently, the audit function has come to incorporate assessment of the outputs generated by spending and suggestions for improving performance (Barzelay 1997). There is scope for citizen participation at this stage, particularly in evaluating performance.

A basic performance benchmark is the satisfaction of citizens and the quality of their interaction with the public sector. By administering surveys on access and satisfaction, NGOs can gauge the success of policies.

In Bangalore, the capital of the state of Karnataka, India, such information is presented in the form of performance report cards (Paul 1998). Citizen surveys in Bangalore were first undertaken in 1993 by an individual, Samuel Paul, with help from a private sector marketing firm. The following year Paul formed the Public Affairs Centre (PAC), an NGO dedicated to improving the quality of governance in India. PAC created report cards in Bangalore in 1999 and 2003. The report cards are based on citizen surveys that examine satisfaction with government services in urban areas in Bangalore. Paul (1998, p. 3) describes the basic logic and validity involved in using report cards that draw on the experience of the users of a service:

> A report card represents an assessment of the public services of the city from the perspective of its citizens. The latter are the users of these services and can provide authentic feedback on the quality, efficiency, and adequacy of the services and the problems they face in their interactions with the service providers. They may not be able to comment on the technical features and standards of the services or to evaluate the overall performance of a provider. But they are eminently qualified to say whether the service meets their needs, and whether

the agency is responsive, corrupt, reliable, etc. When customers rate an agency on different dimensions of the service, it provides a basis for judging its performance as a service provider.

The first round of surveys selected a random sample of homes in each of six regions of the city. It classified respondents as middle or upper income (807 households) or lower income (327 households). Respondents were asked to describe the quality of the services they had received in the past six months: their overall satisfaction, staff behavior, how many visits were required to solve a problem, and whether the problem was actually solved. The 1999 round of surveys expanded the number of participants to 1,339 middle-income households and 839 households from slum areas.

The surveys covered basic services, such as water supply, electricity, garbage removal, hospitals, and police services. The 1993 and 1999 surveys found low overall levels of satisfaction with services. Relative to middle-income households, the poor had to visit agencies more often to solve a problem, were more likely to have to pay a bribe (usually to police), and were less likely to have their problems solved. Despite these problems, the poor tended to show similar levels of satisfaction with services, presumably due to lower expectations.

Upon completion of the 1999 survey, PAC sought a way to increase the impact of the survey results. It developed the report card format and aggressively promoted the report cards to the media. The cards were unveiled at a press conference that generated significant media coverage. All the major newspapers in Bangalore published the findings, and the high-profile *Times of India* ran a weekly feature for two months on issues raised by the cards (PAC 2003). PAC appreciates the importance of the media, which "has become an active stakeholder in making Bangalore citizens more aware and putting the spotlight on issues that need to be addressed. The big change has been the wide involvement of resident associations and civic groups in engaging with city agencies in campaigns and initiatives for improving service delivery" (PAC 2003, p. 9). Paul (1998, p. 17) describes how a reporter from the *Times* of India used report card information to put the spotlight on service quality and corruption in hospitals:

Armed with the information provided by the report card, the reporter concerned went to the public hospitals and interviewed senior officials and doctors to get their side of the story. She then went on to talk to patients to get a confirmation on the report card findings. Her report on the subject in the newspaper was on the front page and generated a public debate ... that went on for several days. The message was loud and clear that the abuses and extortion being practiced in the city's public hospitals should not be tolerated. Within a few weeks, some nurses in one of the public hospitals were arrested on charges of corruption and negligence in a child delivery case.

The report cards also generated a response from the government. "The responses from agency heads and senior government officials were polite but lukewarm except for a few agencies," according to Paul (1998, p. 13). But according to Wagle and Shah (2002), four of the eight agencies responsible for the services attempted to reform themselves or expand citizen feedback mechanisms.

PAC tried to foster both improvement and openness by interacting with agency officials. It briefed the agencies on the survey results and organized workshops. In one session public officials met with one another to discuss the efforts they were making to address criticisms. In another session representatives from the agencies met with the public and discussed the problems raised by the report cards. The chief minister of Karnataka created a "Bangalore Agenda Task Force" that included prominent city residents in an effort to offer responses to the problems identified. The Bangalore City Corporation also promoted an informal network of NGOs and city officials called Swabhimana (self-esteem) (Paul 1998). The network discussed ways of solving problems and identified new problems as they emerged. PAC played a coordinating role in this network. It also advised the corporation on how to establish a system by which citizens can bring their grievances directly to the government and see them redressed. This led to training officials on how to provide citizens with feedback. After a day-long collaboration with PAC, hospitals in Bangalore agreed to establish help desks to provide better customer service to patients.

The 2003 round of report cards surveyed more than 1,700 households. These surveys found increased satisfaction with almost all agencies, a lower incidence of problems, and less corruption (figure 2.2). "The performance of these agencies over the last 10 years is a picture of significant improvement in satisfaction of users of services. Of the nine agencies on which citizens of Bangalore provided feedback, all have received satisfaction ratings above 70 percent this time in contrast to less than 40 percent in 1999" (PAC 2003, p. 3).

PAC argues that the oversight it provided helped matters but that political response to the problems was also important. "It is clear that without the kind of political leadership and vision displayed by the Chief Minister [of Karnataka] in the past four years, this outcome would not have been easy to achieve" (PAC 2003, p. 8).

The report card approach has been expanded to the state level, to other Indian cities, and to other countries, including Bangladesh, the Philippines, Ukraine, the United States, and Vietnam. In the United States, university professors and journalists investigate and grade the capacity of government in a variety of management settings, including financial management, information management, and human resources (Ingraham, Joyce, and Donahue 2003).

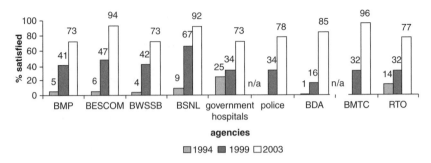

Source: PAC 2003.
Note: Table represents overall satisfaction across three report cards in general households. BMP = Bangalore Municipal Corporation, BESCOM = Bangalore Electric Company, BWSSB = Bangalore Water Supply and Sewerage Board, BSNL = Bharat Sanchar Nigam Limited, BDA = Bangalore Development Authority, BMTC = Bangalore Metropolitan Transport Corporation, n/a = not available, and RTO = Road and Transport Authority.

FIGURE 2.2 Citizen Satisfaction with Government Services in Bangalore, 1994–2003

The Government's Perspective on Public Participation

The normative literature on participation fails to acknowledge the practical aspects of participation and tends to overlook the importance of government administration in implementing participation (Moynihan 2003). This section examines the government viewpoint. It proposes that public officials are less attuned to normative goals of representative and meaningful citizen involvement than to concerns about perceived costs and benefits. They therefore take an instrumental perspective on participation. Efforts to increase public participation need to take into account the factors that shape governmental attitudes toward participation. The government perspective is crucial, as the degree to which public officials either create barriers or promote access to participation forums and public decisions shapes the costs and benefits that citizens consider when deciding whether to participate.

Why Government Matters

Government administrators, even when mandated to implement participation, have a great degree of control over how participatory activities are structured and the impact of the input collected from participation. As Thomas (1995, p. 11) observes:

> Even when they accept the imperative [of participation], public managers and policy planners must still choose when, how often, and to what extent to involve

the public. Despite frequent managerial complaints about the constraining effects of requirements for public participation, these requirements have usually been limited to directing managers to involve the public, leaving the form and extent of that involvement to the discretion of the administrators.

Administrators have substantial power in determining how much influence to share (the level of participation) and which groups or individual citizens to involve (the range of participation). All parties in the participation process—citizens and public officials—are likely to make some judgments as to the relative costs and benefits of participation (Kweit and Kweit 1981). Any individual citizen's choice to participate (or not to participate) is likely to affect only that person. But the decisions of public managers affect the opportunity and nature of participation by all citizens.

The attitude of governments is a major predictor of whether participation will be undertaken and whether it will be meaningful. With respect to participation in PRSPs, Painter (2002) argues that the main determinant of successful participation was the role of government: "Government will and expectations strongly determine the quality of the process. An active, capable, and experienced civil society is helpful in influencing the quality of the participatory process, but not determinative." Governments limited public involvement in developing PRSPs; it is not clear that consultation shaped planning in any way.

Sometimes governmental actors are hostile to participation, viewing it as a threat to their institutional rights and privileges. In other cases governments may not be opposed to participation, but they are skeptical of it, unsure how it works and what benefits it provides beyond symbolic ones.

> A more common perspective among developing-country governments sees participation in the budget process as being politically obligatory, or even politically advantageous, but of little practical significance. Governments use participatory rhetoric and limited gestures toward increased budget transparency and community budget consultations to assuage donors and reduce tensions with civil society, but they may not meaningfully engage with the process—at least initially. (Heimans 2002, p. 15)

In Porto Alegre, Brazil, governments not only welcomed but promoted participatory budgeting. An election platform based on spending changes and enhancing citizen involvement created favorable political conditions. The fact that the government was bankrupt increased the willingness to experiment with new forums, and the disorganization of the bureaucracy weakened resistance to change. The government was also willing to increase revenues that could be applied toward proposals from participation forums, which immediately made participation significant. The Workers' Party changed the municipal revenue system by indexing property taxes, "widening the fiscal space that was a necessary precondition for participatory budgeting" (Robinson 2004, p. 9).

Other Brazilian municipalities that have followed the Porto Alegre model have also tended to be progressive governments that emphasize citizen participation and social justice. The emphasis on citizen involvement is partly a reaction to the military dictatorship that ruled Brazil from 1964 to 1985. While progressive governments initiated participatory budgeting practices, such budgeting practices have been maintained by more conservative governments. They have often been maintained for symbolic purposes and become more prone to "manipulation and mismanagement" (Wampler 2000, p. 7). The Porto Alegre experience points to the importance of political parties in prompting adoption of participation. The parties most likely to adopt participation goals in their platforms are (a) long-term opposition parties reacting to authoritarian regimes or (b) political parties that represent the poor or a social justice agenda.

The success of participation depends in part on administrative capacity. In Porto Alegre the bureaucracy played a positive role in organizing meetings, providing necessary information to citizens about their choices, and offering technical analyses for project proposals. To provide support at the neighborhood level, more government offices were opened in new areas of the city. The decentralization of physical locations was a very visible indicator of government accessibility. Meetings were decentralized and easily accessible to all who wanted to attend.

Wampler (2000) argues that the nature of citizen proposals forces bureaucracies to think more collaboratively. A proposal on health or education requires the departments concerned to work with the planning agency and with community leaders. Technical plans and new investments usually require the approval of participants and foster an ongoing relationship based on open communication.

Shaping the Administrative View: The Instrumental Assessment of Participation

The instrumental perspective suggests that administrators are likely to be concerned mainly with the strain that public participation places on the decision process and the costs it imposes on the administrator. The costs of participation may be classified as direct administrative costs, self-interested administrative costs, and decision process and outcome costs (figure 2.3). Government decision making is characterized by a series of limited opportunities to come to closure within a restricted time period. Increased participation endangers this (Pressman and Wildavsky 1973).

Direct administrative costs refer to the costs of coordinating participation (Kweit and Kweit 1981). Government requirements for participation in Uganda went unheeded because administrators "didn't have the time" to organize participation (Heimans 2002). Administrative self-interest costs arise from the public manager's potential loss of control over the decision agenda, which reduces administrative power and authority over day-to-day activities. Managers who wish to maintain program stability or are concerned with shaping bureaucratic activities and carving out an interesting policy-making role are likely to resist participatory processes that determine the policy agenda

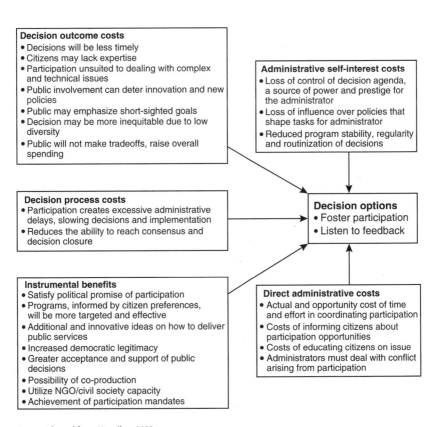

Source: Adapted from Moynihan 2003.

FIGURE 2.3 Administrative Costs and Instrumental Benefits of Participation

(Dunleavy 1991; McNair, Caldwell, and Pollane 1983). Decision process costs are the variable costs involved in making decisions. Administrators view participation as slowing the process of decision making and reducing the potential for reaching consensus (Nelkin 1984). Governments in developing countries may argue that they have limited administrative capacity and cannot afford to create participatory forums.

Administrators may argue that participation reduces the quality of the decision outcome, that poor decisions are made because of lack of knowledge or expertise on the part of the public (Cleveland 1985). A frequently cited explanation for governments' resistance to participatory budgeting is that it will make tough choices on the distribution of resources even more difficult. As governments interact with the public, NGOs, and interest groups, they will have to face explicit demands that cannot be met. "A typical complaint is that participatory budgeting processes or public consultations simply result in 'shopping lists' of demands from communities that do not reflect the scarce resources available" (Heimans 2002, p. 18). Governments may also worry that because participation cannot be made truly representative, important groups may be excluded, distorting policy. In fact, the greater the degree of participation, the more likely it is to be representative. The more limited the range of participation, the more likely that elite interests will gain influence over the budget process in a nontransparent way.

Fölscher, Krafchik, and Shapiro (2000) tracked participation in parliamentary budget hearings during the 1990s in South Africa. They observed broadened involvement beyond a small number of private interests to a relatively high number of presentations from NGOs on poverty and macroeconomic policy. The argument that budgeting can never be made truly representative can also be used as a ploy to question the legitimacy and deflect the input of NGOs—a criticism faced by IDASA in South Africa.

Participation can yield several benefits. Public input can provide managers with information that improves allocative or technical efficiency. Public input may offer innovative solutions that would not have emerged from traditional modes of decision making. Because many public programs require some level of cooperation from citizens, involvement of the public is likely to help government develop more practical goals, raise acceptance of programs, and perhaps even allow citizens to work together with the administration to implement programs (Thomas 1995).

Participation also increases public support of administrators and programs (Brinkerhoff and Goldsmith 2000). Unpopular agencies can use participation to improve their image (Kweit and Kweit 1981; McNair, Caldwell, and Pollane 1983). Participatory forums may be designed to increase the perception that public organizations are more consultative, lending an air of democratic legitimacy to the government's activities (Frederickson 1982).

Conclusions

Participation in developing countries is inadequate. It tends not to be broadly representative of the population, and it fails to involve meaningful dialogue that affects public decision making.

Civil society can play an important role in improving participation. In most of the cases presented in this chapter, an NGO or a team of NGOs effected real change in government decision making by using the budget process. Even in Porto Alegre, where citizen involvement is most direct, an active civil society aided the process of citizen participation. At the same time, NGOs must take into account the government's attitude toward participation and find ways to reduce the perceived costs and increase the perceived benefits of participation.

Notes

1. This section draws on Moynihan (2003).
2. AmericaSpeaks, an NGO, organized the format and handled the logistics of the summit.

References

Andrews, Matthew. 2004. "Are PRSPs Providing a New, Effective and Participatory Development and Poverty Reduction Tool? A Study of Participation in Mozambique's PARPA." In *Rough Diamond: PRSP's and the 60th Anniversary of World Bank and IMF*, ed. Milton Keynes, 7–19. United Kingdom: International World Vision.

Arnstein, Sherry R. 1969. "A Ladder of Citizen Participation." *American Institute of Planners* 35 (4): 216–24.

Barber, Benjamin. 1986. *Strong Democracy: Participatory Politics for a New Age*. Berkeley: University of California Press.

Barzelay, Michael. 1997. "Central Audit Institutions and Performance Auditing: A Comparative Analysis of Organizational Strategies in the OECD." *Governance* 10 (3): 235–60.

Bhatt, Mihir R. 2000. *Alternative Budget Analysis: DISHA's Experience*. Foundation for Public Interest, Ahmedabad, India. http://www.ids.ac.uk/ids/civsoc/final/india/ind14.doc.

Brinkerhoff, Derick W., and Arthur A. Goldsmith. 2000. "Macroeconomic Policy, PRSPs, and Participation." World Bank Participation Group Background Paper, Washington, DC. http://www.worldbank.org/participation/web/webfiles/macrosynthesis.htm.

Budlender, Debbie. 1999. "The South African Women's Budget Initiative." Paper presented at the United Nations Development Programme meeting on Women and Political Participation: 21st Century Challenges. New Delhi, March 24–26. http://magnet.undp.org/events/gender/india/Soutaf.htm.

Cleveland, Harlan. 1985. "The Twilight of Hierarchy: Speculations on the Global Information Society." *Public Administration Review* 45 (1): 185–95.

Cooper, Terry L. 1984. "Citizenship and Professionalism in Public Administration." *Public Administration Review* 44 (Special Issue): 143–49.

Crosby, Ned, Janet M. Kelly, and Paul Schafer. 1986. "Citizen Panels: A New Approach to Citizen Participation." *Public Administration Review* 46 (2): 170–78.

Dunleavy, Patrick J. 1991. *Democracy, Bureaucracy and Public Choice.* Hempstead, United Kingdom: Harvester Wheatshed.

Easton, David. 1990. *The Analysis of Political Structure.* New York: Routledge, Chapman and Hall.

Elliott, Michael. 1995. "America's Worst-Run City." *Newsweek*, March 13, p. 26.

Evans, Gord, and Nick Manning. 2003. "Helping Governments Keep Their Promises: Making Ministers and Governments More Reliable through Improved Policy Management." South Asia Internal Discussion Paper IDP-187, World Bank, Washington, DC. http://unpan1.un.org/intradoc/groups/public/documents/worldbank/unpan013906.pdf.

Fölscher, Alta, ed. 2003. *Budget Transparency and Participation.* Institute for Democracy in South Africa, Ciudad del Cabo, Brazil.

Fölscher, Alta, Warren Krafchik, and Isaac Shapiro. 2000. "Transparency and Participation in the Budgeting Process." Paper presented at the third conference of the International Budget Project, Mumbai, November 4–9.

Forner, Patricia. 2002. "How Is the Next Generation to Live? The Enhanced HIPC II and a Strategy to Reduce Poverty in Bolivia, Honduras and Nicaragua." In *Masters of Their Own Development? PRSPs and the Prospects for the Poor,* ed. Allan Whaites. Monrovia, CA: World Vision.

Fox, Charles J., and Hugh T. Miller. 1996. *Postmodern Public Administration: Toward Discourse.* Thousand Oaks, CA: Sage Publications.

Frederickson, H. George. 1982. "The Recovery of Civism in Public Administration." *Public Administration Review* 42 (6): 501–08.

Fung, Archon, and Erik Olin Wright. 2001. "Deepening Democracy: Innovations in Empowered Participatory Governance." *Politics and Society* 29 (1): 5–41.

Habermas, Jurgen. 1989. *The Structural Transformation of the Public Sphere.* Cambridge, MA: MIT Press.

———. 1996. *Between Facts and Norms: Contributions to a Discourse Theory of Law and Democracy.* Cambridge, MA: MIT Press.

Heimans, Jeremy. 2002. "Strengthening Participation in Public Expenditure Management: Policy Recommendations for Key Stakeholders." Organisation for Economic Co-operation and Development, Paris.

Heller, Patrick. 2001. "Moving the State: The Politics of Democratic Decentralization in Kerala, South Africa, and Porto Alegre." *Politics and Society* 29 (1): 131–63.

Hellström, Tomas. 1997. "Boundedness and Legitimacy in Public Planning." *Knowledge and Policy: International Journal of Knowledge Transfer and Utilization* 9 (4): 27–42.

Hentschel, Jesko. 1996. "Does Participation Cost the World Bank More? Emerging Evidence." In *Participation in Practice: The Experience of World Bank and Other Stakeholders,* ed. Jennifer Rietbergen-McCracken, 25–50. Washington, DC: World Bank.

Inglehart, Ronald. 1997. "Postmaterialist Values and the Erosion of Institutional Authority." In *Why People Don't Trust Government,* ed. J. S. Nye, P. D. Zelikow, and D. C. King. Cambridge, MA: Harvard University Press.

Ingraham, Patricia W., Phillip G. Joyce, and Amy Kneedler Donahue. 2003. *Government Performance: Why Management Matters.* Baltimore, MD: Johns Hopkins University Press.

King, Cheryl Simrell, K. M. Feltey, and B. O' Neill Susel. 1998. "The Question of Participation: Toward Authentic Public Participation in Public Administration." *Public Administration Review* 58 (4): 317–25.

King, Cheryl Simrell, and Camilla Stivers. 1998. *Government Is Us: Public Administration in an Anti-Government Era.* Thousand Oaks, CA: Sage Publications.

Krafchik, Warren. 1999. "The Development of IDASA's Budget Work over the Years." Presentation made at the second conference of the International Budget Project, Cape Town, South Africa, February 21–25. http://www.internationalbudget.org/conference/2nd/idasa.htm.

Kweit, Mary G., and Robert W. Kweit. 1981. *Implementing Citizen Participation in a Bureaucratic Society.* New York: Praeger.

Kweit, Robert W., and Mary G. Kweit. 1980. "Bureaucratic Decision-Making: Impediments to Citizen Participation." *Polity* 12 (4): 647–66.

Lynn, Laurence, Jr. 2002. "Democracy's Unforgivable Sin." *Administration and Society* 34 (4): 447–54.

Maier, Charles S. 1994. "Democracy and Its Discontents." *Foreign Affairs* 73 (4): 48–64.

McGee, Rosemary, with Josh Levene and Alexandra Hughes. 2002. "Assessing Participation in Poverty Reduction Strategy Papers: A Desk-Based Synthesis of Experience in Sub-Saharan Africa." Institute for Development Studies, Brighton, United Kingdom. http://www.ids.ac.uk/ids/bookshop/rr/rr52.pdf.

McGee, Rosemary, and Andy Norton. 2000. "Participation in Poverty Reduction Strategies: A Synthesis of Experience with Participatory Approaches to Policy Design, Implementation and Monitoring." http://www.ids.ac.uk/ids/bookshop/wp/wp109.pdf.

McNair, Ray H., Russell Caldwell, and Leonard Pollane. 1983. "Citizen Participants in Public Bureaucracies: Foul Weather Friends." *Administration and Society* 14 (4): 507–24.

Mistry, M. D. 1999. "The Beginnings of DISHA and Its Budget Training Work in India." Presentation made at the second conference of the International Budget Project, Cape Town, South Africa, February 21–25. http://www.internationalbudget.org/conference/2nd/disha.htm.

———. 2000. "Why DISHA's Public Expenditure Analysis Is Successful in Monitoring the Expenditure and Increasing Participation in Monitoring and Formulation of the Budget in the State of Gujarat, India." Presentation to the World Bank, Poverty Reduction and Economic Management Network, Washington, DC.

Morone, James A. 1998. *The Democratic Wish.* 2nd ed. New Haven, CT: Yale University Press.

Moynihan, Donald P. 2003. "Normative and Instrumental Perspectives on Public Participation: Citizen Summits in Washington, D.C." *American Review of Public Administration* 33 (2): 164–88.

Navarro, Zander. 1998. "Participation, Democratizing Practices and the Formation of a Modern Polity: The Case of 'Participatory Budgeting' in Porto Alegre, Brazil (1989–1998)." *Development* 41 (3): 68–71.

Nelkin, D. 1984. "Science and Technology and the Democratic Process." In *Citizen Participation in Science Policy*, ed. J. C. Petersen, 18–39. Amherst, MA: University of Massachusetts Press.

Olivo, Christiane. 1998. "The Practical Problems of Bridging Civil Society and the State: A Study of Round Tables in Eastern Germany." *Polity* 31 (2): 244–68.

PAC (Public Affairs Centre). 2003. "The Third Citizen Report Card on Public Services in Bangalore." Bangalore, India.

Painter, Genevieve. 2002. "Quality Participation in Poverty Reduction Strategies: Experiences from Malawi, Bolivia and Rwanda." Christian Aid, London. http://www.christian-aid.org.uk/indepth/0208qual/quality.htm.

Pateman, Carol. 1989. *Participation and Democratic Theory*. Cambridge: Cambridge University Press.

Paul, Samuel. 1998. "Making Voice Work: The Report Card on Bangalore's Public Services." World Bank Policy Research Working Paper 1921. Washington, DC. http://www.worldbank.org/html/dec/Publications/Workpapers/WPS1900series/wps1921/wps1921.pdf.

Peters, B. Guy. 1996. *The Future of Governing: Four Emerging Models*. Lawrence: University Press of Kansas.

Pressman, Jeffrey L., and Aaron Wildavsky. 1973. *Implementation: How Great Expectations in Washington Are Dashed in Oakland*. Berkeley: University of California Press.

Putnam, Robert. 1993. *Making Democracy Work: Civic Traditions in Modern Italy*. Princeton, NJ: Princeton University Press.

Reinikka, Ritva. 1999. "Using Surveys for Public Sector Reform." PREM Note 23, World Bank, Poverty Reduction and Economic Management, Washington, DC. http://www1.worldbank.org/prem/PREMNotes/premnote23.pdf

Reinikka, Ritva, and Jakob Svensson. 2001. "Explaining Leakage of Public Funds." World Bank Policy Research Working Paper 2709. Washington, DC.

———. 2004. "The Power of Information: Evidence from Public Expenditure Tracking Surveys." In *Global Corruption Report*, 326–29. Berlin: Transparency International.

Riley, M. 1989. "A Bright Broken Promise. *Time*, June 26, p. 60.

Robinson, M. 2004. "Resources, Citizen Engagement and Democratic Local Governance." Paper prepared for the Resources, Citizen Engagement and Democratic Local Governance (ReCitE) Project Planning Workshop, Trivandrum, Kerala, India, January 4–16. http://www.ids.ac.uk/logolink/resources/downloads/RobinsonResources_en.doc.

Sadan, Mastoera. 2005. "Gendered Analysis of the Working for Water Programme: A Case Study of the Tsitsikama Working for Water Project." Institute for Democracy in South Africa, Pretoria.

Smith, Terence. 2000. "Women and Tax in South Africa." Institute for Democracy in South Africa, Pretoria.

Songco, Dan. 2001. *Accountability for the Poor: Experiences in Civic Engagement in Public Expenditure Management*. Washington, DC: World Bank.

Stivers, Camille. 1994. "Citizenship Ethics in Public Administration." In *Handbook of Administrative Ethics*, ed. Terry L. Cooper, 435–55. New York: Marcel Dekker.

Tauxe, Caroline S. 1995. "Marginalizing Public Participation in Local Planning: An Ethnographic Account." *Journal of the American Planning Association* 61 (4): 471–82.

Thomas, John Clayton. 1995. *Public Participation in Public Decisions: News Skills and Strategies for Public Managers.* San Francisco: Jossey Bass.

Wagle, Swarnim, and Parmesh Shah. 2002. "Participation in Public Expenditure Systems: An Issue Paper." World Bank, Participation and Civic Engagement Group, Washington, DC.

Wampler, Brian. 2000. "A Guide to Participatory Budgeting." Paper presented at the third conference of the International Budget Project, Mumbai, November 4–9. http://www.internationalbudget.org/cdrom/papers/systems/ParticipatoryBud-gets/Wampler.pdf.

Wamsley, Gary L., and James F. Wolf. 1996. "Introduction: Can a High Modern Project Find Happiness in a Postmodern Era?" In *Refounding Public Administration: Modern Paradoxes, Postmodern Challenges,* ed. G. L. Wamsley and J. F. Wolf. Thousand Oaks, CA: Sage.

World Bank. 1998. *The Public Expenditure Management Handbook.* Washington, DC: World Bank.

———. 2001. "Case Study 3: Gujarat, India. Participatory Approaches in Budgeting and Public Expenditure Management." Participation Group Social Development Department, World Bank, Washington, DC. http://siteresources.worldbank.org/INTP-CENG/1143372116506093229/20511035/sdn72.pdf.

Zajac, Gary, and John G. Bruhn. 1999. "The Moral Context of Participation in Planned Organizational Change and Learning." *Administration and Society* 30 (6): 706–73.

Regional Surveys

3

Lessons from Latin America's Experience with Participatory Budgeting

BENJAMIN GOLDFRANK

Within a relatively short period (1990–2005), participatory budgeting has evolved from an obscure process of popular participation championed by a few leftist parties in South America to a "best practice" for reducing poverty and improving governance. Depending on how strictly participatory budgeting is defined, it has expanded from about a dozen cities, most of them in Brazil, to 250–2,500 locales in Latin America alone.[1]

Whether this diffusion of participatory budgeting is seen as cause for celebration or alarm depends on both how participatory budgeting is interpreted and how it is implemented. Interpretations of participatory budgeting, especially as practiced in Porto Alegre, the Brazilian city that named and publicized it, abound. Yet studies of how participatory budgeting is practiced, especially outside of Brazil, are only beginning to appear. Systematic comparisons of the ways in which participatory budgeting is designed and implemented are rare.

This chapter analyzes recent efforts to introduce participatory mechanisms into local government budget processes in Latin America. After defining participatory budgeting and outlining its history, it presents the major normative perspectives on participatory budgeting as well as a number of analytical perspectives. The broad hypothesis advanced is that the design and results of participatory budgeting depend on both the designers' intentions and local conditions. This hypothesis is first tested at the national level by comparing experiences in Bolivia, Brazil, Guatemala, Nicaragua, and Peru. The chapter then presents case studies of 14 municipalities outside Brazil. The last section draws conclusions from the case studies and identifies future directions for participatory budgeting in Latin America.

History of Participatory Budgeting

A broad definition of participatory budgeting usually describes it as a process through which citizens can contribute to decision making over at least part of a governmental budget.[2] Narrow definitions usually derive from particular experiences of participatory budgeting, especially that of Porto Alegre. According to these definitions, participatory budgeting is a process that is open to any citizen who wants to participate, combines direct and representative democracy, involves deliberation (not merely consultation), redistributes resources toward the poor, and is self-regulating, such that participants help define the rules governing the process, including the criteria by which resources are allocated (see, for example, Avritzer 2002, Genro and Souza 1997, and Santos 1998).

Neither the broad nor the narrow definitions are ideal for constructing a history of participatory budgeting. The broad definition would include too many cases, such as lobbying, general town hall meetings, and special public hearings or referendums on specific budget items; the narrow definition would include too few examples. A more wieldy definition might be that participatory budgeting is a process by which citizens, either as individuals or through civic associations, can voluntarily and regularly contribute to decision making over at least part of a public budget through an annual series of scheduled meetings with government authorities.

Much of the literature on participatory budgeting credits the Workers' Party with having created it in Porto Alegre in 1989. Its origins are actually more complicated and disputed. During the late 1970s and early 1980s, municipal governments in Lages (Lesbaupin 2000), Boa Esperança (Baiocchi 2001b), and Pelotas (Goldfrank and Schneider 2006), all controlled by the Party of the Brazilian Democratic Movement, submitted their budgets for public discussion (a former mayor of Pelotas claims to have invented participatory budgeting). For its part, the Workers' Party experimented with citizen budget councils not only in Porto Alegre but in several of the 36 municipalities it won in the 1988 elections, including Ipatinga, João Monlevarde, Piracicaba, Santo André, and Santos (Abers 1996).

The design of participatory budgeting in Porto Alegre was developed by both community associations and the Workers' Party municipal administration (Baierle 1998; Baiocchi 2002). Both sides were aware of earlier experiments by the Brazilian Democratic Movement Party. Before the implementation of participatory budgeting, Porto Alegre's Union of Neighborhood Associations produced a report demanding participation in formulating the budget. That report described eight municipalities in which participatory budgeting had been attempted in the past (Goldfrank 2005). Workers' Party publications such as *Teoria & Debate* published discussions of various forms of participatory governance in the run-up to the 1988 municipal elections. At least two other political parties on the left—the Radical Cause in Ciudad Guayana, Venezuela (and shortly after in Caracas) and the Broad Front in Montevideo, Uruguay—were implementing very similar participation programs at roughly the same time as the Workers' Party in Brazil.[3]

It was not until 1990 that the process in Porto Alegre was dubbed "participatory budgeting." Both the label and the practice (albeit in modified forms) began to be adopted in other cities under the Workers' Party in the early 1990s.[4] Local governments throughout Latin America began using participatory budgeting shortly thereafter, especially after 1996, when the United Nations Habitat II Conference in Istanbul recognized Porto Alegre's participatory budgeting as one of 42 best practices in urban governance.

All of the early experiences of participatory budgeting were implemented by parties that opposed the party in power at the national level. Experiments first occurred in Brazil largely because Brazil was the only authoritarian country—and one of the only countries in the region—that simultaneously allowed an opposition party to exist, gave significant spending responsibilities to municipalities, and held relatively fair mayoral elections (except in strategic cities such as state capitals and major ports). The twin waves of decentralization and democratization that swept Latin America in the 1980s and 1990s encouraged similar experimentation within and beyond Brazil, especially where political parties similar to the Workers' Party were allied with social movements demanding both democracy and improved urban services.

In contrast, many of the later experiences of participatory budgeting (which generally do not adopt the participatory budgeting label) were legislated into existence by national power-holders on the center or right of the political spectrum. Examples include the 1994 Popular Participation Law in Bolivia, sponsored by President Gonzalo Sánchez de Lozada; Nicaragua's municipal reforms in the late 1990s, under President Arnoldo Alemán; and the decentralizing reforms in Guatemala outlined in the 1996 Peace Accords under President Alvaro Arzú and codified in 2002 under President Alvaro Portillo. In all three cases, the requirements of citizen participation in order to receive debt relief funds from the Heavily Indebted Poor Countries (HIPC II) program starting in 2000 seem to have stimulated increased efforts to ensure that municipalities were implementing national laws.

Peru's 2003 Participatory Budgeting Law appears to be somewhat different, both because it uses the participatory budgeting label and because an ostensibly center-left president, Alejandro Toledo, pushed it forward. Within Brazil, while the majority of recent participatory budgeting experiences continue to be under leftist administrations, primarily the Workers' Party, parties of all political stripes have now used participatory budgeting, including the Party of the Liberal Front, an outgrowth of the official party of the military dictatorship. Participatory budgeting is thus no longer exclusively a leftist project.

Normative and Analytical Approaches to Participatory Budgeting

The early ideological motivations for adopting participatory budgeting represent only one of four distinct normative approaches to the subject (a radical democratic approach). The others might be termed orthodox leftist, liberal, and conservative. The radical democratic and liberal perspectives derive from the foremost proponents of participatory budgeting, that odd combination of leftist parties and international development agencies. These views are more evident in the debate surrounding participatory budgeting and in academic analyses than are conservative and orthodox leftist critiques of participatory budgeting, which come mostly from parties on the center and the right and from Leninist factions or parties. Conservative and orthodox leftist critiques should not be ignored, however, because these actors can play important roles in weakening or defeating participatory budgeting experiments.

The original normative reasons for implementing participatory budgeting given by the Workers' Party in Porto Alegre—as well as by the Radical Cause Party in Caracas and the Broad Front Party in Montevideo— were closely tied to the general transformation that much of the Latin American left sought in the 1970s and 1980s.[5] The new, "renovated," or postauthoritarian left that emerged out of failed guerrilla movements and repressive military dictatorships discarded the traditional teleological view of socialism along with traditional instrumental or dismissive views of democracy. Socialism was no longer seen as inevitable but as an open-ended process to be constructed; democracy was no longer seen as a way station along the path to true socialism or a formula for bourgeois domination but as fundamental to any socialist project. The guiding construct became "radical democracy" (also called "deepening democracy" and "democratizing democracy"). In the campaign proposals and government documents of the Workers' Party, Radical Cause Party, and Broad Front Party, four key elements guide their approach to participatory budgeting: direct citizen participation in government decision-making processes and oversight; administrative and fiscal transparency to prevent corruption; concrete improvements in urban infrastructure and services, with an emphasis on aiding the poor; and changing political culture, conceived as the transformation of urban residents into citizens, from political objects of clientelist practices into political subjects aware of their democratic rights (Goldfrank 2002).

In calling for a new participatory state, those guided by this radical democratic vision rejected both the Soviet-style all-powerful centralized state and what they called the neoliberal or minimal state advocated by international financial institutions and by most national governments in the region (Dutra 2002). Participatory budgeting, in this view, would help relegitimate the state by showing that it could be effective, redistributive, and transparent. The more Gramscian-inspired proponents believed that participatory budgeting would be an arena in which empowered citizens could construct an alternative "hegemony" (Dutra 2002; Sader 2002).[6] Olívio Dutra (2002), the former mayor of Porto Alegre, who first introduced participatory budgeting there (later extending it to Rio Grande de Sul after being elected governor of that state), describes the process as revolutionary and links it to socialism:[7]

> we are fully conscious that this revolutionary process is situated in a context of heightened struggle between two distinct projects. The traditional elites know perfectly well that this practice gives real content to democracy, ending privileges, clientelism, and ultimately the power of capital over society. This is a political struggle with a clear class (or class bloc) content which will continue to develop for a long time. That is why if anyone claims, and some do, that participatory budgeting is just a more organized form for the poor to fight over the crumbs of capitalism, or at best, that it is a slight democratic improvement totally unrelated to socialism, they would be completely mistaken. Besides deepening and radicalizing democracy, participatory budgeting also is consti-tuted by a vigorous socialist impulse, if we conceive socialism as a process in which direct, participatory democracy is an essential element, because it facilitates critical consciousness and ties of solidarity among the exploited and oppressed, opening the way for the public appropriation of the State and the construction of a new society.

In this statement, Dutra alludes to the critique of participatory budgeting by the orthodox left.[8] From this perspective, participatory budgeting is at best insignificant because of its excessively local focus; its multiclass character (that is, the fact that it is not an instrument solely of workers); and its inability to transform the fundamental structures of capitalism or harm bourgeois interests. At worst participatory budgeting helps the bourgeoisie cope with the "crisis of capitalism" by taming popular movements and teaching them to cooperate with elites rather than engage in direct action to destroy the bourgeois state. A crucial complaint of these critics is that national issues such as debt repayment are not discussed within the participatory budgeting process. Most of these critics point to the support given participatory budgeting by "imperialist organizations" such as the United Nations and the Inter-American Development Bank as evidence that the process is a Trojan horse used to undermine revolutionary aspirations.

Indeed, the United Nations (through its Habitat division), the Inter-American Development Bank, and numerous other international development agencies have promoted participatory budgeting in various ways, ranging from publishing books and articles to financing workshops and studies to requiring participation as a condition for aid and providing assistance to individual participatory budgeting projects.[9] Although much of the discourse used by the development agencies closely resembles the radical democratic language and many of the goals—reducing poverty and extending service provision, ending corruption and clientelism, promoting transparency and accountability, improving government efficiency and legitimacy—are similar, the agencies' liberal approach to participatory budgeting differs from the radical democratic approach in several ways. While the leftist parties initially behind participatory budgeting view the process as contributing to the reconceptualization of socialism, development agencies see it as one among several tools for reconceptualizing development.

Two factors appear to have contributed to the adoption of participatory budgeting by the development community in the 1990s. One was the rising influence of the notion of participation in development; the other was the notion of good institutions, or good governance, as necessary for economic growth.[10] For many proponents of the liberal perspective, participatory budgeting is a potential institutional remedy within a second round of market-oriented economic and administrative reforms in Latin America, following the failure of the first round to reduce poverty or increase growth rates despite bringing down inflation. As Campbell (2003, p. 8) argues, "The next stage of reforms in the region was shifted to the local level, where new models of governance were being invented. These models were marked by innovation in the governance contract, by widespread participation, and by new forms of accountability in spending."

From this perspective, participatory budgeting exists alongside and in support of other public sector reforms, such as privatization and streamlining state employment.[11] Whereas the radical democratic approach views participatory budgeting as legitimating the state's role to protect it against privatization, the liberal approach sees it as co-existing with strategies for reducing the state's role. Whereas the radical democratic approach views participatory budgeting as involving citizens in participating in budgetary decision making and monitoring results, the liberal approach views participation more broadly, to include consultations between governments and citizens; provision of information to citizens; use of labor, materials, and money contributed by citizens to implement projects; and payment of taxes.

In some ways the liberal and orthodox leftist approaches to participatory budgeting coincide. Both see participatory budgeting as facilitating market-oriented, or capitalist, development by encouraging citizens to trust government (and therefore stabilizing democracy). Both ignore or dismiss what radical democrats see as participatory budgeting's potential as a counterhegemonic or socialist project. This is precisely the danger that the conservative approach to participatory budgeting highlights. When participatory budgeting experiments were initiated in Porto Alegre, Montevideo, and Caracas, they were criticized as dangerous for the stability and even persistence of representative democracy by established political parties, particularly in Montevideo and Caracas (see Goldfrank 2002).[12] From the conservative perspective, rather than deepening democracy and promoting government efficiency, participatory budgeting is antidemocratic and unstable. Two somewhat contradictory positions can be found within this view. One is that unrepresentative volunteer participants are given greater power than democratically elected (and therefore representative) municipal council members and technically trained professional municipal employees. Participatory budgeting thus undermines the legitimacy of the municipal legislature and leads to poor service provision and urban planning. The other position is that participatory budgeting participants are politically manipulated by the local ruling party and deceived into thinking that they have decision-making power. In both cases many within the conservative perspective explicitly link participatory budgeting to totalitarianism. They see participatory budgeting as the creation of a parallel power aimed at replacing representative, multiparty democracy and capitalism with single-party socialist domination, effected through a direct relationship between the executive branch and the masses.

Participatory budgeting is not a neutral, technical instrument—notwithstanding development agencies' inclusion of it as part of a "toolkit" for development. Much of the now extensive academic literature on participatory budgeting, while often influenced by one of these normative approaches, either ignores the ideological and political battle surrounding it or fails to incorporate this battle into the analysis. Many scholars have focused on showing that participatory budgeting embodies concepts such as participatory publics (Wampler and Avritzer 2004), co-governance for accountability (Ackerman 2004), progressive pragmatism (Rhodes 2003), deliberative development (Evans 2004), or empowered participatory governance (Baiocchi 2001b; Fung and Wright 2001; Miños Chavez 2004b).[13] They and other scholars have produced rich analyses of participatory budgeting, focused almost entirely on Brazilian experiences, especially Porto Alegre. They have shown that participatory budgeting can achieve many of the goals envisioned by both the radical democratic and liberal perspectives, especially in terms of redirecting public resources toward poor neighborhoods (Marquetti 2002; Serageldin and others 2003); extending service provision (Navarro 2004; Santos 1998); democratizing existing and spurring the creation of new civic associations (Abers 2000; Baierle 1998; Baiocchi 2001a, 2001b; Wampler and Avritzer 2004); and increasing transparency and accountability (Ackerman 2004; Fedozzi 1997; Wampler 2004), while reducing clientelism (Abers 2000) and enhancing democratic representation for the formerly excluded (Nylen 2003; Souza 2001). They show that these outcomes are by no means guaranteed by participatory budgeting and that even well-regarded cases show some contradictory results (Baierle 2003; Nylen 2003; Souza 2001; Wampler 2004).

Preconditions and Design Features

To explain the success and failure of different participatory budgeting experiments, scholars propose a long list of potentially important design features and enabling conditions. Navarro (2004) provides one of the most comprehensive inventories, which he divides into political, administrative, economic, legal, geographical, and "controversial" issues.[14]

Most scholars agree that political will, sufficient resources, and political decentralization are necessary for successful participatory budgeting; many believe that preexisting societal organization is also necessary. Other conditions cited below can be helpful but are not considered preconditions.

- ▪ *Political will:* The incumbent party and especially the mayor should have a commitment to opening channels of citizen participation in order to share decision-making power.

- *Sufficient resources:* The municipal government should control revenues sufficient to enable investments in public works projects and social programs.
- *Political decentralization:* Municipal officeholders should be democratically elected.
- *Social capital:* The locale should possess civil society associations, preferably disposed to participate in municipal affairs, organized in networks, and relatively autonomous.
- *Bureaucratic competence:* The municipal administration should be staffed by a substantial number of technically qualified employees.
- *Small size:* The locale, or at least the decision-making units of participatory budgeting (which might be considered a design feature), should not be so large as to discourage collective action.
- *Legal foundation:* Existing laws should allow and preferably promote citizen participation in budget decisions.

There is less consensus on which features of institutional design are most important and even whether certain features facilitate or weaken participatory budgeting. Features that have been discussed include the following:

- *Deliberation:* Participants should engage in face-to-face discussion and debate and be given at least some decision-making power over at least some part of the budgetary process, usually the establishment of investment priorities.
- *Centralized supervision:* The mayor's office should be directly involved in coordinating the participatory budgeting process.
- *Accessible rules and information:* The rules governing the process, including the criteria used to allocate resources across neighborhoods and make decisions, as well as all the budgetary and planning information necessary to make informed decisions and monitor results, should be publicly available and provided in an accessible format.
- *Focus on immediate versus long-term planning:* Some scholars argue that focusing on immediate, practical needs is key to stimulating participation. Others argue that a narrow focus undermines discussion of broader, long-term issues and weakens urban planning.
- *Informal versus formal structure:* Some scholars argue in favor of an informal structure for participation that is open to individuals and groups without privileging existing organizations and that is capable of being modified by the participants themselves. Others suggest that in order to avoid political manipulation of participatory budgeting by incumbents and ensure representation of important political and social actors, the process should be regulated by law.

Gaps in the Literature

Despite the growing attention given to participatory budgeting, at least three gaps remain in the literature. First, no rigorous, cross-national analytical testing of which design features and preconditions are most important for producing the desired outcomes has been conducted. Cabannes (2004) provides a valuable review of participatory budgeting experiences in 25 cities across 10 countries. Torres Ribeiro and de Grazia (2003) present useful data on more than 100 cases of participatory budgeting in Brazilian cities. Both studies are based on self-reporting by municipal officials, however, and neither conducts causal analysis.

Second, the design of participatory budgeting and the conditions under which it is introduced have not been linked theoretically. Though many scholars suggest generically that the design of participatory budgeting should be adapted to local circumstances, there is little theorizing about how context affects designs.[15]

Third, the competitive, or nonneutral, aspect of participatory budgeting has not been thoroughly examined.[16] Insufficient attention has been devoted to opposition parties.

I addressed these lacunae in previous research (Goldfrank 2002, 2005) with a structured comparison of participatory budgeting in Caracas, Montevideo, and Porto Alegre. That work led me to conclude that "the design features that ultimately aided the deepening of democracy in Porto Alegre—a high degree of participant decision-making power, a wide range of issues under debate, and an informal structure—were contingent upon a decentralized national state that afforded resources and responsibilities to the municipal government and a set of weakly institutionalized local opposition parties that failed to resist the participation program forcefully" (Goldfrank 2005, p. 9). In this chapter I examine 14 case studies to determine whether they support this statement.

Participatory budgeting is a political institution that is part of normal partisan competition (Goldfrank and Schneider 2006). Political leaders strategically introduce and attempt to design participatory budgeting to serve multiple ends, including gaining electoral support, weakening opponents, forming or consolidating alliances, and fulfilling ideological commitments. The results are not necessarily as originally intended. Outcomes depend not only on the designers' intentions and the local contexts but on the intentions and strategies of other actors, including opponents. This point is especially important when examining the national cases, where the political projects and ambitions of power-holders at different levels of government come into direct conflict.[17]

National Case Studies

The recent expansion of citizen participation in subnational budget processes across Latin America—driven in Bolivia, Guatemala, Nicaragua, and Peru by mandates from the national government—provides an excellent opportunity to examine the full range of hypotheses about preconditions, design features, and strategic objectives.[18] Before these countries are examined individually, some broad comparisons based on the preceding discussion can be made with the locally driven cases in Brazil.

All five countries are politically decentralized, in the sense that municipal executives are directly elected.[19] However, regional governors are elected in Brazil and Peru (at the provincial and regional levels) but appointed in Bolivia, Guatemala (at the regional and departmental levels), and Nicaragua. In Bolivia, Guatemala, and Nicaragua, some national administrations have concentrated "decentralized" resources in the regional governments in order to avoid supporting municipalities held by the opposition.

No national law requires participatory budgeting in Brazil. As a result, in the few hundred cities where it exists, mayors are more likely to be at least somewhat committed to citizen participation than their counterparts in countries that mandate participatory budgeting. In 1997–2000, 73 of the 140 Brazilian cities using participatory budgeting had Workers' Party mayors and 33 had mayors from other parties on the left. In many of the remaining cities, the deputy mayor belonged to the Workers' Party and was often in charge of participatory budgeting (Paiva 2001).

Because Brazil is both wealthier and more fiscally decentralized than the other countries, its municipalities generally have more revenues to spend. Most Brazilian cities spend $240–$400 per resident (Cabannes 2004). In the Central American and Andean cases studied here, most municipalities spent orders of magnitude less (as little as $11 per capita in Nandaime, Nicaragua [WBI 2004f]). Brazilian municipalities are also more likely to have civil society organizations that can work together than are municipalities in Guatemala, Nicaragua, and Peru, where recent civil wars have polarized the population.

The only precondition that might benefit the non-Brazilian cases is the legal foundation. While Brazilian laws require large cities to create municipal administrative councils for health, education, and other social sectors in order to receive federal transfers, they do not require budget councils. In contrast, national laws in the other four countries require development or oversight councils with responsibilities for contributing to municipal budgets and monitoring implementation. Peru's laws go furthest. Guatemala's laws on participation are contradictory: the Development Councils Law requires budgetary proposals from community development councils, the Municipal Code does not.

The two remaining preconditions—bureaucratic competence and small size—vary within and across countries. They may help balance each other because larger cities, which tend to have lower participation rates in various local civic activities, also tend to have larger, more professional bureaucracies, although in general, municipal employees in Latin America do not have a reputation for efficiency (Nickson 1995).

The institutional design of Brazil's participatory budgeting differs from that of other countries in several important ways. First, its programs tend to focus more on immediate needs.[20] Indeed, in the four other countries, the participatory budgeting processes either grew out of or are linked to more long-term municipal development planning.

Second, participatory budgeting is generally less formally structured in Brazil. Individuals rather than representatives of organizations are more likely to participate (Cabannes 2004).[21] In most Brazilian cities participatory budgeting is internally regulated; outside Brazil "participatory budgeting has been regulated and institutionalized by municipal resolution, decrees, laws or constitutions" (Cabannes 2004, p. 40).[22]

Third, participatory budgeting is more deliberative in Brazil than in other countries. Community assemblies debate and set investment priorities on an annual basis; regional and sectoral forums of delegates from these assemblies and a municipal council of delegates meet throughout the year to negotiate budget details with city officials before the budget is sent to the municipal legislature for approval. In other countries the deliberative character of participatory budgeting is often difficult to perceive.[23] The laws in Bolivia, Guatemala, and Nicaragua suggest more consultative roles for the development councils. The Peruvian participatory budgeting law requires that 60 percent of participatory budgeting coordination council members be government officials.[24] Roughly half of the members on the development councils in Guatemala and Nicaragua are also from the government.

Fourth, municipalities in Brazil do a better job of disseminating information than municipalities in other countries, partly because they have greater resources, which allows them to print and distribute rulebooks and pamphlets and to advertise meeting times and places. In Porto Alegre city buses serve as mobile calendars for announcing participatory budgeting assemblies, which are also advertised in newspapers and on a government-produced television program. Even in poor municipalities, information is made accessible: in the impoverished Brazilian fishing village of Icapuí, for example, the mayor painted monthly budget figures—both revenues and expenditures—on the side of his house.

How have the contrasting designs and preconditions affected the results of participatory budgeting? Outside Brazil implementation of national laws on citizen participation in subnational budgeting has been slow and uneven. This seems to reflect the indifference or hostility toward participatory budgeting by many mayors and the lack of bureaucratic competence of many municipal governments, especially the smaller ones. Regional and local authorities have often used undemocratic procedures in composing the development councils, feeding the view that clientelism and corruption persist. The lack of clear criteria for distributing resources has led to an urban bias in many cases, even in predominantly rural areas, undermining poverty reduction efforts. Actual citizen participation rates have been low, not only in decision-making processes but even in consultation exercises. As a World Bank Institute summary report notes, "The lack of information, interest, capacity, time, and financial resources constrains direct participation" (WBI n.d.-a, p. 40).

Some observers have expressed concern that participatory budgeting in Brazil fails to integrate into effective long-term urban planning, generates antagonisms with municipal legislatures, and is not legally required of all 5,507 municipalities, which means that even in cities that have tried participatory budgeting, it may not continue in future administrations. Indeed, a study of 103 Brazilian cities with participatory budgeting during the 1997–2000 period shows that in 28 percent of the cases, participatory budgeting was discontinued by the initiating or the subsequent administration (Chaves Teixeira n.d.).

What features account for the diverging results across countries? Political will, bureaucratic competence, sufficient resources, and an informal, deliberative, and needs- and rules-based design appear to increase the chance that participatory budgeting will be successful.

Preconditions, strategic objectives, and institutional design seem to be linked. Where national governments try to legislate participation rather than design public, deliberative processes, they tend to create overly formal institutions that privilege existing political and social organizations.[25] Determining which organizations are privileged depends on the goals of power-holders at both the national and subnational levels of government.

Locally driven participatory budgeting processes tend to be more informal and deliberative, for two possible reasons. One is that mayors who implement participatory budgeting are often responding to demands by social movements for deliberative public spaces. The other is that open formats potentially allow mayors to attract new constituents. It is probably not a coincidence that most cases of successful participatory budgeting in Peru exhibit more informal and deliberative designs and were started by mayors before the 2003 law went into effect.[26]

Bolivia

Institutions designed at the national level have been modified (or rejected) by local authorities in Bolivia, based on local conditions, with widely varying results. President Gonzalo Sánchez de Lozada introduced decentralization measures and the Popular Participation Law in 1994. Since then the experience of citizen participation in subnational budgeting in Bolivia has been mixed.

Most observers find fault with both the design and the implementation of the participatory institutions, although some believe living standards in rural communities have improved.[27] It seems likely, however, that any improvements were due more to the increased funds made available to municipalities than to increased citizen participation. Revenue transfers to all local governments more than tripled between 1993 and 1997; allocations for noncapital expenses jumped from about $4 million a year to roughly $112 million (Altman 2003). In addition, HIPC II funds became available in 2000.

President Sánchez de Lozada's motivations for implementing the Popular Participation Law are a source of debate. Many analysts suggest that in addition to seeking to strengthen democracy, reduce poverty, and reinforce the structural adjustment program adopted in the 1980s, Sánchez de Lozada sought to design the law strategically so as to reap political benefits. First, his party was weakest in departmental capitals, and he feared that the elite's desire for autonomy in Santa Cruz would sow national disunity. For this reason, the participation and decentralization laws emphasized the municipal rather than the departmental levels of government. Sánchez de Lozada's successor, Hugo Banzer, whose party dominated the departmental capitals, reversed this trend (Altman 2003).

Second, participatory institutions under Sánchez de Lozada seemed intended to break the power of leftist labor and peasant unions, elitist "civic committees," and political parties and perhaps construct a new alliance with indigenous movements. On the one hand, he appointed an indigenous leader as his vice president. On the other hand, the Popular Participation Law gave municipal planning and budgeting participation rights only to territorial-based organizations, which were conceived as traditional indigenous and peasant community organizations in rural areas and neighborhood associations in urban areas. The territorial-based organizations were supposed to use customary practices to elect an oversight committee to monitor budget implementation in each municipality. The Popular Participation Law thus ignored the unions and civic committees, creating a competitor for the party representatives in the municipal legislature.

It is not surprising, then, that the major union confederations (the Bolivian Labor Central [COB], linked to Evo Morales, and the United Union Confederation of Bolivian Peasant Workers [CSUTCB], linked to Felipe Quispe); the civic committees; departmental elites; and opposition parties all opposed the Popular Participation Law (Altman 2003). The unions referred to it as the *ley maldita* (damned law) and called on indigenous peasants not to participate (their call was not always heeded) (WBI 2004b).

The Popular Participation Law appears to have functioned most effectively in small, homogeneous, indigenous communities with strong traditional organizations. In many municipalities, opponents of the law obstructed, delayed, and tried to subvert the new participatory institutions. In the first years after the law went into effect, local party elites manipulated it to adapt it to their own use, designating oversight committee members from the top down rather than through participatory processes and sometimes creating fictitious territorial-based organizations rather than work with existing organizations. Although the law stipulates that municipal governments should hold workshops and consultations to hear community demands, this has not occurred systematically or democratically across the 327 municipalities. In rural areas the "culture of consultation" is "not exempt from the political system's behavior patterns, nor from those of social movements, which, like the parties, maintain authoritarian traits" (WBI 2002, p. 12). The situation is even worse in urban areas, where implementation of the law has been delayed and the consultation processes co-opted. As Bartholdson, Rudqvist, and Widmark (2002, p. 28) argue, political parties "divide indigenous and local community members" using traditional clientelist tactics: "Particularly in the Bolivian lowlands, municipalities have been controlled by elites in the urban centres, and the needs of the rural indigenous population have been marginalized."

The political manipulation of the new ostensibly participatory institutions has had negative effects on the practice of citizen participation in municipal budgeting. In many municipalities, territorial-based organizations and oversight committees either do not function at all or are not effective at transmitting community demands into budgets or monitoring budget implementation in order to reduce corruption (Altman 2003; Bartholdson, Rudqvist, and Widmark 2002; Krekeler, Quezada, and Rea 2003). Channels for direct participation by community members appear to be lacking, and the representativeness of the territorial-based organizations has been questioned. According to Krekeler, Quezada, and Rea (2003, p. 25), the annual budget process "has been reduced to a mere listing of needs of each neighborhood or community expressed by the presidents of the neighborhood associations or territorial-based organizations, which generally do not coincide with the demands of the majority of the residents because, often, the territorial-based organization leaders do not consult the residents; on the contrary, they prioritize the demands using personal criteria."

Nonetheless, at least one aspect of the Popular Participation Law seems unambiguously to have enhanced democracy. In one of the only majority-indigenous countries in Latin America, a country with a long history of the exclusion of this majority, the law has increased the number of indigenous mayors, municipal councillors, and, in turn, national representatives. It is ironic that while Sánchez de Lozada may have pushed the law as a way of winning indigenous support, the indigenous union leaders who vilified the law ended up benefiting most from it, eventually using their strength to force Sánchez de Lozada from office.

Guatemala

Less political controversy has accompanied decentralization and participation laws in Guatemala. Reform was linked to the mid-1990s peace process, agreed to on a more consensual basis, and strongly encouraged by international organizations.[28]

Despite these advantages, of the five countries studied here, Guatemala has probably seen the least success with participatory budgeting. According to a study by the World Bank Institute (2004a, p. 56), "the concept of community participation in the municipal budget . . . is just a discourse raised as an initiative, not a process." This view is supported by other studies, which find that the municipal development councils appear "to have been created mainly to cover administrative obligations and not as a forum for participation" and that they only rarely overcome a "merely formal scope" (Puente Alcaraz and Linares López 2004, p. 249). A number of problems prevent the effective functioning of participatory budgeting in Guatemala, starting with the apparent lack of genuine commitment on the part of national leaders, who seem to have adopted participation laws largely under pressure from international organizations.

Although fiscal decentralization has increased in recent years, Guatemalan municipalities remain relatively poor, dependent on less than transparent national transfers, and heavily indebted. Transfers have increased since 2000, with the availability of HIPC II funds. Departmental governments, whose leaders are appointed, receive the largest share of these investment funds; they can—and often do—withhold funding from municipalities in which the elected mayor is from a different political party (Puente Alcaraz and Linares López 2004). Mayors must produce three separate budgets to obtain transfers for public investments, and political criteria determine the distribution of funds for two of these transfer sources (Miños Chavez 2001). In addition to lacking sufficient funds, municipal governments generally lack qualified personnel; both factors undermine participatory budgeting processes (Centro Pluricultural para la Democracia 2005). Observers have noted a lack of citizen interest in the community and municipal development councils; civil society organizations are either absent or unwilling to work together (Centro Pluricultural para la Democracia 2005). One study argues that the weak and fragmented nature of civic participation in Guatemala stems from "the survival of authoritarian traits, the internal armed conflict, and the introduction and application of policies that encourage individualism and social atomization" (WBI 2004e, p. 3).

Perhaps the most important reason for the general failure of participatory budgeting in Guatemala is the dearth of mayors committed to sharing power with citizens. Since 1999 between a third and almost half of all mayors have belonged to the Guatemalan Republican Front, the party of ex-military dictator Efraín Rios Montt; they have not been considered committed to participatory ideals. Where community and municipal development councils are more than fictive, mayors have often shaped them for political benefit. The community councils have not generally been composed of representatives elected in open public assemblies, as they are supposed to be. The municipal development councils are open only to sector representatives summoned by the mayor (WBI n.d.-a). Municipalities with mayors from locally based, nonpartisan civic committees (which are often headed by indigenous leaders) appear more committed to participatory budgeting. A notable case was Quetzaltenango, one of the four largest cities in Guatemala, during the 2000–03 term (Selee 2004). These civic committees won in 25 municipalities in 2003 (though a traditional party took back Quetzaltenango), less than 10 percent of the total and the same number they won in 1999. Future success for participatory budgeting in Guatemala may depend partly on whether civic committees gain popularity in more municipalities.

Nicaragua

At first glance Nicaragua in the late 1990s might appear to have been an auspicious arena for introducing participatory budgeting reforms.[29] A leftist party with a rhetorical commitment to participatory democracy and a history of alliances with social organizations—the Sandinista Front for National Liberation (FSLN)—controlled a third of all municipalities; the new president, Arnoldo Alemán, had been mayor of the capital city; and international agencies committed large sums of aid after Hurricane Mitch, followed by HIPC II funding in 2000. Building partly on the FSLN's municipal autonomy laws of the late 1980s and encouraged by international donors, Alemán introduced further decentralization and participation reforms in 1997, 2000, and 2001. The laws compel municipal governments to consult with citizens in the budget process through town hall meetings and neighborhood and municipal development committees. In practice, the major political actors' will to share decision-making power, use international funds transparently, and implement the reforms is questionable.[30]

Even some sympathetic observers do not consider the FSLN to have reformed along the lines of other Latin American parties on the left. Scholars highlight the FSLN's continued tendencies to co-opt and control social movement allies and to close off spaces for dissenting opinions instead of promoting meaningful participation processes (Hoyt 1997; LaRamée and Polakoff 1999).

Legal reforms, which were meant to strengthen municipal government and were agreed to by the FSLN as part of a governing pact, also faced problems. One was that they included measures to strengthen the dominance of the two-party system under the FSLN and Alemán's Liberal Alliance. Another was that the reforms were not accompanied by adequate resources. Between 1997 and 2003, central government transfers to municipalities represented about 1 percent of the central government's budget. Transfers increased to 4 percent in 2004 and should increase annually by 1 percent over the next six years, depending in part on the country's economic performance (Pineda Gadea 2003). It is unclear whether these incremental increases will be sufficient. Municipal governments in Nicaragua are vastly underfunded, with some receiving less than $9,000 a year in central transfers in 2003 and many forced into bankruptcy (Grigsby 2003). Furthermore, central transfers were biased based on political criteria, as were investment funds allocated through a separate government entity, the Nicaraguan Institute of Municipal Promotion (Grigsby 2003; Howard 2002; Ortega Hegg 2001).

The climate of political polarization and the weakness of municipal bureaucracies also worked against participatory budgeting. As in Guatemala, failure to achieve successful participatory budgeting practices in Nicaragua seems overdetermined. While the laws requiring participation seem worthy, "in practice, the attendance and dialogue in the town hall meetings have been neither constant nor massive, like the use of the other established procedures" (Pineda Gadea 2003, p. 17). Open town hall meetings are sparsely attended, chaotic, and unproductive (Ortega Hegg 2003). Development committees tend to be convened by the mayor and are thus often exclusionary, favoring only the mayor's social allies (Howard 2002).

Peru

As national policy, participatory budgeting is still nascent in Peru, though a number of local governments implemented participatory budgeting reforms before passage of national laws in 2003. These laws obligate all regional, provincial, and district governments to promote citizen participation in the formulation, debate, and "concertation" (or agreement) of their development plans and budgets through the creation of coordination councils and through public assemblies.

While Peru shares a top-down model of participatory budgeting with the other countries examined here, the designers of its laws did take local experiences into account. This may be because some members of the ruling party, Perú Posible, came from the United Left, with its history of municipal participation programs in the 1980s before Alberto Fujimori's decade of centralized and clientelist authoritarian rule.[31] A desire for decentralization as part of democratization emerged on the part of party representatives and civil society organizations in opposition to Fujimori; decentralization was also supported by international agencies, such as the U.S. Agency for International Development. Most decentralizing reforms were thus fairly consensual. However, the related citizen participation laws were contested by many congressional representatives and nearly failed to pass (Chirinos Segura 2004). Echoing the conservative approach to participatory budgeting, many traditional parties, especially the Aprista Party (the second-largest party in Congress), argued that citizen planning and budget councils undermined representative democracy. It is perhaps not surprising that the Apristas had the largest share of power at the subnational level, controlling nearly half of the 25 regions. Faced with opposition resistance, the government passed a compromise hybrid bill in mid-2003 that gave local authorities 60 percent of the seats on the councils.

The first two years of participatory budgeting are not considered to have succeeded in promoting participation, transparency, effective planning, or improvements in public infrastructure and service provision (Chirinos Segura 2004; Díaz Palacios 2004; Monge 2004; Ricci López and Bravo 2004). A host of factors have undermined participatory budgeting, from problems in design to resistance and manipulation by the opposition, insufficient resources, and lack of civil society initiative.

Unlike Bolivia, in Peru all legally registered social organizations (not just territorial organizations) with at least three years of proven existence are allowed to participate in elections for the regional and local councils meant to coordinate the development plan and budget. The restrictions were meant to avoid the top-down creation of phantom organizations; in practice, they excluded many organizations of the poor, which lacked legal standing. Civil society representatives hold only 40 percent of the seats on the coordination councils, and a third of those are slated for business representatives, reducing participation by the poor.

The participation laws contradict the guidelines from the Ministry of the Economy and Finance, which allowed individuals to participate and reduced the importance of the coordination councils. This contradiction caused confusion, and, as in other countries that nationally legislated participatory budgeting, many local and regional leaders chose to ignore the rules.

As of mid-2004, only about a third of the 1,821 district municipalities had created local coordination councils (Díaz Palacios 2004). In his study of more than 30 provincial and district participatory budgeting experiences, Díaz Palacios (2004, pp. 233–34) finds that mayors seemed to be complying "with constituting the local coordination council more for formal reasons than out of democratic conviction," given that the local coordination council were not taking on the planning and budgeting roles allowed for in the law. Chirinos Segura (2004) reports that the Congress had to pass additional laws in order to force the regional governments to establish their coordination councils, which even then were rarely convened. In some cases they were convened but could not reach a quorum. Elections for the coordination councils were either never held or not very democratic (Chirinos Segura 2004; Díaz Palacios 2004; Ventura Egoávil 2003). In place of a general election process, the mayor or regional presidents often invited certain organizations to assemblies in order to select representatives. At the other extreme, many local authorities ignored the rules about legal registration and being in existence for three years in order to allow more social organizations to participate.

Problems remain even where mayors are committed to participatory budgeting and try to work around the restrictions in national laws. Local governments remain dependent on unreliable and stingy central government transfers; civil society is weak and fragmented, with little interest in institutionalized participation; and little information is disseminated about the recent laws. Municipal governments in Peru have the authority to create local taxes, but only those in larger, wealthier cities have the capacity to do so. On the whole, then, municipalities depend on transfers, which represented about

4 percent of the national government's budget in 2004 and have risen since then (Schneider and Zuniga-Hamlin 2005). Divided among 2,000 municipal budgets, however, funding is low. Of the six municipalities examined below, four had investment budgets of $4–$13 per capita. Moreover, to receive transfers of investment funds, municipalities have to follow strict but little publicized budgeting guidelines set by the national Ministry of Economy and Finance. Several regional and local governments had to return revenues to the central government for failing to comply with these rules (Monge 2004).

At the same time, interest in participation appears to have declined. According to Chirinos Segura (2004, p. 200), in "post-Fujimori Peru . . . the demand for participation has reached its lowest levels in modern history." According to Díaz Palacios (2004), citizens are not well organized, organizations that do exist lack formal structures, and organizational representatives are unrepresentative, poorly qualified, and divided.

One bright spot in Peru is that the Ministry of Economy and Finance has revised the participatory budgeting guidelines every year, seemingly in response to criticisms of the original laws formulated by mayors, governors, and civil society organizations. In 2004, for example, the criteria for municipal spending were relaxed, so that mayors are no longer forced to allocate 70 percent of funding to capital spending. Changes in 2005 seem to have corrected other design problems as well (see Sánchez Velarde 2005). The new guidelines are guidelines rather than legal norms, thus allowing for local adaptations. They emphasize that the budgets agreed to by the coordination councils should be respected by the municipal authorities; more clearly establish the links between the multiyear development plans and the annual budgets, as well as between the regional and local coordination councils; and give greater powers to the coordination councils in terms of organizing the participatory budgeting process. Perhaps most important, the 2005 guidelines stress that the participatory budgeting process be open to all who want to participate and that the participating organizations consult with their members about budget priorities.

Local Case Studies

While national outcomes appear not to have lived up to expectations, there are a number of remarkably successful local cases. Some of the success stories, particularly the Peruvian cities of Ilo and Villa El Salvador, could have been expected, given that the efforts were locally initiated, United Left administrations were in power, and highly organized civic associations with a tradition of local participation were active. Others, such as Curahuara de

Carangas in Bolivia and Huaccana in Peru, are more surprising. In Curahuara de Carangas, an isolated and extremely poor Aymara village in the Andean highlands, participatory budgeting has not only reinvigorated traditional indigenous organizations, it has helped transform them to be more inclusive of women, more engaged with broader indigenous movements, and more focused on long-term sustainable development. In Huaccana, another rural indigenous town, the Shining Path guerrilla movement had destroyed traditional customs and divided the community. Despite very limited resources, the Quechua mayor stimulated high rates of participation in participatory budgeting, helped revitalize civic associations, and redistributed public works and programs in favor of the poor.

This section compares participatory budgeting in 14 municipalities in an attempt to tease out which combinations of preconditions, institutional design, and political competition generate successful experiences like these. Given the variation in the precision of the case study data, these are necessarily rough categorizations.

All of the municipalities suffer from deficiencies in public services. These are especially pronounced in rural areas, where even basic services such as water and electricity are scarce. Resources available for municipal capital spending vary tremendously, from about $5 to $50 per capita.

The municipalities were governed by a wide spectrum of parties, from ideologically motivated parties on the left, particularly the United Left in Peru, to Nicaragua's Liberal Party on the right. The degree of opposition from traditionally powerful political parties or elites varied from virtually none (often in rural villages) to relatively strong, especially where old ethnic divisions were reinflamed by the rise to power of indigenous leaders.

Successful participatory budgeting has occurred under a variety of conditions (table 3.1). Highly successful participatory budgeting emerged even where resources were minimal, opposition from rival political parties was relatively strong, and outside NGOs played no role. Certain conditions appear to be especially advantageous, particularly a reasonably high level of resources, a weak opposition, a high level of social capital, a very strong NGO presence, and a mayor from a leftist, indigenous, or union background. Levels of social capital are categorized based on the number of associations, whether they work cooperatively with one another, and whether they engage in clientelist exchanges. Huaccana is rated as having "weak+" social capital because it had few civic associations following years of guerrilla warfare but some land was communally held, which created trust and collaboration. Tarabuco and Limatambo are rated "medium+" rather than "high" because, although each has a long tradition of peasant organizing, even longer

TABLE 3.1 Characteristics of Case Study Municipalities in Bolivia, Guatemala, Nicaragua, and Peru

Level of success/location	Population	Ethnicity	Level of financial resources	Incumbent party	Opposition party	Level of social capital	NGO presence
High level of success							
Curahuara de Carangas, Bolivia	5,937	Aymara	High	Indigenous	None	Strong	Very strong[a]
Huaccana, Peru	11,289	Quechua	Low	Indigenous	None	Weak+	Very strong[a]
Ilo, Peru	60,053	Mixed	High	Left	Weak	Strong	Weak
Limatambo, Peru	9,264	Quechua	Low	Indigenous/left	Medium+	Medium+	None
Santo Domingo, Peru	10,209	Quechua/mixed	Medium	Peasant Union	None	Strong	Strong
Villa El Salvador, Peru	344,657	Mixed	Very low	Left	Weak	Strong	Strong
Moderate level of success							
El Alto, Bolivia	632,372	Aymara/mixed	Medium?	Center	Medium	Medium	Weak
Tarabuco, Bolivia	20,000	Quechua	Medium	Peasant Union	Strong	Medium+	Medium
Estelí, Nicaragua	110,000	Mixed	Low	Left	Weak	Medium	Strong
Santo Tomás, Nicaragua	19,778	Mixed	Low	Right	Weak?	Weak	Weak
Independencia, Peru	210,807	Mixed	Very low	Center	Weak?	Medium	Weak
Low level of success							
La Union, Guatemala	24,213	Ladino	Low	Center	Medium	Weak	Weak?
Panajachel, Guatemala	10,919	Maya/mixed	Medium	Nonpartisan civic committee	Medium	Weak	Weak?
Nandaime, Nicaragua	38,800	Mixed	Very low	Right	Weak	Weak	Strong

Source: Bolivia: WBI (2002, 2003, 2004b, 2004c, n.d.-b); Guatemala: Fundemos (2003), WBI (2004a, 2004d, 2004e); Nicaragua: Pineda Gadea (2003, 2004), WBI (2004f, 2004g); Peru: Ventura Egoávil (2003, 2004a, 2004b, 2004c, 2004d, 2004e, 2004f).
a. Internationally and nationally based NGOs provided extensive funding and technical aid and encouraged the mayor to implement participatory budgeting.

traditions of animosity between indigenous peasants and the nonindigenous population persist.

The high success rate in Peru contrasts with the relative lack of success in Guatemala. While these cases are only illustrative and do not constitute a representative sample, this difference probably stems from two related issues. The highly successful Peruvian experiences began because of local initiative (except in Huaccana, where Care-Peru chose the town as a pilot project and Oxfam and the Department for International Development supported it). These efforts began before the national participatory budgeting law was passed. In contrast, the Guatemalan experiences followed the national laws and are much more recent, having begun only in 2003.

Table 3.2 lists key aspects of the institutional design and various measures of success. The formality of the structure refers to how open the participatory budgeting process is to individual citizens and how much it privileges existing organizations and local authorities. The two cases assessed to have formal structures relied exclusively on existing organizations and authorities. The cases rated "formal–" also included spaces for individuals to participate.[32]

Municipalities rated "informal" had open public processes that did not privilege preexisting groups. Decision-making power refers to whether the participants debate and decide on spending priorities, how much of the budget is affected by these decisions, and whether authorities respect the decisions. The participation rate includes the number of individuals participating and the number of organizations participating through representatives.

Table 3.2 provides some support for the assertion that outcomes tend to be better where participatory budgeting is less formalized and more deliberative. In the two purely formal cases of participatory budgeting (Tarabuco, Bolivia, and Nandaime, Nicaragua), achievements were meager. In Tarabuco there were ongoing claims of corruption and clientelism, and the quality of these services did not improve (although some investments were made in education and health care). In Nandaime, where the criteria for determining spending allocations are opaque, an extreme urban bias persists. While a little less than half the population lives in the urbanized area, which has relatively good basic services, 89 percent of municipal investments were made there.

In Peru and in Curahuara de Carangas, Bolivia, where the structures were less formal, participants had more decision-making power, participation rates were higher, policies were more redistributive, and government was more transparent. Even the most prosperous city using participatory budgeting in Peru (Ilo) used highly redistributive criteria that allocated nearly twice as much investment funding to the largest and poorest area as it did to the smaller, wealthier zone.

TABLE 3.2 Key Aspects of Institutional Design and Measures of Success of Participatory Budgeting in Case Study Municipalities

Country/municipality	Formality of structure	Decision-making power	Participation rate	Expansion/redistribution of services	Transparency
Bolivia					
Curahuara de Carangas	Formal –	High	High	High	High
El Alto	Formal –	Medium	High	Some	Improved
Tarabuco	Formal	Medium	High	Some	Low
Guatemala					
La Union	Informal	Medium	Low?	Some	Improved
Panajachel	Formal –	Medium	Low?	Some	Improved
Nicaragua					
Estelí	Formal –	Medium	High	Some	Improved
Nandaime	Formal	Low	Low/medium?	Low	Low
Santo Tomás	Formal –	Medium	High?	Some	Improved
Peru					
Huaccana	Informal	High	Very high	High	High
Ilo	Informal	High	Very high	High	High
Independencia	Formal –	High	Medium	Some	Improved
Limatambo	Informal	High	High	High	High
Santo Domingo	Formal –	High	High	High	High
Villa El Salvador	Informal	Medium	Very high	High	High

Source: Bolivia: WBI (2002, 2003, 2004b, 2004c, n.d.-b); Guatemala: Fundemos (2003), WBI (2004a, 2004d, 2004e); Nicaragua: Pineda Gadea (2003, 2004), WBI (2004f, 2004g); Peru: Ventura Egoávil (2003, 2004a, 2004b, 2004c, 2004d, 2004e, 2004f).

This analysis of local cases reinforces the notion that preconditions, competitive contexts, and design features are important to successful participatory budgeting. It also suggests that no particular combination of these factors seems necessary.

Conclusions

The conclusions that can be drawn from these case studies are necessarily preliminary because the precision, type, and quality of data in the studies vary; the studies were not randomly selected; and many of the experiences lasted only a year or two. Nonetheless, several general lessons and indications about future directions of participatory budgeting are apparent.

First, national legal mandates for participatory budgeting have not created widespread local success in encouraging citizen participation, fiscal transparency, or effective municipal government. This is partly because designers of national laws had other goals in mind (possibly in addition to these goals) and partly because of local obstacles, including reluctant mayors or opposition parties, the weak fiscal and administrative capacity of municipal governments, and fragmented, conflict-ridden civic associations.

Second, despite problems, participatory budgeting has succeeded in some remarkably diverse locales—from small, poverty-stricken, indigenous, rural villages to large cities—with residents with various ethnic and class identities. While carefully identifying necessary or sufficient conditions will require further study, success seems correlated with several factors, in varying combinations:

- the mayor is indigenous, from a party on the left, or both;
- opposition from local political elites is weak or nonexistent;
- national or international aid organizations provide project funding, technical assistance, or both;
- the municipality has sufficient revenues to make significant investments in public works or programs;
- there is a tradition of participation and cooperation within and among local civic associations or indigenous customary organizations that has not been destroyed by guerrilla warfare or clientelist politics.

Third, even where participatory budgeting succeeds on some dimensions, it does not dramatically reduce poverty (especially income poverty) on its own. For poverty reduction to occur, fundamental principles of participatory budgeting as originally conceived (transparency, direct participation, redistribution toward the poor) need to be applied not only to national levels of government but to international policy-making institutions as well, under conditions similar to those associated with the local success cases. While at first glance these conditions seem unlikely to be in place in the near future, the current wave of left-leaning presidents in much of Latin America, the democratizing pressure from social movements organizing in venues such as the World Social Forum, and the recent moves toward rethinking on the part of international financial institutions and aid agencies are positive signs.

Fourth, none of the normative approaches to participatory budgeting accurately captures its results, which vary extensively across cases. Participatory budgeting does not always strengthen the state with respect to the market, as radical democrats hope and conservatives fear, nor does it necessarily insulate pro-market reforms, as liberals hope and the orthodox left fears. Recent adoption of participatory budgeting by pro-market parties of the center and the right both inside and outside Brazil challenges the assumption about weakening the market, while recurring anti-privatization protests in countries requiring subnational participatory budgeting—Bolivia, Nicaragua, and Peru—undercut the assumption about insulating the market.

Fifth, the ideological contests surrounding participatory budgeting continue and are likely to persist. On the one hand, certain international development agencies with a liberal approach are promoting participatory budgeting more emphatically and more broadly than ever. Development agencies are advocating and local governments adopting participatory budgeting from Albania to Zambia. On the other hand, participatory budgeting has old and new champions in the recently ascendant Latin American left. Uruguay's Tabaré Vázquez, the former mayor of Montevideo who introduced participatory budgeting reforms there with a radical democratic approach, was elected president in 2004; at least one current within the governing alliance there is pushing for a national participatory budgeting process.[33]

In Venezuela citizen participation in local budgeting and planning councils is enshrined in articles 168, 182, and 184 of the new "Bolivarian" Constitution (Nunes 2004). Most of the planning councils in Venezuela seem not to be functioning as envisioned by the law and may be operating in a politically biased manner (as in many of the other cases of nationally mandated subnational participatory budgeting). Still, after a 10-year hiatus, participatory budgeting has returned to Caracas (Harnecker 2005), and Hugo Chávez recently began advocating participatory budgeting as well, which will surely evoke protests from conservative traditional parties.

Sixth, the liberal approach to participatory budgeting is currently dominant: the open, informal, deliberative design pioneered by Porto Alegre's radical democrats seems to be out of fashion. In Bolivia, Nicaragua, and Peru parties with a more liberal perspective have implemented more regulated, formal, consultative designs that work with preexisting civil society organizations. This trend is evident even within Brazil, where some had hoped that President Luiz Inácio da Silva would implement national-level participatory budgeting. Instead, Silva's major participatory endeavor was the series of meetings for the multiyear federal budget that took place across Brazil's 27 states in 2003. The government invited 70 NGOs to participate in each meeting. The process, as well as Silva's government more generally, has been criticized by Brazil's largest NGO confederations for not providing open, deliberative spaces of participation.[34]

In Porto Alegre itself, after four consecutive victories the Workers' Party lost the 2004 municipal election. Though the new mayor promised to maintain participatory budgeting, his administration seems to be deemphasizing it. Unlike his predecessors, he has not attended participatory budgeting assemblies, and he has announced a new model, Solidarity Local Governance, based on government and civil society organizations. As the Secretary of Political Coordination and Local Governance notes, "Local governance is a nondeliberative executive forum; it is a networked articulation that seeks to create co-responsibility pacts. In this space, there is no dispute, no voting, and no delegates" (CIDADE 2005, p. 1).

Last, to strengthen the future chances of successful participatory budgeting at the local level, its original principles should be applied to higher levels of national and international governance. Even in the small number of municipalities that improved local service provision with participatory budgeting, low incomes and joblessness remain serious problems. This is also true of cities with longer traditions of participatory budgeting, such as Porto Alegre. One of the earliest and most insightful observers of participatory budgeting, Sérgio Baierle, cites a municipal study comparing the 1981–85 period in Porto Alegre (before participatory budgeting) with the 1995–99 period (after several years of participatory budgeting) (Baierle 2003). While education and health care improved, the unemployment rate shot up 78 percent, the number of poor people increased almost 20 percent, and income inequality rose by 16 percent. Local participatory budgeting is not untouched by national economic policies. As Baierle (2003, pp. 303–04) notes, "It is impossible to avoid the consequences of macro-politics of adjustment imposed at the federal level. No matter how fiercely the deconstruction of the public sector is fought at the local level . . . cities still control only a thin slice of the national public budget."

Applying participatory budgeting principles of transparency, participation, and redistribution to decision-making spheres where larger sums of money are at stake, may encourage local participatory budgeting efforts in two ways. First, by producing more universal, egalitarian social policies, it may strengthen local social capital, allowing citizens in very poor countries to think beyond their next meal. Second, by convincing mayors and citizens that participatory budgeting is indeed about these principles— and not politically motivated subterfuge—it may persuade them that it is worth trying.

Notes

1. The lower figure includes cities in which participatory budgeting began as a local government initiative; the higher figure includes all municipal governments required by national laws to consult civil society organizations on budget priorities. It includes Bolivia's 327 municipalities, Nicaragua's 153 municipalities, and Peru's 1,821 districts, 194 provinces, and 25 regions.
2. This formulation borrows from the definition of UN-Habitat (2004).
3. Both parties were elected in 1989 and started their participation programs in 1990. For a comparison of the two Venezuelan cases, see Maya López (1999). For a comparison of Porto Alegre and Montevideo, see Miños Chavez (2004b). For comparisons of Caracas, Montevideo, and Porto Alegre, see Goldfrank (2001, 2002, 2005). The United Left in Peru experimented with similar participation programs in the mid- to late 1980s (see Schönwälder 2002).
4. In Brazil participatory budgeting spread gradually, from 12 cities in 1989–92 to 36 in 1993–96, 140 in 1997–2000, and about 300 in 2001–04. The figures correspond only roughly to the increase in the number of Workers' Party mayors (36 in 1989–92, 53 in 1993–96, 115 in 1997–2000, and 187 in 2001–04).
5. The most thorough account of the left's rethinking is in Roberts (1998).
6. Ruckert (2005) claims that international development agencies promote participatory planning in order to defend "neoliberal hegemony" by co-opting "counterhegemonic" ideas.
7. Other Workers' Party leaders also link local-level participatory democracy and participatory budgeting to socialism (Daniel and others 2002).
8. This view is promoted by the Unified Socialist Workers' Party as well as some minority factions within the Workers' Party in Brazil and by a few key peasant and labor leaders, such as Felipe Quispe, in some Andean countries. For an example of this approach, see Fontana and Flores (2001). For Quispe's view of Bolivia's Popular Participation Law, see Altman (2003).
9. For examples, see UN-Habitat (2004), UN-Habitat and Transparency International (2004), Schneider (2004) on USAID, and Drosdoff (2000) on the Inter-American Development Bank.
10. The notion of good institutions is related to that of effective state institutions. As the *World Development Report 1997* notes, structural reforms in the 1980s and 1990s were an "overzealous rejection of government. . . . Development without an effective state is impossible" (World Bank 1996, p. 25).
11. The UN-Habitat division, which vigorously critiqued the structural adjustment programs of the 1980s and 1990s and the "retreat of the state," is an exception (UN-Habitat 2003).
12. Coordinated attacks on participatory budgeting in Porto Alegre did not occur until the late 1990s, after participatory budgeting was adopted at the state level,

where it was subjected to much greater criticism (Goldfrank and Schneider 2006). For details on the arguments summarized here, see Goldfrank (2002), Nylen (2003), and the sources cited in Goldfrank and Schneider (2006).

13. Space does not allow all of the relevant works on participatory budgeting to be cited here. The literature in Portuguese is especially vast. For a review of the literature on participatory budgeting in Brazil, see Souza (2001). For a compendium of studies of Workers' Party subnational administrations using participatory budgeting, see Baiocchi (2003).

14. See also Cabannes (2004), Miños Chavez (2001), and UN-Habitat (2004). In my view, the discussion of the Peruvian participatory budgeting experience by Chirinos Segura (2004) provides the best conceptualization of the most important factors affecting participation programs.

15. The UN-Habitat (2004) guide does suggest conditions under which implementing participatory budgeting is not advisable.

16. Many scholars cite the conflict between the executive and legislative branches that participatory budgeting sometimes produces; Wampler (2004) focuses on this conflict. Observers of citizen participation programs in Peru have made the same point about the nonneutral character of participation programs and the likely backlash against them from existing power-holders (Chirinos Segura 2004).

17. Chirinos Segura (2004) makes a similar point about nationally legislated participation programs. He argues that the most common problem with top-down models is the resistance they tend to produce from lower levels of government, which see their authority diminished.

18. Unless otherwise noted, the discussion of the national and local cases is based on the following sources: Bolivia: WBI (2002, 2003, 2004b, 2004c, n.d.-b); Guatemala: Fundemos (2003), WBI (2004a, 2004d, 2004e); Nicaragua: Pineda Gadea (2003, 2004), WBI (2004f, 2004g); and Peru: Ventura Egoávil (2003, 2004a, 2004b, 2004c, 2004d, 2004e, 2004f). The discussion of Brazil is based on the literature cited above as well as Villas-Boas (2003) and my own field research on various occasions from 1997 to 2005.

19. In Bolivia if no party wins a majority of the votes, the city council chooses between the top two lists, which is similar to the rule for electing the national executive.

20. One notable exception in Brazil is Santo André.

21. In Belo Horizonte, as well as in a few other Brazilian cities, individual participation and organizational participation are combined.

22. Santo André and Icapuí are exceptions. Both have municipal statutes governing participatory budgeting.

23. Cabannes also finds more deliberative types of participation in Brazil than in the non-Brazilian cases.

24. In Santo André, Brazil, half of all participatory budgeting council members are from the municipal executive branch, and the mayor presides.

25. Some local governments do this as well, with similarly disappointing results in terms of citizen participation (Peterson 1997).

26. More generally, Chirinos Segura (2004) argues that the most successful experiences of citizen participation in Peru have been designed and carried out by local governments.

27. Bartholdson, Rudqvist, and Widmark (2002, p. 47) claim that "no real progress has been reported with respect to poverty and exclusion, which continue being as

ubiquitous as ever." For an excellent, balanced review of the literature on the Popular Participation Law, as well as interesting original research, see Altman (2003).

28. Input from a wide range of actors was important to the peace process, but Mayan organizations complained of being excluded (Warren 1998).

29. The author thanks Yann Kerevel for providing several of the sources for this section.

30. President Alemán had a reputation for corruption while mayor of Managua. In 2003 he was convicted of money laundering and misappropriation of funds, among other charges, after allegedly stealing more than $100 million from the national government. For Nicaragua's struggles with corruption, see the Global Integrity Web site (http://www.globalintegrity.org/2004/country.aspx?cc=ni&act=notebook).

31. Henry Pease García, for example, who was active in the United Left's administration of Lima in the 1980s, became president of the Congress for Perú Posible and was a strong supporter of participatory budgeting.

32. One exception is Curahuara de Carangas, where the structure of participation is based on all 10 preexisting indigenous organizations (ayllus) and the one neighborhood association, which included everyone in the central village. These organizations cover the entire population and are thus representative, unlike many of the organizations in other municipalities.

33. For a discussion of the national participatory budgeting proposal, see Miños Chavez (2004a).

34. For examples, see the critique by the coordinator of IBASE (Dantas 2004) and the summary of the NGOs' reaction in Goldfrank and Schneider (2006).

References

Abers, Rebecca. 1996. "From Ideas to Practice: The Partido dos Trabalhadores and Participatory Governance in Brazil." *Latin American Perspectives* 91 (23): 35–53.

————. 2000. *Inventing Local Democracy*. Boulder, CO: Lynne Rienner.

Ackerman, John. 2004. "Co-Governance for Accountability: Beyond 'Exit' and 'Voice.'" *World Development* 32 (3): 447–63.

Altman, David, with Rickard Lalander. 2003. "Bolivia's Popular Participation Law: An Undemocratic Democratisation Process?" In *Decentralisation and Democratic Governance: Experiences from India, Bolivia and South Africa*, ed. Axel Hadenius. Stockholm: Expert Group on Development Issues.

Avritzer, Leonardo. 2002. "New Public Spheres in Brazil: Local Democracy and Deliberative Politics." http://www.democraciaparticipativa.org/files/LeonardoAvritzer-NewPublic-SpheresinBrazil.pdf .

Baierle, Sérgio. 1998. "The Explosion of Experience: The Emergence of a New Political Ethical Principle in Popular Movements in Porto Alegre, Brazil." In *Cultures of Politics, Politics of Cultures: Revisioning Latin American Social Movements*, ed. Sonia Alvarez, Evelina Dagnino, and Arturo Escobar. Boulder, CO: Westview.

————. 2003. "The Porto Alegre Thermidor? Brazil's 'Participatory Budget' at the Crossroads." *Socialist Register* 300–22.

Baiocchi, Gianpaolo. 2001a. "Brazilian Cities in the Nineties and Beyond: New Urban Dystopias and Utopias." *Socialism and Democracy* 30 (2): 43–63.

————. 2001b. "Participation, Activism, and Politics: The Porto Alegre Experiment and Deliberative Democratic Theory." *Politics and Society* 29 (1): 43–72.

————. 2002. "Synergizing Civil Society: State-Civil Society Regimes in Porto Alegre, Brazil." *Political Power and Social Theory* 15: 3–86
————, ed. 2003. *Radicals in Power: The Workers' Party (PT) and Experiments in Urban Democracy in Brazil.* New York: Zed Books.
Bartholdson, Örjan, Anders Rudqvist, and Charlotta Widmark. 2002. "Popular Participation in Bolivia, Colombia and Peru: A Synthesis of Three Studies." Stockholm: Swedish International Development Cooperation Agency. www.kus.uu.se/SAdelstudie.pdf.
Cabannes, Yves. 2004. "Participatory Budgeting: A Significant Contribution to Participatory Democracy." *Environment and Urbanization* 16 (1): 27–46.
Campbell, Tim. 2003. *The Quiet Revolution: Decentralization and the Rise of Political Participation in Latin American Cities.* Pittsburgh, PA: University of Pittsburgh Press.
Centro Pluricultural para la Democracia. 2005. "Presupuesto participativo: Reflexiones y propuestas en el ámbitoz municipal." *Quetzaltenago* (March). www.cpdguatemala.org/DoctoPresupuestoParticipativo.pdf.
Chaves Teixeira, Ana Claudia. n.d. "O orçamento participativo em pequenos municípios rurais: Contextos, condições de implementação e formatos de experiência." http://www.democraciaparticipativa.org/files/AnaClaudiaOor%E7amentoparticipativoempequenosmunic%EDpiosrurais.pdf.
Chirinos Segura, Luis. 2004. "Participación ciudadana en gobiernos regionales: El caso de los consejos de coordinación regional." In *La participación ciudadana y la construcción de la democracia en América Latina,* ed. Grupo Propuesta Ciudadana. Lima: Ser, Consode, Oxfam, Grupo Propuesta Ciudadana, Participa Peru, DFID, EED, and USAID-Peru.
CIDADE (Centro de Assessoria e Estudos Urbanos). 2005. "¿Como fica o orçamento participativo com a governança solidária local (GSL)?" *Boletim CIDADE* 5 (14). www.ongcidade.org/site/arquivos/boletim/14425eb1c905068.pdf.
Daniel, Celso, Marina Silva, Miguel Rossetto, and Ladislau Dowbor. 2002. *Poder local e socialismo.* São Paulo: Fundação Perseu Abramo.
Dantas, Iracema. 2004. "Brasil: Laboratorio de participación ciudadana." In *La participación ciudadana y la construcción de la democracia en América Latina,* ed. Grupo Propuesta Ciudadana. Lima: Ser, Consode, Oxfam, Grupo Propuesta Ciudadana, Participa Peru, DFID, EED, and USAID-Peru.
Díaz Palacios, Julio. 2004. "Los consejos de coordinación local." In *La participación ciudadana y la construcción de la democracia en América Latina,* ed. Grupo Propuesta Ciudadana. Lima: Ser, Consode, Oxfam, Grupo Propuesta Ciudadana, Participa Peru, DFID, EED, and USAID-Peru.
Drosdoff, Daniel. 2000. "From the Ballot Box to the Ledger Sheet." IDB-América January–February. http://www.iadb.org/IDBAMERICA/Archive/stories/2000/eng/JAN00E/e200e1.htm.
Dutra, Olívio. 2002. "El presupuesto participativo y la cuestión del socialismo." www.cta.org.ar/docs/prespart/PPysocialismo.doc.
Evans, Peter. 2004. "Development as Institutional Change: The Pitfalls of Monocropping and the Potentials of Deliberation." *Studies in Comparative International Development* 38 (4): 30–52.
Fedozzi, Luciano. 1997. *Orçamento participativo: Reflexões sobre a experiência de Porto Alegre.* Porto Alegre and Rio de Janeiro: FASE/IPPUR/Tomo.

Fontana, Mariúcha, and Júlio Flores. 2001. "Presupuesto participativo: En los límites del orden burgués." *Revista Marxismo Vivo* 4 (December).

Fundemos (Fondo de Desarrollo Democrático). 2003. "Sistematización de la metodología: Participación ciudadana para el control presupuestal." Fundemos, Centro Canadiense de Estudios y Cooperación Internal and Agencia Canadiense para el Desarrollo Internacional, Guatemala City.

Fung, Archon, and Erik Olin Wright. 2001. "Deepening Democracy: Innovations in Empowered Participatory Governance. *Politics and Society* 29 (1): 5–41.

Genro, Tarso, and Ubiratan de Souza. 1997. *OrÇamento participativo: A experiência de Porto Alegre*, 2nd ed. São Paulo: Fundaçao Perseu Abramo.

Goldfrank, Benjamin. 2001. "Deepening Democracy through Citizen Participation? A Comparative Analysis of Three Cities." Paper presented at the annual meeting of the American Political Science Association, San Francisco, August.

———. 2002. "Urban Experiments in Citizen Participation: Deepening Democracy in Latin America." Ph.D. dissertation, University of California, Department of Political Science, Berkeley.

———. 2005. "The Politics of Deepening Local Democracy: Decentralization, Party Institutionalization, and Participation." Paper presented at the annual meeting of the Midwest Political Science Association, Chicago, April.

Goldfrank, Benjamin, and Aaron Schneider. 2006. "Competitive Institution Building: The PT and Participatory Budgeting in Rio Grande do Sul." *Latin American Politics and Society* 48 (3): 1–31.

Grigsby, William. 2003. "The Bankruptcy of Municipal Governments and the Swindle of Municipal Autonomy." *Envío* 264 (July). www.envio.org.ni/articulo/2103.

Harnecker, Marta. 2005. "Presupuesto participativo en Caracas: La experiencia del Gol." Caracas: La Burbuja and Alcaldía de Caracas. www.rebelion.org/docs/14418.pdf.

Howard, Joanna. 2002. "Write-Ups on Estelí's Participatory Planning Initiative." Paper presented at the LogoLink International Workshop in Participatory Planning: Approaches for Local Governance, Bandung, Indonesia, January 20–27.

Hoyt, Katherine. 1997. *The Many Faces of Sandinista Democracy*. Ohio University Center for International Studies, Athens, OH.

Krekeler, Jorge, David Quezada, and Oscar Rea. 2003. "Planificación participativa municipal: Apuntes sobre el contexto Boliviano." In *Memoria del Seminario Internacional: Presupuestos participativos en el contexto boliviano*, ed. Red Nacional de Participación Ciudadana y Control Social. Quito: UN-Habitat.

LaRamée, Pierre, and Erica Polakoff. 1999. "The Evolution of the Popular Organizations in Nicaragua." In *The Undermining of the Sandinista Revolution*, ed. Gary Prevost and Harry Vanden. New York: St. Martin's Press.

Lesbaupin, Ivo. 2000. *Poder local X exclusão social: A experiência das prefeituras democráticas no Brasil*. Petrópolis, Brazil: Vozes.

Marquetti, Adalmir. 2002. "Democracia, eqüidade e eficiência: O caso do orçamento participativo em Porto Alegre." In *Construindo um novo mundo: Avaliaçáo da experiência do orçamento participativo em Porto Alegre, Brasil*, ed. João Verle and Luciano Brunet. Porto Alegre, Brazil: Guayí.

Maya López, Margarita. 1999. "Alcaldías de izquierda en Venezuela: Gestiones locales de la causa radical (1989–1996)." In *Gobiernos de izquierda en América Latina: El desafío del cambio*, ed. Beatriz Stolowicz. Mexico City: Plaza y Valdés Editores and Universidad Autónoma Metropolitana-Xochimilco.

Miños Chavez, Daniel. 2001. "El presupuesto participativo: ¿Es viable en Guatemala?" Paper presented at the Inter-American Forum on Municipal Capacity, Organization of American States, August 7, Guatemala City.

———. 2004a. "Democratizar la democracía: Hacia una propuesta de presupuesto participativo nacional." August. Transnational Institute, Amsterdam. www.tni.org/archives/chavez/democratizar.htm.

———. 2004b. *Polis and Demos: The Left in Municipal Governance in Montevideo and Porto Alegre*. Maastricht, Netherlands: Shaker Publishing and Transnational Institute.

Monge, Carlos. 2004. "Participatory Budgets: The Peruvian Experience." Paper presented at the World Bank International Conference on Local Development, Washington, DC, June 2–4. www1.worldbank.org/sp/ldconference/Materials/Parallel/PS1/PS1_S5_PPT3.pdf.

Navarro, Zander. 2004. "Participatory Budgeting in Porto Alegre, Brazil." In *Leadership and Innovation in Subnational Government: Case Studies from Latin America*, ed. Tim Campbell and Harold Fuhr. Washington, DC: World Bank Institute.

Nickson, Andrew. 1995. *Local Government in Latin America*. Boulder, CO: Lynne Rienner.

Nunes, Luis. 2004. "Participación ciudadana y construcción de la democracia en América Latina: El caso Venezuela." In *La participación ciudadana y la construcción de la democracia en América Latina*, ed. Grupo Propuesta Ciudadana. Lima: Ser, Consode, Oxfam, Grupo Propuesta Ciudadana, Participa Peru, DFID, EED, and USAID-Peru.

Nylen, William. 2003. *Participatory Democracy versus Elitist Democracy: Lessons from Brazil*. New York: Palgrave Macmillan.

Ortega Hegg, Manuel. 2001. *Cultura política, gobierno local, y descentralización: Nicaragua*. San Salvador: FLACSO El Salvador.

———. 2003. "La conversion de un 'canal formal' en un 'espacio real' de participación social." In *Participación ciudadana y desarollo local en Centroamérica*, ed. Ricardo Córdova and Leslie Quiñónez Basagoitia. San Salvador: FUNDAUNGO.

Paiva, Uilson. 2001. "Orçamento participativo atrai do PT ao PFL." *O estado de São Paulo*, March 5, p. A7.

Peterson, George. 1997. *Decentralization in Latin America: Learning through Experience*. Washington, DC: World Bank.

Pineda Gadea, Claudia. 2003. "Condiciones del marco nacional para los procesos de preparación participativa de presupuestos municipales en Nicaragua." World Bank Institute, Managua.

———. 2004. "Las experiencias de participación cívica en políticas y procesos de preparación del presupuesto municipal en Estelí." World Bank Institute, Managua.

Puente Alcaraz, Jesús, and Luis Felipe Linares López. 2004. "A General View of the Institutional State of Decentralization in Guatemala." In *Decentralization and Democratic Governance in Latin America*, ed. Joseph Tulchin and Andrew Selee. Washington, DC: Woodrow Wilson Center.

Rhodes, Sybil Delaine. 2003. "Progressive Pragmatism as a Governance Model: An In-Depth Look at Porto Alegre, Brazil, 1989–2000." In *What Justice? Whose Justice? Fighting for Fairness in Latin America*, ed. Susan Eckstein and Timothy Wickham-Crowley. Berkeley and Los Angeles: University of California Press.

Ricci López, José, and Elisa Wiener Bravo. 2004. "Planeamiento y el presupuesto partici- pativo regional 2003–2004: Enfoque de desarrollo, prioridades de inversión y roles de los agentes participantes." Cuadernos Descentralistas 11, Grupo Propuesta Ciudadana, Lima.

Roberts, Kenneth. 1998. *Deepening Democracy? The Modern Left and Social Movements in Chile and Peru.* Stanford, CA: Stanford University Press.

Ruckert, Arne. 2005. "(Re-)producing Neoliberal Hegemony? The Poverty Reduction Strategy in Nicaragua." Paper presented at the annual meeting of the Canadian Political Science Association, London, Ontario, June 2–4.

Sader, Emir. 2002. "Apresentação: A democracia como chave da hegemonia." In *Construindo um novo mundo: Avliação da experiência do drçamento participativo em Porto Alegre, Brasil,* ed. João Verle and Luciano Brunet. Porto Alegre, Brazil: Guayi.

Sánchez Velarde, Jimena. 2005. "Cambios en el nuevo instructivo para el año fiscal 2006." *Boletín Electrónico, Campaña Nacional del Presupuesto Participativo* 2 (May). www.participaperu.org.pe/novedades/campa_presu.doc.

Santos, Boaventura de Sousa. 1998. "Budgeting in Porto Alegre: Toward a Redistributive Democracy." *Politics and Society* 26 (4): 461–510.

Schneider, Aaron, and Rebecca Zuniga-Hamlin. 2005. "A Strategic Approach to Rights: Lessons from Clientelism in Rural Peru." *Development Policy Review* 23 (5): 567–84.

Schneider, Mark. 2004. "Promoting Democracy through Decentralization and Strengthening Local Governance: USAID's Approach and Experience." In *Leader- ship and Innovation in Subnational Government: Case Studies from Latin America,* ed. Tim Campbell and Harold Fuhr. Washington, DC: World Bank Institute.

Schönwälder, Gerd. 2002. *Linking Civil Society and the State: Urban Popular Movements, the Left, and Local Government in Peru, 1980–1992.* University Park, PA: Pennsylvania State University.

Selee, Andrew. 2004. "Exploring the Link between Decentralization and Democratic Governance. In *Decentralization and Democratic Governance in Latin America,* ed. Joseph Tulchin and Andrew Selee. Washington, DC: Woodrow Wilson Center.

Serageldin, Mona, John Driscoll, Liz Meléndez San Miguel, Luis Valenzuela, Consuelo Bravo, Elda Solloso, Clara Solá-Morales, and Thomas Watkin. 2003. "Assessment of Partici- patory Budgeting in Brazil." Center for Urban Development Studies, Harvard Univer- sity, Cambridge, MA, and Inter-American Development Bank, Washington DC.

Souza, Celina. 2001. "Participatory Budgeting in Brazilian Cities: Limits and Possi- bilities in Building Democratic Institutions. *Environment and Urbanization* 13 (1): 159–84.

Torres Ribeiro, Ana Clara, and Grazia de Grazia. 2003. *Experiências de orçamento participativo no Brasil: Período de 1997 a 2000.* Petrópolis, Brazil: Fórum Nacional de Participação Popular and Vozes.

UN-Habitat. 2003. *The Challenge of the Slums: Global Report on Human Settlements 2003.* London: UN-Habitat.

———. 2004. "72 Frequently Asked Questions about Participatory Budgeting." Urban Governance Toolkit Series, UN-Habitat, Quito.

UN-Habitat, and Transparency International. 2004. "Tools to Support Transparency in Local Governance." Urban Governance Toolkit Series, UN-Habitat, Nairobi.

Ventura Egoávil, José. 2003. "Condiciones del marco nacional Perú." World Bank Institute, Lima.

————. 2004a. "Estudio de caso: Distrito de Independencia-Lima, Perú." World Bank Institute, Lima.

————. 2004b. "Estudio de caso: Distrito de Limatambo-Cuzco, Perú." World Bank Institute, Lima.

————. 2004c. "Estudio de caso: Distrito Santo Domingo-Piura, Perú." World Bank Institute, Lima.

————. 2004d. "Estudio de caso: Huaccana-Chincheros, Perú." World Bank Institute, Lima.

————. 2004e. "Estudio de caso: Provincia de Ilo-Moquega, Perú." World Bank Institute, Lima.

————. 2004f. "Estudio de caso: Villa El Salvador-Lima, Perú." World Bank Institute, Lima.

Villas-Boas, Renata. 2003. "Experiencias de presupuesto participativo en Brasil." World Bank Institute, São Paulo.

Wampler, Brian. 2004. "Expanding Accountability through Participatory Institutions: Mayors, Citizens, and Budgeting in Three Brazilian Municipalities." *Latin American Politics and Society* 46 (2): 73–99.

Wampler, Brian, and Leonardo Avritzer. 2004. "Participatory Publics: Civil Society and New Institutions in Democratic Brazil." *Comparative Politics* 36 (3): 291–312.

Warren, Kay. 1998. *Indigenous Movements and Their Critics: Pan-Maya Activism in Guatemala.* Princeton, NJ: Princeton University.

World Bank. 1996. *World Development Report 1997: The State in a Changing World.* New York: Oxford University Press.

WBI (World Bank Institute). n.d.-a. "Civic Participation in Subnational Policies and Budgeting: Systematization of National and Subnational Case Studies from Latin America." World Bank Institute, Washington, DC.

————. n.d.-b. "Informe de Trabajo: Estudio de caso del municipio de El Alto." World Bank Institute, La Paz.

————. 2002. "Condiciones del marco nacional Bolivia." World Bank Institute, La Paz.

————. 2003. "Experiencias de Participación Cívica en Políticas y Procesos de Preparación de Presupuestos Municipales en Bolivia." World Bank Institute, La Paz.

————. 2004a. "Condiciones del marco nacional para los procesos de preparación de presupuestos subnacionales en Guatemala." World Bank Institute, Guatemala City.

————. 2004b. "Experiencias de participación cívica en políticas y procesos de preparación de presupuestos municipales en Curahuara de Carangas." World Bank Institute, La Paz.

————. 2004c. "Experiencias de participación cívica en políticas y procesos de preparación de presupuestos municipales en Tarabuco." World Bank Institute, La Paz.

————. 2004d. "Experiencias subnacionales en participación cívica en la preparación de presupuestos en Guatemala: Municipio de Panajachel, Sololá." World Bank Institute, Guatemala City.

————. 2004e. "Experiencias subnacionales en participación cívica en la preparación de presupuestos en Guatemala: Municipio de La Unión, Zacapa." World Bank Institute, Guatemala City.

————. 2004f. "Las experiencias de participación cívica en políticas y procesos de preparación del presupuesto municipal en Nandaime, Granada." World Bank Institute, Managua, Nicaragua.

————. 2004g. "Las experiencias de participación cívica en políticas y procesos de preparación del presupuesto municipal en Santo Tomás, Chontales." World Bank Institute, Managua, Nicaragua.

Participatory Budgeting in Central and Eastern Europe

ALTA FÖLSCHER

In a democratic context and from a human rights perspective, civic engagement in public affairs is a desirable end, valued for itself. Civic engagement is also seen as instrumental to state effectiveness. When citizens have the opportunity to make their needs known and hold public institutions to account, public resources are likely to be used more efficiently to deliver public goods and services that are better aligned with citizens' needs.

Recognition of the potential of civic engagement in public affairs is widely shared. There is less consensus on what level of engagement is desirable and what form it should take. Increasingly, it is argued that participation in public affairs through elected representatives is insufficient, that the aims of social accountability, functional democracy, and optimization of public resources are best served if citizens also engage with public processes between elections and do so directly.

Participatory budgeting in the broad sense refers to citizens' engagement with public budgets, including such mechanisms as analysis by civil society of spending policies as an input to public debate. A narrower use of the term denotes instances in which citizens provide direct input into decisions about public resource use, usually at the local level of government.

In addition to electing representatives to local councils, citizens in some local municipal and submunicipal areas of Central and Eastern Europe are participating in public resource decisions. This chapter discusses selected examples of such participation. It focuses on the environments within and the mechanisms through which citizens engage with the allocation and use of public resources and on the impact such initiatives have had. The chapter draws on studies on the Russian Federation and Ukraine undertaken for this volume, as well as other studies.

Because of their shared history during much of the 20th century, the countries of Central and Eastern Europe share many similarities. These countries also differ in important ways, as a result of local economic, social, cultural, and political dynamics, both before and after the collapse of the Soviet Union.

All accessible and reasonably well-developed examples from Albania, Armenia, Bulgaria, Moldova, Poland, Romania, the Russian Federation, and Ukraine were included in the analysis. A range of countries and case studies allows preliminary conclusions to be drawn about how differences in the environment may affect the impact and sustainability of participatory budgeting.

The use of case studies is limiting in several ways, however. First, relying solely on cases that are in the public domain means that other instances of citizen participation are not examined. Second, the literature focuses on cases in which citizen participation resulted from an initiative funded by donors or international nongovernmental organizations (NGOs). Third, the source material for some cases (Albania and Romania) was prepared by project staff, which may bias findings. Fourth, the selection of case studies may be biased in favor of initiatives that achieved some success: there are no assessments of initiatives that failed.

The chapter is organized as follows. The next section examines common features in the environment that affect the nature and impact of participatory budgeting practices in the region. The second section groups examples by the nature of participation, examining the relations among environmental factors, initiative features, and impact. The last section distills lessons from the examples. An annex provides details on participatory budgeting from each case study.

The Central and Eastern European Context

Until the early 1990s, power in most of the states in the region was centralized, with little formal discretionary power at the local level. For several generations central governments kept tight control over most aspects of public life: citizens' economic, social, cultural, and political lives were largely directed from the center, with implementation through local offices of the central state. The role of the state was pervasive and prescriptive, and freedom of association and access to information were limited. The state provided citizens with a range of goods and services, but citizens had little control over which services were provided and at what level and quality. Ordinary people were passive receivers of public goods. This affected the local government environment, citizen attitudes toward the state and service provision, and the size, nature, and depth of organized civil society.

With the collapse of the Soviet Union, the structure of central-local intergovernmental relations and state-citizen relationships changed. States passed new constitutions providing for autonomous local governments. Constitutional change was often followed by development of the legislative framework at the national, state, and local levels of decision making to provide for an independent level of local government and for citizen participation. At the same time, Western countries, multilateral institutions, and international NGOs extended development aid and undertook democratization activities in the region. These activities influenced the development discourse.

The history of the region means that participatory budgeting initiatives operate in contexts characterized by the following conditions:

- Citizens have historically been detached from decisions that affect them, are mistrustful of collective action, and are passive receivers of public services.
- Collective forms of political and social organization, such as political parties and civil society organizations (CSOs), are relatively new, as is an elected, independent, and autonomous local level of government.
- Intergovernmental fiscal relations systems are still being developed; roles and responsibilities are weakly and ambiguously assigned to local levels.
- The expenditure responsibilities of local governments do not match their revenue capacity, and transfers from upper levels are nontransparent and unreliable.
- Local governments have insufficient authority to make decisions and often are still developing the capacity to use resources effectively and efficiently to solve local problems.
- Citizens are dissatisfied with local services but do not believe that they can affect them or that local governments are able to do anything to alleviate or solve problems.

The literature on participatory budgeting highlights the need for capacity on both sides of the equation (governments and citizens) in order to achieve positive and sustainable impact (Abers 2003; Goetz and Gaventa 2001). What institutional environment do local governments in the region face? What capacity do citizens and nonstate actors in the region have to participate in participatory budgeting?

The Institutional Environment of Local Governments

Despite an improving legislative environment for local government, in most of the case study countries, policy implementation occurs within an ambiguous legal framework in which roles and responsibilities are unclear. Local governments have limited authority over and limited discretion in their expenditure responsibilities, both because of their weak fiscal capacity and because of the intergovernmental system. In some countries the roles of local governments are not clarified through the further development at lower levels of the national framework legislation. Most countries also lack legislated mechanisms for participation (a notable exceptions is Bulgaria [box 4.1], where national legislation elaborates the mechanisms for participation). Conflicting provisions in different legislative instruments are also common. This results in ambiguous legal frameworks in Albania (Banks and Pigey 1998; Urban Institute 2004); Armenia (Doane, Simpson, and Rabenhorst 2000); Bulgaria (Novkirishka-Stoyanova 2001); Moldova (Viitorul 2004); Poland (Levitas 1999); the Russian Federation (Krylova 2005a; Savranskaya 2003); and Ukraine (Krylova 2005b).

In all countries in the region, the principle of local self-government is a driving factor in the framework legislation. Many countries are signatories to the European Charter of Local Self-Government, which envisages local governments as independent, autonomous local organs of government elected through equal universal suffrage and with meaningful provision for citizen participation in decision making.

In practice, local governments remain constrained in carrying out their public service delivery functions. Expenditure responsibilities are not matched with revenue capacity. Local governments are assigned very few taxes, and even then the rates are often set by a different level of government. Local taxes, particularly land and property taxes, are often difficult to assess and collect. The transfers from shared revenue sources, such as income tax, are not transparently assigned or reliable.

In many countries the first (municipal or village) or second (typically *rayon* [regional]) levels of local government have delegated expenditure functions for which they are accountable to state or national functional departments of expenditure. Local government budgets are reviewed or

BOX 4.1 The Bulgarian Legal Framework for Citizen Participation in Local Self-Government

Like many other countries in the region, Bulgaria is a signatory to the European Charter of Local Self-Government. Unlike other countries, its Constitution and national legislation set out mechanisms for citizen participation in local self-government, including referendums, community meetings, subscription mechanisms, and regulated contact with the mayor. Bulgarians also have the right to demonstrate, to attend meetings of standing committees of the municipal council, and to attend open municipal council meetings.

The Bulgarian Constitution provides for indirect and direct participation in local referendums and community meetings. Referendums can be called by one-quarter of registered voters in a locality or by at least one-quarter of councillors. The outcomes of referendums are binding on local government.

Local meetings can be called on issues of local importance, such as sanitation, public works, use of municipal property, and protection of the environment. These meetings can be initiated by the city council, by the mayor, or by one-quarter of voters. Decisions are legitimate if more than half of all voters attend the meetings and the majority of participants vote in favor of a proposal. The municipal council can reform or revoke the decisions of meetings on request of the mayor, but only after deliberation and voting.

The subscription mechanism can be used to bring decisions to the attention of the municipal council. A subscription can by initiated by 100 or one-fifth of all voters, whichever is smaller. A steering committee must be set up to manage the process. The framework allows the initiators of a subscription one month to collect signatures; the subscription is recognized if at least one-quarter of voters support it. The municipal council has one month to consider the subscription; the final decision rests in its hands.

Source: Novkirishka-Stoyanova 2001.

approved at higher levels. This is the case in Albania and Ukraine. The authority and discretion to make expenditure decisions in line with local needs are therefore limited. Roles and responsibilities are opaque, reducing accountability.

As relatively recent structures operating in a murky intergovernmental environment, local governments have little capacity to plan, budget, or implement expenditure responsibilities or to motivate higher levels of government to increase the level of resources. Local governments in some countries have been restructured more than once in an effort to create viable units or to adjust the emerging power balances between central and territorial governments. Restructuring destroys the emerging capacity to design viable budgets, advocate for funds at higher levels, raise financing, and manage and evaluate budget implementation.

These factors reduce citizens' belief that local government can solve their problems, and they diminsh their interest in participating in decisions (Doane, Simpson, and Rabenhorst 2000; Urban Institute 2004). Citizen participation is further discouraged by limited access to information and lack of knowledge of local government responsibilities and citizen rights. Local own revenues are usually the least significant portion of local government revenues and the least significant portion of taxes paid. This undermines the development of citizen interest to track how their tax contributions are used locally. Citizens are generally dissatisfied with services, but they mistrust local governments and are unwilling to pay taxes, adding momentum to the vicious cycle. Local governments lack the support of local citizens when advocating for more resources at higher levels of government or claiming their right to autonomy.

Citizens and Organized Civil Society

Several factors make citizen participation in government difficult in the region. First, governments developed in a context in which government was traditionally opaque and harshly discouraged citizen participation in public affairs. Second, in rural areas, citizens are often poor, disempowered, and involved in a daily struggle for basic household survival, limiting their interest in communal affairs. Third, many urban residents have little access to power and resources and are excluded from key decisions affecting them. Fourth, fixed attitudes within government and citizens' beliefs about government often hinder enabling environmental factors from developing. Citizens do not perceive social infrastructure to be their responsibility. Indeed, in Moldova and the Russian Federation, citizens are suspicious of activities that are collective and contribute to the public good (see, for example, Ovchintseva 2003, Tiurin 2003, USAID 2001).

The literature on governance and social development suggests that intermediary organizations, such as NGOs (or nonstate organizations) and community-based organizations (CBOs), have a key role to play in encouraging socioeconomic development, improving state effectiveness, and spurring the growth of meaningful democracy (Azfar and others 1999; Dongier and others 2002; Krishna 2003; Malena, Forster, and Singh 2004). Organized civil society provides citizens and governments with information, acts as a conduit for voice, holds government actors to account, and organizes collective action. It can mitigate citizens' own weak capacity for meaningful participation and help develop that capacity.

Organized civil society started emerging in the case study countries only after the collapse of communism. Several patterns are evident (Karatnycky, Motyl, and Schnetzer 2001; Krylova 2005a; Kuts 2001; Ovchintseva 2003; Preci 2002; Urban Institute 2004; USAID 2001; World Bank 2003):

- Civil society has developed more rapidly and is better able to play a mean-ingful role in decision making in countries that faced a range of transition issues and were not focused on independence from the Soviet Union (Albania, Bulgaria, Poland, Romania).
- In all countries, national CSOs have more sophisticated organizational structures, better infrastructure, and better capacity in larger cities than in smaller cities, towns, or villages.
- The role of organized civil society is still often viewed as replacing government in the delivery of services.
- CSOs face major obstacles to financial sustainability. In countries where civil society development is still low (such as Moldova), the lack of funding is acute.
- Many countries (such as Ukraine) lack enabling legal frameworks for citizen participation. In others the existing frameworks hinder the devel-opment of civil society.
- Competition for scarce resources strains relationships among local CSOs, preventing them from forming coalitions.
- Not all CSOs adhere to standards of ethics, transparency, and good governance, hindering the development of trust between citizens and organized civil society and between local government institutions and organized civil society.
- The development of organized civil society benefits from cross-border exchanges and exposure to international successful practice.

The Political Context

According to Goetz and Gaventa (2001), the nature and organization of the political system help determine the level and quality of participation of citizen groups or lobbies (the civil society environment) and the nature and power of the state (the local government environment). An interest group may be equipped with all the preconditions for effective engagement (social organization, relationships with powerful actors, sympathy in the broad population, and "even a crisis event to concentrate public concern on the group's needs"), but the political environment may frustrate success if "the group does not contribute to prevailing political agendas or patronage systems" (p. 11). Informal political systems affect the incentive structure for citizen engagement: if citizens perceive that participation is likely to be ineffective given the nature of power and the distribution of power in society, they are unlikely to engage. Fox (2000) claims that the political system can also undermine public accountability.

The regional case study literature rarely provides an assessment of the impact of local or national political institutions on the level and quality of citizen participation. It does, however, indicate the importance of a functional multiparty system. In many of the case study countries, political party institutions are still weak. When parties are still based on "personalism and clientelism," lack policy platforms, and rely instead on the politics of identity, civil society groups are less likely to gain an effective voice (Goetz and Gaventa 2001, p. 11). Development partners and international NGOs often initiate participatory budgeting practices in the region in the hope that improving citizen participation at the local level will improve service delivery and contribute to accelerated democratization of these societies. An assessment of the political dimension is therefore important.

The negative institutional and political context of local government—together with the absence of countervailing forces of citizen interest and capability to act and the lack of vibrant organizations able to mobilize and support citizen action—should have hindered the development of participatory budgeting practices in the region. Yet as the case studies show, citizens are participating in resource decisions of local governments across the region.

Case Studies of Participatory Budgeting

Very different types and levels of citizen engagement with public resource decisions are called participatory budgeting. McGee (2003) distinguishes four types of participation: information sharing, consultation, joint decision making, and initiation and control by stakeholders. As participatory practices move up this ladder, the argument goes, they become more effective instruments of participation.

This chapter uses this typology of participation, with one addition, information generation. In some countries in the region, CSOs have used applied budget analysis as a policy advocacy tool and disseminated their findings publicly. These activities typically generate information on public policy and services outside the state in order to influence state actions. This form of participation represents a first level of participation, which can be positioned on the ladder one level below shared information.

These five types of participation in the budget process can be grouped into two broad categories: initiatives that are dependent on the state's providing information and space for engagement (information sharing, consultation, and joint decision making) and initiatives that can survive more independently from local government administrations (information generation and direct initiation and control). As the case studies show, sustainable and effective participatory budgeting is contingent on some willingness on the side of local governments to provide information and to engage.

Information Generation

CSOs around the world have gained voice in the public arena by analyzing public policy, budgets, and service delivery (see Falk 2001 for examples). The results are made available to decision makers and stakeholders either directly or through the media, in an effort to influence decision making and build capacity elsewhere for engagement with public policies. The public policy and service benefits include enrichment of the public debate and improved accountability for policy making and implementation. Such work can serve as a catalyst for public participation and collective action.

Many of the case studies discussed in the next section (on information sharing, consultation, and joint decision making) include information-generation activities by civil society as an input into joint local government-citizen activities. The two case studies described in this section are unique in that they originated locally within strong CSOs, without consultation with or negotiation space provided by local government. In both cases such spaces were eventually created, perhaps suggesting that CSOs faced with poor local governance practices could initiate participatory processes through applied budget work.

These two cases described here employed three different types of information generation activities that can be used to make room for space for engagement in the public arena: analysis of the quality of policy and budgeting institutions at the local level, analysis of public policy and budgeting decisions, and research on the quality of public service delivery. In both cases the organizations made efforts to:

- ensure the legitimacy of the work by using rigorous methods and generating good-quality information;
- build local coalitions with other CSOs;

- raise public awareness and support by using local media channels;
- build understanding and capacity in the cities and media through seminars;
- ensure successful dissemination of the results, through the media, special events, and other means.

Both of the organizations had contact with international NGOs that facilitated the adaptation of successful practices from elsewhere. Both also had access to external funding (from the Ford Foundation in the case of Strategiya, from the World Bank and the Canadian International Development Agency in the case of the People's Voice Project). Both CSOs increased the public space for engagement and built a functional partnership with local municipalities.

Access to this space is not broad based, however. A common criticism of public participation initiatives is that because of the need for specialized capacity to undertake technical work, such initiatives tend to limit participation to those who already have access to power and resources. While the development of partnerships between local government organizations and local citizen organizations should be seen as a positive development, and the more diverse analysis of public policy issues may improve the quality of outcomes, there is a risk of co-option by the state of scarce civil society capacity when the public space for participation is not meaningfully extended to a broader base.

Tsentr Strategiya's activities in the Russian Federation

In 1998 the NGO Tsentr Strategiya initiated its program in St. Petersburg and eight other Russian cities (Krylova 2005a). At first the project, which drew on successful practices used elsewhere in the world, focused on research on budget transparency at the city level and mechanisms for citizen participation. The logic was that without good information and some access to decision processes and decision makers, engaging with the allocation and use of public funds would be of limited value. The initial research drew on international assessment frameworks and built support among local NGOs, academic communities, and the mass media to advocate for improved transparency. Tsentr Strategiya and its partners in other cities built capacity to engage with budgets and shed light on how municipal governments were using resources. In 2002 the project achieved enough legitimacy that it expanded its activities, working with local municipalities to develop joint mechanisms for participation.

The People's Voice Project in Ukraine

The People's Voice Project, a local NGO, initiated analysis and policy advocacy on women's issues, education, and public budget and economic issues in two

Ukrainian cities, Ternopil and Ivano-Frankivsk, in coalition with local partners. It started its work by raising public awareness and educating local municipalities on citizens' rights, the need for responsiveness, and the benefits of building local voice (Zakharchenko 2002). In partnership with other local NGOs, in 2000 it created a program of citizen report cards, which measure citizens' attitudes toward public service delivery and specific services. The project organized a national conference to discuss the results of the report cards. The findings of the survey have been used extensively in public debate on municipal resources and public service issues as well as in subsequent budget and policy formulation (Holdar 2002). Building on this earlier work, the People's Voice Project and its partners are now developing local strategic plans.

Information Sharing, Consultation, and Joint Decision Making

In the case studies discussed in this section, information sharing, consultation, and joint decision making often occur together. Budget hearings take place in localities where municipalities provide better information on their resource use. The hearings are frequently accompanied by other mechanisms that draw citizens into decision making, such as capital investment planning committees. Efforts are initiated by local governments. However, different localities use very different mechanisms to achieve these three aims, and localities focus on different aspects of public resource decisions.

The cases in this section describe two mechanisms for soliciting citizen input in a systematic way, both of which increased participation. In Armenia the project was initiated by a third party and encountered resistance from city officials. The high expectations of citizens were difficult to manage, particularly given local governments' lack of administrative and fiscal capacity. In contrast, in Zwolen, Poland, the mayor initiated the program, reducing resistance by city officials, who participated in the initiative. Care was taken to ensure that resources were available, giving citizens an incentive to participate. In both cases the information-gathering effort was largely one-directional: citizens provided information on preferences but did not necessarily engage in dialogue with the local government.

Participatory urban assessment in Armenia

Save the Children and the Urban Institute undertook a pilot project of participatory urban assessment in nine cities in Armenia. The aim of the assessment was to bring more citizen voice into capital planning. A team of consultants initiated the project by conducting research on each of the cities to generate a preliminary list of problems that could be addressed in the capital budget. The cities were divided into districts, each representing a community. A series of meetings was then held with each of the districts. At the first meeting, the initiative was explained. Citizen action groups were elected in each community through direct voting at the meetings. Representatives from these groups were subsequently elected to serve on the city capital planning committee. In a second meeting, participants were asked to rank problems. The results from all meetings were submitted to the city capital planning committee for consideration for the capital plan. The process resulted in 277 proposals to the committee, putting significant pressure on city officials. The initiative involved more than 10,000 citizens, out of a population of about 500,000, in the nine cities.

Capital investment cards in Zwolen, Poland

Zwolen is a small city in eastern Poland. Its 17,000 inhabitants are represented by 22 city councillors. Both the local authorities and citizens are open to new ideas and new management tools. On the mayor's initiative, in 1998 they developed a multiyear capital investment plan that involves citizens at all stages of the process. The city distributed capital investment cards widely to citizens, inviting them to express their development priorities.

At the outset, the city made the rules of the process known, setting out a detailed schedule for implementation and a method for prioritizing and ranking proposed projects. Three criteria were emphasized: improving the city's economy, creating work, and increasing city revenues. The city also appointed an implementation committee to oversee the process and mediate the decisions. The implementation committee worked closely with the city treasurer to ensure that expectations for resources were realistic. Existing projects were also emphasized and considered. The final draft of the budget was approved by the implementation committee, the city board, and the city council (Natkaniec 2002).

Advisory Groups, Bodies, and Committees

Local governments sometimes engage citizens on their priorities and needs indirectly, through some form of representation. Citizen advisory groups offer local governments a mechanism with which to "bring some of the technical expertise and opinions of communities to bear on solving local government problems" and "enhance the dialogue on relevant issues in order to resolve conflicts" (Serban 2002, p. 4). Advisory groups also demonstrate local governments' commitment to transparent and democratic government. They are, however, more exclusive than initiatives that combine information gathering with more intensive efforts at engagement to collect information on citizens' opinions.

In the Gatchina Rayon, in the Russian Federation, the municipality appointed local leaders to provide them with advice. In the Maikop Rayon, nine villages were pro-active in making their affairs more transparent and inviting citizen participation. In some Russian cities, budget roundtables have been held at which selected expert members of civil society have met with municipalities on specific issues. Citizen groups have also been successful in Albania and Romania.

Participatory budgeting councils in Albania

A World Bank–funded project in Albania, implemented through the Urban Institute in partnership with local NGOs, used participatory budgeting councils and a redesigned budget process to improve citizen participation in budgeting. The project selected municipalities in which the local governments were willing to include participatory mechanisms in the budget process, development partners were already active, and a minimum base of organized civil society groups existed.

The project began with an awareness campaign on citizen and local government rights and responsibilities. It then divided each locality into zones. At a first public meeting in each locality, local government officials presented budget forecasts and information on the implementation of the current budget. At a second meeting, representatives to the participatory budgeting council for the locality were elected. This meeting also identified priorities for the neighborhood. The council and local government staff subsequently conducted field visits (a "bus caravan") in order to evaluate priorities, constraints, and possible solutions with citizens. The caravan process exposed officials and citizens to each other's pressing issues and problems. The council then underwent intense training on priority setting and financial planning before proposing plans to the city councils, which made the final decision.

One of the shortcomings of the project was the difficulty of getting broad-based participation. Participation of women was uneven, and outlying localities were difficult to reach effectively (Urban Institute 2004).

Citizen advisory groups in Brazov, Romania

Brazov is a city with 350,000 inhabitants. In 2000 it held its first budget hearings, attracting fewer than 50 people. The following year participation increased to 600 participants; advisory groups (on transport, education, and general issues) were established; and the Brazov Citizen Information Center was created.

The main purpose of the transport committee is to assist the transport authority in developing city transport modalities and to provide input into budgeting for transport. The committee is made up of citizens from various user groups, who were elected. The education committee is tasked with assessing the infrastructure needs of schools, making recommendations on priorities, and monitoring the transfer of education functions from central to local government. The Citizen Information Center supports the committees by explaining the capital budget and providing technical support. It operates as the hub of a network of 35 neighborhood committees, which monitor the use of the capital budget against neighborhood needs. Brazov learned and developed expertise by doing, and the quality of participation improved every year (Serban 2002).

Public Meetings and Budget Hearings

Several countries have legal frameworks that provide for public meetings and budget hearings as mechanisms for operationalizing local self-government. These mechanisms have increased participation in Bulgaria and Ukraine.

The literature on social investment funds includes many examples of development benefits accruing from competition among communities for resources, particularly if the rules of competition are transparent and enforced and the program includes community-level education and capacity building. The Svishtov case study described below is not unlike a social investment fund, except that communities compete for public resources within the city budget.

Capital investment planning in Svishtov, Bulgaria

Svishtov, a port city of 49,000 on the Danube River, is a fishing and agricultural center. In the early 2000s the city created a capital investment plan that distinguished between large infrastructure projects, which are financed externally, and smaller, community-specific projects, which are funded by the city budget through a participative process. This two-part investment planning is now an institutionalized part of budgeting in the city (Driscoll 2002).

Svishtov has also implemented other strategic budgeting mechanisms. It has a forward planning horizon on its capital budget, enabling tradeoffs to be made over time, and it has moved planning from a project-by-project to a programmatic basis. Citizen inputs are used to determine which programs receive attention in the budget (upgrading sidewalks, improving city parks, maintaining child care centers). Citizen applications for funding under the budget, within the selected programs, are invited through a series of community-based public hearings. Clear criteria and procedures have been set for selecting projects, and communities can offer co-financing. A steering committee, with municipality and civil society representation, decides which projects within the programs will be proposed to the council. Criteria include the participative nature of the project, the level of co-financing, the economic and social benefits, the maintenance costs and responsibilities, and technical considerations. The steering committee prepares the plan for approval by the city council.

Svishtov applied good budgeting principles (resource-constrained, forward-horizon, programmatic planning; rationality in decision making and transparent rules; and sustainability of forward recurrent costs) to ensure that participation is engaged on real issues and provides real payoffs to citizens who participate. The fact that participation has been growing suggests that its efforts to involve citizens have been successful. Additional resources for capital investment have been provided within the city budget, and citizen interest in maintaining the resulting infrastructure has grown, adding to sustainability and reducing city costs in future years. This is the only case study that provides concrete evidence that the initiative had any impact beyond improving participation.

Public budget hearings in Kemyanets-Podilski, Ukraine

Kemyanets-Podilski (population 99,000) was the first city in Ukraine to adopt public budget hearings as an integral part of the budget process. This mechanism is part of the legal framework for local self-government in Ukraine. The mechanism is mandatory, but compliance is low.

The first hearings were initiated by a CSO, in partnership with the local government. Clear rules govern the initiation and management of hearings: public hearings can be initiated by a group of residents (1 percent of the entire population or 5 percent of a neighborhood's population), by the town council, or by the mayor. A written initiative is registered and then announced in the media. Within five days the preparation plan needs to be approved. This includes establishing a hearing committee, forming expert groups, and setting the schedule. Government officials and members of the initiating group serve on the hearing committee, together with municipal council members and representatives of NGOs. The hearing is advertised through local media. Budget hearings are often supported by research conducted by local academics. Surveys (that include the most vulnerable populations) are conducted on citizens' priorities for local budget allocations.

Within a month of initiation, the public meeting is conducted. The budget hearing is held in December, before the local council meets to decide the budget. The meeting is chaired by the head of the hearing committee and is attended by representatives of the municipal council and executive, lower-level (village or neighborhood) self-government organizations, and NGOs.[1] Budget hearings start with a report on the previous year's budget and presentation of the following year's plan. Local officials then explain different aspects of the plan before fielding questions. If disagreement occurs, organizers attempt consensus. The minutes of the meeting register all opinions. Within three days, copies of the minutes are sent to the municipal council secretariat and the initiating group and are posted on the municipal information board. The secretary of the council summarizes the outcomes and submits them for consideration at the next council assembly for budget planning (this assembly is open to the public). The outcomes of the supporting polls and surveys are also reported to council members. The results of the meeting are published in the official municipal newspaper.

Initiation and Control by Stakeholders

Following capacity building and technical assistance from development professionals, some communities have actually initiated public projects, raised the funds to finance them, and managed implementation.

Village responsibility for finances in Maikop Rayon, Russia

Villagers in the municipality of the Maikop Rayon are responsible for their own finances. They identify priorities, raise and allocate funds, and operate the village bank account. Villages in the rayon are now more active in local public infrastructure development as a result of community efforts, seven of the original nine villages in the project now have a gas supply, trade has been reorganized, and working phones have been installed.

Community solutions to problems in Zaozerie, Russia

Zaozerie is an impoverished village in the Mezen Rayon, Arkhangelsk Oblast. After the local collective farm was closed, the village of about 25 homesteads faced high unemployment, the collapse of social services, and ongoing emigration.

A participative project was implemented by the Institute for Public and Humanitarian Initiatives, the Mezen Rayon administration, and the Arkhangelsk Oblast government. The institute started with a series of seminars with the rayon administration on the principles of rural self-government. This was followed by meetings, speeches, and discussions with village residents to educate them on their rights and responsibilities. Villagers were at first unwilling to take any action. They got involved when the institute acted in cooperation with village leaders and raised funds for small infrastructure projects (repairing the village well and renovating the local clinic). As citizens' interest and confidence grew, villagers decided to provide a center for the elderly. Completion of this center was an important turning point for the villagers, who have since hired a midwife, repaired the local school, and improved the clinic. The project has changed the village mindset about who is responsible for solving the village's problems.

Conclusions and Lessons Learned

With few exceptions, development agencies or international NGOs were the initiators of participatory budgeting mechanisms in Central and Eastern Europe. Even where initiatives resulted from local action, international organizations funded the key organizations and contact with networks of CSOs worldwide preceded local action. While this does not necessarily detract from the value of the initiatives, it may have implications for sustainability.

Local government autonomy and resource availability, citizen organization and interest, and developed political party systems are often seen as prerequisites for successful participatory budgeting. In Central and Eastern Europe, these mechanisms are proposed as entry points to overcome governance weaknesses.

Three sets of questions are relevant when assessing the value of participatory budgeting mechanisms in the case study settings:

- Did the initiatives improve the ability of citizens to participate in government decision making? Did they improve citizens' capacity? Did they expand public space for engagement?
- Did the initiatives improve the effectiveness of local government? Did they increase the investment and the quality of public services? Did the initiatives lead to more equitable investments? Were better and more relevant decisions about resource use made?
- Can participatory budgeting initiatives function as an effective entry point to catalyze national change and build good governance systems? Did the reviewed initiatives bring about more and better participation?

In all cases, the introduction of participatory mechanisms increased participation. Even where citizens were passive providers of information about their preferences, the initiatives signaled a changed mindset and offered more opportunity for participation than existed before. It is not clear, however, whether the nature of participation was sufficient to ensure its sustainability: if participation does not result in real change, it discourages future participation.

It is also not clear that the mechanisms in place ensure inclusiveness: while participation by those who already have the capability to engage is perhaps better than no participation at all, it is inferior to mechanisms that draw in those who have traditionally been excluded. The case studies suggest that inclusive participation is difficult to achieve: women, vulnerable groups, and people living in remote areas are easily excluded. Interestingly, cases toward the upper end of the participatory scale seem to have provided more opportunity for good-quality, broad-based participation.

Did the reviewed initiatives result in more effective local government? The evidence is not clear. As Krylova (2005a, 2005b) notes, it is difficult to assess the degree to which citizen participation contributes to changes in resource allocations, as the counterfactual is not readily available.

Where information on citizens' preferences is collected at the local level and the activity was initiated by the local government, the results are included in future plans. The extent of this inclusion is not clear, but it seems to be contingent on subsequent decision-making mechanisms (such as implementation committees). Whether narrower interests determine which citizens' preferences are included when decisions are finally made is not clear.

There is some evidence that advisory groups produced real effects. In Brazov, Romania, the advisory group on education had real input into decisions on which schools were upgraded and in which sequence. Whether limited participation (only a few citizens can be elected to committees) leads to better resource decisions is not clear. The value of advisory groups depends on the incentives in place for citizens who get to participate. If members of citizen advisory groups are likely to be held to account by their fellow citizens for the outcomes of their participation, they may be more likely to provide good-quality, nonpartisan inputs. In the absence of such accountability— which may be likely, given citizen apathy—the value of such participation mechanisms may be limited. Members of participatory structures will be absorbed easily into the existing power structures. This may mean that these mechanisms' usefulness in addressing broader governance weaknesses depends on a robust citizen-state governance environment.

The extent to which public budget hearings and meetings increase local government effectiveness (measured as improved service delivery that better reflects citizen preferences) seems to depend on the institutional arrangements accompanying the hearings. In Svishtov, Bulgaria, outcomes were good: citizens competed for real resources and exercised real choice, and cofinancing resulted. In Ukraine, where the hearings were more general, the outcomes seemed to be more indirect: participation was greater, and there was more engagement with local government decisions, which may lead to improved accountability and better service delivery in the longer term.

Where citizens initiate and control outcomes, infrastructure and services are provided that would not otherwise have been available. In three of the cases—Svishtov (Bulgaria), Zaozerie (Russia), and Maikop Rayon (Russia)— the opportunity for citizens to initiate projects led to an increase in the volume of resources available for local development.

Can these initiatives improve governance? Evidence from the case studies is weak. In Strategiya, Russia, advocacy on governance issues resulted in institutional changes. Elsewhere both local government officials and citizens became better informed of their rights and responsibilities as a result of participatory efforts.

Are these initiatives scalable? Can there be a shift from isolated initiatives, often introduced or supported by development agencies and international partners, to overarching programs that are a defining element of public action for citizens in the region? More important, can these initiatives produce results if capacity in government is low, the citizen-state relationship is not rooted in state accountability, and the center of government is weak? There is no evidence in the case studies that this is possible. In fact, at least in countries that are homogeneous and the center holds the balance of power but has weak governance, there may be an opportunity cost of investing in local-level governance and a real cost in terms of citizens' disillusionment in trying to engage government.

The following conclusions can be drawn from the case studies:

- Initiatives create opportunities for participation. Questions remain about whether the quality of participation is sufficient to ensure lasting interest and whether participation is sufficiently broad based.
- Initiatives can break down barriers between citizens and government, improving mutual understanding and communication.
- Initiatives strengthen local CSOs, which may improve local governance over the long term. However, it is not clear that the organizations that gain access to decision making and forge partnerships with local government do not themselves become arms of local government.
- Initiatives can direct resources to more relevant infrastructure and services.
- Initiatives can increase additional revenue for local development.

These benefits do not result automatically. Certain conditions facilitate effective participation. NGOs, local governments, and development agencies may need to establish these conditions before attempting to introduce participatory budgeting.

Several lessons can be drawn from the case studies: *Better information produces better results.* It is an axiom of participation that citizens need access to information to participate. The case studies provide concrete examples of the fact that good information not only precedes participation but enhances its effectiveness. In the Bulgarian case, good information on future resource flows enhanced the realism and therefore the effectiveness of participatory planning. In Ternopil and Ivano-Frankivsk, Ukraine, the generation of good information on citizens' attitudes to local government and specific services added weight to participatory practices in decision-making forums.

Single participation mechanisms are less effective than combinations of mechanisms. Combining budget hearings with information-generation activities, for example, makes it more difficult for municipal governments to ignore citizen inputs, which in turn gives citizens reasons to participate. Similarly, setting up citizen advisory groups as an extension of budget hearings may create minimum accountability of advisory group members. Consultation is also likely to be more meaningful when combined with some measure of joint decision making.

Awareness raising and education of stakeholders are necessary. Almost all the case studies cite the need to raise awareness of citizens and local government officials, to increase their capacity as part of a participatory budgeting initiative, or both. Some note that such activities enhanced the quality of decision making.

Incentive structures count. Citizens participate in budgeting only if they expect some results to flow from their efforts. Clear resource ceilings must be set, so that real choices have to be made and wish-list planning does not lead to disillusionment down the line. A medium-term budgeting framework is needed, so that multiyear capital projects can be included and tradeoffs made among projects over time. Real participation and results were evident in Svishtov, Bulgaria, where some of these rules were put in place.

Clear rules for participation and decision making are required. The more successful case studies all include references to the clear articulation of the rules of engagement at the outset. (In Zwolen, Poland, for example, the municipal council agreed to the rules and made them public before commencing the consultation process.) These rules must cover who may initiate participatory events and how, what the roles and responsibilities of different actors are, how the government needs to respond to the results of decision making, and what the criteria are for choosing among priorities following consultation. The time frame of participatory processes also needs to be determined and publicized up front.

Partnerships contribute to more effective arrangements. Partnerships between local governments and key CSOs help make participation work. In many cases, particularly where budget hearings and public meetings are used as key mechanisms, the institutional arrangements themselves call for partnerships. In other cases, such as the participatory assessment in Armenia, where local government involvement was low, mistrust by local government officials limited the effectiveness of the initiative.

Localities learn by doing. Learning by doing can occur only where real benefits flow from participation, so that the initiative is continued. The sustainability of participatory activities, which depend on funding from CSOs, is still in question. Only when citizens demand participatory mechanisms as a right and local governments have less discretion over their continuation will participatory mechanisms be institutionalized. Participation, even in the form of information generation by CSOs, can catalyze further participatory practices, such as consultation or some form of joint decisions.

Ownership by local leadership is critical. Success requires strong local leadership by the government (many initiatives were initiated by progressive mayors) and civil society organizers (whose organizational capacities are required).

Leading CSOs and local government officials need specific skills. They need to be adept at facilitation, conflict resolution, and technical budgeting.

Public relations campaigns and media involvement are vital. In all of the case studies, either the local government or CSOs identified the need for informing citizens about the initiative and used the media to elicit participation and publish the results of the process. Independent, robust media institutions are needed to fulfill this function and build trust in the initiatives.

Coalition building by local NGOs strengthens initiatives. In the Strategiya initiative, the People's Voice Project, and the other Ukraine initiatives, participatory initiatives depended on building coalitions with local NGOs. Working together increased their influence with local authorities and brought together various types of expertise. In Ivano-Frankivsk, Ukraine, for example, the local academic community conducted surveys of citizens' priorities, providing credible and legitimate information that was much harder for local governments to ignore.

External catalysts play a key role in initiating and developing participatory practices. All but two of the initiatives studied were initiated by external development agencies or CSOs.

Participatory budgeting initiatives offer the potential not only to change citizen attitudes about their rights and responsibilities and their views of local government but also to improve the effectiveness of local government. Ideally, over time such developments contribute to more robust governance practices, as citizens' understanding of their voice and how to make it heard grows. The initiatives studied are still fragile, however, and they are limited to locations where strong CSOs were able to take the lead or progressive local governments were already in place.

Annex: Achievements, Challenges, and Lessons from Participatory Budgeting Processes in Case Study Countries

TABLE 4A.1 Achievements of and Lessons from Citizen Participation in Central and Eastern Europe

Case study	Achievements and challenges	Lessons
Albania	**Achievements** Local governments' understanding of citizens increased. Citizens' understanding of tradeoffs increased. Citizens' interest in results of spending rose, and accountability improved. **Challenges** Local governments have little financial autonomy. All local government budgets are approved by the Ministry of Finanace, and local officers of the ministry exercise significant control. Development of organized civil society is relatively new, and capacity remains low. Information at the local level is not easily obtainable.	Citizens need good information. Participative budgeting needs to be aligned to local fiscal realities. A conflict resolution process must be in place, and rules must be clear from the outset. Public understanding needs to be built. Participation of women and residents of remote areas is difficult to achieve. Generation of sustainable results takes time.
Armenia	**Achievements** Ten thousand citizens got involved in identifying priorities.	A high level of technical input is required. Building capacity of local governments, CSOs, and communities to make the initiative sustainable is critical.

Challenges
City officials resisted participation.
Sustainability is difficult to achieve.

Svishtov, Bulgaria	**Achievements** Learning through doing took place. Citizen awareness of government duties grew. Participation improved. Co-financing emerged. Sustainability of capital projects increased. Planning should focus only on what is possible. Incentives are needed to induce citizen interest. Local leaders and interest groups must advocate, initiate actions, organize funding, and manage the process. Education of citizens on rights and responsibilities and the workings of the intergovernmental system is critical. Participation develops as capacity builds. Participation attracts co-financing and increases sustainability. **Challenges** Risk remains that elites may capture process.
Zwolen, Poland	**Achievements** Participation increased local government's sense of citizen priorities. A transparent process with transparent rules was adopted to allocate capital resources to priorities. Media campaigns to inform citizens about initiative are very important. **Challenges** Involvement of local communities and private sector in local development is low. Citizens do not see getting involved as their responsibility.

(continued)

TABLE 4A.1 (*continued*)

Case study	Achievements and challenges	Lessons
Brazov, Romania	**Achievements** Budget hearing process resulted in the formation of smaller, more effective and more involved committees. Neighborhood committees were active in monitoring neighborhood needs and implementing small infrastructure projects. **Challenges** Building citizen trust in the meaningfulness of the mechanisms of engagement was difficult.	Sustaining efforts over the first few years is critical, as the participation process takes a long time to institutionalize.
Russian Federation Zaozerie, Mezen Rayon, Archangelsk Oblast	**Achievements** Social services in village improved. More resources were available. Capacity of villagers to plan, raise funds, and implement solutions to their own problems increased. Mindset regarding where solutions should originate changed. **Challenges** Rural local authorities have insufficient resources to undertake local development. Local citizens are not informed about changes in local government structures and opportunities for participation. Local citizens are initially distrustful about collective efforts.	Local leadership by the teacher can be important. Building the capacity of villagers to understand their rights to seek their own solutions is important.

Nine villages in Maikop Rayon, Krasnodar Kray	**Achievements** Villages planned, financed, and developed their own infrastructure, in line with their own priorities. Seven villages now have gas pipes, trade has been organized, phone communication has been installed in some villages, and transport infrastructure has improved. **Challenges** Building trust between local government and citizens is difficult.	Empowered participation processes facilitate the generation of additional revenue to use at the local level. Legal framework that allows for public meetings to make binding legal decisions of self-government in small villages facilitates innovative solutions.
Gatchina Rayon, Leningrad Oblast	**Achievements** Expenditures are controlled closer to beneficiaries. Local administrators are more involved in budgeting and revenue calculation. **Challenges** Local administrators initially saw their role as mainly controlling expenditures and not managing local development.	Capacity building in local administrations is vital.
St. Petersburg	**Achievements** Capacity and confidence of local NGOs were built. Participation increased modestly over time. Interactive mechanisms were established among NGOs, the expert community, and local authorities that may yield fruit in the future. Joint programs were developed; joint budgeting mechanisms are being institutionalized in some cities. Joint reviews of policies were conducted in some cities. Civil society capacity supplemented the low capacity of local authorities. Participation increased.	Involvement by academics resulted in strong conceptualization and ability to communicate at a sophisticated level. Independent budget analysis contributed to the success of hearings. Hearings and other transparency institutions evolved as mutually reinforcing mechanisms. Murky roles and responsibilities in intergovernmental relations negatively affected participation.

(*continued*)

TABLE 4A.1 (*continued*)

Case study	Achievements and challenges	Lessons
		Low level of capacity in local NGOs, lack of NGO coalitions, and low level of consolidation hindered local organization and effective participation.
		Other mechanisms of influence and interaction that exist between local elites and authorities resisted the introduction of transparent public hearings.
		Illiteracy and a low level of awareness among the public, NGOs, and elected council members hindered participation.
		Low level of transparency and weak media limited impact.
	Challenges	Analysis by NGOs was more useful than analysis by academics.
	Access to information remains deficient; demand for information remains low.	Poor communication about hearings limited impact.
	The regulatory basis for public involvement in decision making is not clear.	History affects how citizens respond to participatory initiatives.
	The divide between NGOs funded from the budget and others was difficult to bridge.	The quality of moderation is important.
	Local government perceived participation as consisting only of information sharing and consultation.	
	Mutual distrust detracted from hearings.	

| Ukraine

Kemyanets-Podilski, Khmelnitsk Oblast, and 31 other cities | Low level of capacity in local NGOs, lack of NGO coalitions, and low level of consolidation hindered local organization and effective participation.
Actors who benefited from existing nontransparent mechanisms of influence and access resisted open public hearings.
Low level of expertise or apprehension of local experts created a high level of mutual distrust. | **Achievements**
Participation in hearings to set local budget priorities grew to 600 people, with many representing entire communities.
Hearings offered an avenue for groups working with vulnerable groups to bring their concerns into budget deliberations.
Trust between citizens and government increased.
Citizens' priorities and opinions were integrated into the budget process.
Local government was able to draw on citizens' support to advocate at higher levels of government.
An initiative was launched to approach oblast and national governments to secure local budget revenue from income taxes.
As a result of introducing public hearings, municipal spending patterns changed.
Projects' experience has been disseminated to other cities through the Internet. | Participatory processes developed with experience.
Technical capacity in town (local university) facilitated the use of more sophisticated instruments, such as opinion surveys.
Leadership by the local mayor and the dynamism of town leadership with values of pluralism and political activism were important.
More transparency on budget issues preceded participation practices.
Better background information (budget and budget execution information on the Web site, for example) enabled participation.
Surveys and opinion polls supporting budget hearings made it more difficult for council to ignore citizens' priorities.
Public hearings need to be backed with other mechanisms of engagement, such as public planning committees. |

(continued)

TABLE 4A.1 *(continued)*

Case study	Achievements and challenges	Lessons
		The switch to program budgeting was effective, changing the nature of questions asked in the budget process.
		Significant capacity building support is needed before successful mechanisms can be replicated elsewhere.
	Challenges	
	Quality of participation was not ideal, with women underrepresented.	
	Mechanisms were captured by elites.	
	Although the legal framework makes hearings obligatory, not all cities have statutes in place.	
	Capacity remains low in both local governments and civil society in some cities.	

Note

1. The legal framework includes provisions under which citizens can organize themselves into units of local self-government.

References

Abers, Rebecca. 2003. "Reflections on What Makes Empowered Participatory Governance Happen?" In *Deepening Democracy: Institutional Innovations in Empowered Participatory Governance*, ed. Archon Fung and Eric Wright. London: Verso.

Azfar, Omar, Satu Kähkönen, Anthony Lanyi, Patrick Meagher, and Diana Rutherford. 1999. "Decentralization, Governance and Public Services: The Impact of Institutional Arrangements." IRIS Center, University of Maryland, College Park.

Banks, Christopher, and Juliana Pigey. 1998. "Republic of Albania: Opportunities and Issues for Municipal Reform." Report prepared for the U.S. Agency for International Development, Urban Institute, Washington, DC.

Doane, John, Malcolm Simpson, and Carol Rabenhorst. 2000. "Baseline Study for Armenia Local Government Program." Report prepared for the U.S. Agency for International Development, Urban Institute, Washington, DC.

Dongier, Phillipe, Jenny Litvack, Keith Mclean, and Anirudh Krishna. 2002. "Forging Partnerships between Elected Local Governments and Community-Based Organizations." Paper presented at a meeting on Strengthening Operational Skills in Community Driven Development, April 15–19, World Bank, Washington, DC.

Driscoll, John. 2002. "Introducing Community-Based Capital Investment Planning in Bulgaria." Local Government Initiative, Research Triangle Institute, Washington, DC.

Falk, Stevan. 2001. *A Taste of Success: International Budget Project.* Center for Public Policy Priorities, Washington, DC.

Fox, Jonathan. 2000. "Political Accountability and Civil Society: Propositions for Discussion." Paper presented at the conference on Institutions, Accountability, and Democratic Governance in Latin America, sponsored by the Helen Kellogg Institute for International Studies, University of Notre Dame, Paris, May 8–9.

Goetz, Annemarie, and John Gaventa. 2001. "Bringing Citizen Voice and Client Focus into Service Delivery." IDS Working Paper 128, Institute for Development Studies, University of Sussex, Brighton, United Kingdom.

Holdar, Gina. 2002. "Report Cards." In *Citizen Participation Handbook*, ed. B. Coe. Kiev: People's Voice Project.

Karatnycky, Adrian, Alexandra Motyl, and Amanda Schnetzer, eds. 2001. *Nations in Transit.* Washington, DC: Freedom House.

Krishna, Anirudh. 2003. "Partnerships between Elected Local Governments and Community-Based Organizations: Exploring the Scope for Synergy." Social Development Paper 52, World Bank, Washington, DC.

Krylova, Elena. 2005a. "Civil Participation in Subnational Budgeting in Russia." Background paper prepared for *Participatory Budgeting*, ed. Anwar Shah. Washington, DC: World Bank.

———. 2005b. "Civil Participation in Subnational Budgeting in Ukraine." Background paper prepared for *Participatory Budgeting*, ed. Anwar Shah. Washington, DC: World Bank.

Kuts, Svitlana. 2001. "Deepening the Roots of Civil Society in Ukraine." Finding from an Innovative and Participatory Assessment Project on the Health of Ukrainian Civil Society, Civicus, Kiev.

Levitas, Tony. 1999. "The Political Economy of Fiscal Decentralisation and Local Government Reform in Poland, 1989–1999." Research Triangle Institute, Washington, DC.

Malena, Carmen, Reiner Forster, and Janmejay Singh. 2004. "Social Accountability: An Introduction to the Concept and Emerging Practice." Social Development Paper 76, World Bank, Washington, DC.

McGee, Rosemary. 2003. "Legal Frameworks for Citizen Participation: Synthesis Report." LogoLink report, Institute for Development Studies, University of Sussex, Brighton, United Kingdom.

Natkaniec, Agnes. 2002. "Citizen Participation and Capital Investment Planning." In *Citizen Participation Handbook*, ed. B. Coe. Kiev: People's Voice Project.

Novkirishka-Stoyanova, Malina. 2001. "Legislative Framework Supporting Citizen Participation in Local Government in Bulgaria." Local Government Initiative, Research Triangle Institute, Sofia, Bulgaria.

Ovchintseva, Liubov. 2003. "The Current State of the Social Sphere in the Village." In *Local Self-Government and Civic Engagement in Rural Russia: A Collection of Papers.* World Bank, Eastern Europe and Central Asia Region, Washington, DC.

Preci, Zef. 2002. "Dialogue and Partnership between Government and Civil Society in Albania." Albanian Centre for Economic Research, Tirana.

Savranskaya, Olga. 2003. "Legal Foundations of Rural Self-Governance." In *Local Self-Government and Civic Engagement in Rural Russia: A Collection of Papers.* World Bank, Eastern Europe and Central Asia Region, Washington, DC.

Serban, Daniel. 2002. "Community Involvement in Public Service Delivery. A Challenge for Both Local Authorities and Citizens: The Romanian Experience." Organisation for Economic Co-operation and Development, Paris.

Tiurin, Gleb. 2003. "House of Hope for Zaozerie." In *Local Self-Government and Civic Engagement in Rural Russia: A Collection of Papers.* World Bank, Eastern Europe and Central Asia Region, Washington, DC.

Urban Institute. 2004."Participatory Budgeting Initative in Albania." Tirana.

USAID (U.S. Agency for International Development). 2001. "Assessment of Nongovernmental and Civil Society Organizations in Ukraine and Moldova." USAID Regional Mission Report, Kiev.

Viitorul. 2004. *General Report on the Situation with Autonomy of Local Government in the Republic of Moldova.* Viitorul, Chisinau, Moldova.

World Bank. 2003. *Local Self-Government and Civic Engagement in Rural Russia: A Collection of Papers.* Eastern Europe and Central Asia Region, Washington, DC.

Zakharchenko, Olha. 2002. "The Role of Citizen Involvement, Policy Development and Implementation." In *Citizen Participation Handbook*, ed. B. Coe. Kiev: People's Voice Project.

5

Participatory Budgeting in Asia

ALTA FÖLSCHER

The chapter examines the use of participatory budgeting by subnational governments in Bangladesh, India, Indonesia, the Philippines, and Thailand.[1] In some of these countries, participatory budgeting was initiated by the government. In others, local nongovernmental organizations (NGOs) or third parties initiated the process. Some of the efforts described aim to improve transparency and accountability, others seek to provide citizens with direct participation in public decision making. Some operate in the formulation phase of the budget cycle, others engage in participative monitoring and even auditing.

Do the case studies provide evidence of benefits from participation? If so, can useful conclusions be drawn about necessary and supporting factors for replicating such initiatives elsewhere?

To answer these questions, the chapter begins by showing how participatory budgeting can enhance development. It then reviews the Asian context, examining how broad trends of democratization, decentralization, and participatory practices have played out in the five case study countries. The third section describes the types of participatory budgeting initiatives and examines how well they performed in each of the five countries. The fourth section draws lessons from the Asian experience. The last section draws conclusions about participatory budgeting based on the case studies.

How Can Citizen Participation Enhance Development?

Citizen participation in the allocation and use of local public funds can enhance development outcomes, for several reasons. First, citizens have the best knowledge of their needs, their preferences, and local conditions. Their participation in decision making makes it more likely that available funds will be used to deliver the goods and services most needed, thereby improving government effectiveness. Participation contributes to better public policy and better policy implementation.[2]

Second, citizen participation improves vertical, or social, accountability. When citizens are engaged in planning, funding, delivering, and monitoring public goods and services, the incentives and pressures on public officials and officeholders change. Officials become more accountable for the choices they make on behalf of citizens; as a result corruption is less likely and effectiveness and efficiency increase. Citizens' perceptions change as they learn to see themselves as the clients of government. Development partners emphasize these changes as objectives of participatory programs, particularly in countries with poor governance environments, such as Bangladesh and Indonesia. As Edstrom (2002, p. 2) notes, the aim is to "institute transparency and democracy from the bottom up in a country [Indonesia] where serious abuse of office and top-down planning have been endemic. [Participatory governance] calls on villagers to demand accountability from both the government and their neighbors, and to take responsibility for the investments they deem important." Participatory governance systems "embody the aspiration of making government at local levels more responsive to citizens and more effective in service delivery through building in participation and accountability" (McGee 2003, p. 6).[3]

Third, participatory budgeting has the potential to improve the quality of democracy. Participation in public decision making is a form of direct democracy that allows for a more meaningful democratic relationship between citizens and government than that provided by representative democracy (McGee 2003). Participation can also provide marginalized groups with access to policy makers. In any political system, already powerful and economically advantaged groups have easier access to the state than marginalized groups. Purely representative democracies are unlikely to address this imbalance, particularly if they are already highly unequal. When participatory elements are introduced into governance systems, the opportunities for redress increase, as institutionalized participatory mechanisms lower the entry barriers for engagement with the state and allow disadvantaged groups a voice in policy making. This is in contrast to purely representative democracy, which presupposes absolute bureaucratic efficiency. A combination of direct and representative democratic governance institutions is likely to be the most functional. As Edwards notes, "Without sustained public pressure (as in participatory democracy), governments rarely fulfill the promises they make on election day. But without elections, it is difficult to reconcile the different interests and agendas that exist in civil society" (2002, cited in McGee 2003, p. 9).

Effective participatory democracy depends on the quality of deliberation in the process. Deliberation emphasizes "eliciting broad public participation in a process which provides citizens an opportunity to consider the issues, weigh alternatives, and express a judgment about which policy or candidate is preferred . . . . It is distinguished from ordinary, thin modes of public involvement by the breadth and quality of participation" (Weeks 2000, cited in McGee 2003, p. 10).

Participatory democracy is not tokenistic. It presupposes decision-making processes that are not dictated primarily by interest group politics but by rationality. If participative practices are to deliver on the promise of improving the quality of democratic governance, enabling conditions for good-quality deliberative processes should be in place. These include the incentives citizens face, their skill levels, and the quality of information available in the process.

Meaningful and effective citizen participation in public choices also improves trust in government and commitment to the tradeoffs made. Together with improved budget transparency, participation can build social cohesion, which can lead to the very tangible benefit of increased tax collection.

The Asian Context

Russell-Einhorn (forthcoming) distinguishes between background factors affecting the effectiveness of citizen voice initiatives and factors that have to do with institutional design, resource availability, and capacity. The first set of constraints is usually embedded in the social and political environment and includes sociocultural, political, and administrative traditions, legacies, and reforms. In this regard, the Asian context is marked by supportive legal frameworks, active civil societies, and a relatively recent history of citizen-led constitutional change, often set against a longer history of political patrimony and elitism.

Political, Constitutional, and Legislative Contexts for Participation

All the countries in the sample are democracies. Two (Bangladesh and India) were founded as a result of secession and independence movements; three (Indonesia, the Philippines, and Thailand) recently underwent constitutional change after civil society uprisings against authoritarian rule. All have legal provisions for direct democracy, although they are not always embodied in governance practice (table 5.1). In all five countries, traditional social structures coexist with liberal democracy and provisions for participation

TABLE 5.1 Constitutional and Legal Provisions for Decentralization and Participation in Bangladesh, India, Indonesia, the Philippines, and Thailand

Country	Political and constitutional context	Constitutional and legal provisions for decentralization and participation
Bangladesh	Democracy since 1971, following secession of East Pakistan from West Pakistan. The constitution includes a bill of rights and "pledges ownership of the republic to the people."	A recent government review recommended a four-tier system of local government, including village-level councils, but the recommendation has not been implemented. The legal framework for assigning roles and responsibilities across levels of government is weak, as is the fiscal capacity of local governments.
India	Federal democratic republic since 1947, born out of the Gandhian independence movement. The constitution has a strong focus on fundamental rights. The 73rd and 74th amendments introduced village-level autonomy to promote democracy at the grassroots level.	The constitution assigns clear roles and responsibilities to local government. Local governments are largely dependent on transfers from national government: their own revenue sources are limited to property and professional taxes and a limited set of license fees. Transfer criteria for recurrent spending are determined by the Finance Commission; the national Planning Commission allocates funds to major capital investment projects. The financial autonomy of local governments to initiate new programs and projects remains limited.

(continued)

TABLE 5.1 (*continued*)

Country	Political and constitutional context	Constitutional and legal provisions for decentralization and participation
Indonesia	Demonstrations and riots in 1998 led to the resignation of Suharto after 32 years of dictatorship. The constitution was enacted in 1945. Since then piecemeal change has been made toward making it more progressive.	Indonesia has passed two decentralization laws since 1999. In 2001 it passed implementation legislation. Bureaucratic opposition has succeeded in rolling back many of the gains made in the legislation.
Philippines	The Marcos regime fell in 1987, following mass demonstrations. The constitution is progressive, containing a strong bill of rights and recognition of civil society.	The Local Government Code of 1991 embodies a comprehensive decentralization program. In accordance with the constitutional provisions, the code institutionalizes the participation of civil society at the local level, envisaging a partnership between NGOs and local administrations, in terms of both joint planning and partnering in service provision. The code creates local development councils, with guaranteed seats for NGOs.
Thailand	Demonstrations in 1992 ended 60 years of military rule. The constitution is progressive, containing a strong bill of rights, enacted with support from a broad civil society coalition.	The constitution provides for decentralization. The Local Government Code places strong emphasis on participation.

Sources: Brillantes 2005; McGee 2003; Paul 2005b; Rahman, Kabir, and Razzaque 2004; Suwanmala 2004.

and accountability to the larger population. In practice this means that meaningful participation is not the norm; access to political power and the organs of state is still largely elitist.

Experience around the world suggests that legal provisions for decentralization and participation are necessary to create an enabling environment for these institutions. Legal frameworks regulate the terms of actors' engagement and their scope for influencing behavior in the arenas of other actors (McGee 2003). This holds both for how subnational governments influence national governments and how civil society influences government. Experience also suggests that legal frameworks are not sufficient to ensure that effective decentralization and participation mechanisms develop. Despite numerous constitutional and legal provisions for direct democracy and accountability, restrictions to democracy are in place in the case study countries, where undemocratic traditional social norms underpin the political systems (McGee 2003). Decentralization will be effective only if it is supported by a clear assignment of roles and responsibilities in a legal framework, but such a framework alone is not enough.

This mismatch between the legal framework and practice plays out in various ways in the case study countries. In Bangladesh local government elections are hotly contested and draw high voter turnout, but the roles and responsibilities of local governments are not well defined and implementation capacity is very weak. Fiscal capacity is also limited, with local governments largely dependent on transfers from the center. A weak framework for local government, coupled with a strong national nexus between politicians, bureaucrats, and business, results in a government that remains highly centralized (Rahman, Kabir, and Razzaque 2004). As a result, local government institutions are ill equipped to provide basic services. At the national level, vulnerable groups are largely excluded from access to budget decision makers. The state is not entirely closed to participation, however. Organized and well-resourced interest groups have direct access to political power and bureaucracy, and they lobby for their interests. In contrast, the poor have virtually no control over policy changes, with profound implications for their livelihoods (Rahman, Kabir, and Razzaque 2004). The Bangladesh case study describes an instance in which development partners are joining forces with other stakeholders to create demand from citizens for better local government.

In India the assignment of roles and responsibilities to local government is clear, but local governments have only limited financial autonomy to initiate new programs and projects. The financial (and therefore policy) autonomy of local governments is nominal rather than real (Paul 2005b). In addition, traditional social norms hinder effective broad-based participation. It is therefore interesting that in the case studies from India, all initiatives except one were initiated by civil society, with at least two cases involving groups representing the lowest tiers of society.

In Indonesia implementation of the decentralization legislation is slow and has met with bureaucratic resistance, rolling back many of the gains made in the legislation (McGee 2003). In the Indonesian case study of participatory decision making at the local level, government is a key partner. According to Edstrom (2002), choosing to work with local rather than national government reflects the recognition that radical interventions are needed to improve state effectiveness in an environment of severe corruption.

In the Philippines implementation of the local government framework is uneven: the case of Naga City suggests that national legal provisions for participation may need to be supplemented with more-detailed legal instruments to regulate the direct participation interface between citizens and the state. Politics has not favored strong accountability or local constraints on central power (Azfar, Kähkönen, and Meagher 2001). The traditional system has been described as neopatrimonial, combining the decentralized power of families and clans with a centralized bureaucracy that coordinates the implementation of policy. These dynamics put civic participation in local government at risk. Still, several social changes have facilitated effective democratization and decentralization, including civic participation in local government.

In Thailand the implementation of the Local Government Code, with its provisions for participation, has been uneven (Suwanmala 2004). The Thai case nevertheless illustrates how enactment of a national framework can stimulate change at the local level.

State of Civil Society

Civil society has been successful in bringing about large-scale political change in some Asian countries by deploying conflict-driven mechanisms of protest and mass action. The region is also characterized by large national NGOs that deliver services parallel to those provided by the state. This phenomenon developed in reaction to the state's failure to deliver basic services on the ground. In Bangladesh, for example, the strength of civil society delivery organizations is a feature of national life.

Citizen participation in a cooperative relationship with government in local-level public decision making is relatively new. However, there is some evidence in the case studies that a history of exercising public voice may have left citizens with some capacity to take up a meaningful role.

This is perhaps best illustrated if the case studies in this chapter are contrasted with those from Central and Eastern Europe (see chapter 4). The first striking difference is that the Asian case studies illustrate activities that are almost exclusively initiated and carried out by domestic actors (the local government or local civil society). International actors play a much smaller role as initiators and managers of initiatives than they do in Eastern Europe, where almost all initiatives have been sponsored by development partners or international NGOs. This difference may relate to Asia's longer traditions of accountable governance and civic engagement, which have given citizens and (local) governments a different view of the relationship between citizens and the state. Civic engagement in local decision making occurs in a context in which citizens already have an understanding of their roles in local governance. In contrast, years of centrist communist rule in Central and Eastern Europe disempowered civil societies. An important contribution of participatory budgeting in that region may be building citizens' awareness of their rights and obligations. In Asia this "platform" of awareness was already in place.

The Philippines offers a good example of a country in which civil society's role has developed along two mutually reinforcing paths. Before 1986 increasing centralization, graft, and lack of resources left a vacuum in local service delivery, which civil society filled (Brillantes 2005). The overthrow of the Marcos regime in 1986 resulted in a constitution that provides a strong framework for civil society participation in the process of governance. The constitution tasks the state to encourage NGOs that promote the welfare of the nation. It guarantees the right of people's organizations to effective participation at all levels of social, political, and economic decision making. The Local Government Code provision translates this provision into explicit mechanisms for participation. NGOs are allocated a minimum of one-quarter of the seats on local development councils, as well as seats on local pre-bid and awards committees, local health and school boards, and the local peace and order councils.

Governments in the Asian case study countries may also be better equipped to maximize the benefit from citizen-state partnerships than their counterparts in other regions. In Rajasthan, India, the state government has recognized the role communities can play in ensuring that public funds are used effectively: it is replicating the social audit methodology initiated by a CSO in other districts in the state. In the Thai cases and in Naga City in the Philippines, local governments have seen the potential in the national legal frameworks for participation and initiated participatory practices.

Types of Participatory Budgeting Initiatives

Very different types and levels of citizen engagement with public resource decisions and service delivery are referred to as "participatory budgeting." Two broad types of citizen engagement can be distinguished based on the degree to which citizens enter the action space of the state in planning, allocating, and monitoring the use of public resources.

In the first set of participatory budgeting initiatives, citizens do not attempt to take over or partner with the state in these phases of the budget process. They undertake activities in the broader public domain that are aimed primarily at improving the transparency of governments' actions and the accountability of state actors. This type of participation occurs within the boundaries of representative democracy: making public decisions is still the purview of government agencies and elected office holders. However, citizens do not take the bureaucratic effectiveness of these institutions for granted but undertake activities to bolster transparency and accountability. Put differently, these activities typically generate information on public policy and services outside of the state in order to influence what happens in the state. Activities in this broad category are usually initiated by NGOs.

In the second set of initiatives, citizens engage in the decision-making processes of public agencies. Examples of this type, which could be seen as a form of direct democracy, can be observed throughout the budget process. In addition, the mechanisms deployed represent different intensities of participation, because governments have discretion over the degree of access to traditional state-controlled action spaces they provide in setting up or taking over participatory mechanisms. McGee (2003) sets out four types of participation: information sharing, consultation, joint decision making, and initiation and control by stakeholders. As participatory practices move up this ladder, the argument goes, they become more effective instruments of participation: direct initiation and control by stakeholders are more powerful than joint decision making, which in turn is more powerful than consultation and information sharing.

Initiatives that Improve Transparency and Accountability

Civil society achieves the first level of engagement with the budget when it attempts to bring information on citizens' opinions and preferences to the attention of subnational governments or to initiate dialogue and influence public decision making through budget analysis. This level of participation relies on the quality of the information needed to persuade decision makers to change development and funding priorities and to improve the quality of services. However, as Paul (2005a) argues, budget analysis and dissemination by skilled professionals are often aided when broad-based movements, or "people power," get behind it. Paul emphasizes the need for coalitions of different types of NGOs, including organizations that have broad-based membership.

Getting ordinary citizens involved requires that the analysis be easy to understand and relevant to the concerns of average citizens. Participation can occur in a variety of ways, such as involving citizens in publicity campaigns and events or inviting them to express their preferences by voting on policy and service delivery issues. The involvement of ordinary citizens also strengthens civil society groups' efforts at monitoring and auditing public projects and services in a systematic way.

In all five case studies presented below, the NGOs use mechanisms for transparency and accountability to influence what happens within the state. They often bring important new information on public services into the public domain. They bring "people power" to bear on the accountability of elected representatives and public officials by drawing in ordinary citizens and coalitions of NGOs. To do so, they make effective use of the media to reach citizens, legislators, and officials. They know how to capitalize on the aversion of public figures to exposure. The organizations are inventive when it comes to translating technical information into ordinary terms and making what may seem distant relevant to people's ordinary lives.

Paul (2005a) argues that programs like these can be successful only in societies that adhere to democratic governance, are open to public debate and criticism of those in authority, have relatively free media, and have independent NGOs in place. One could take this argument further to add that the quality of democratic governance counts. Goetz and Gaventa (2001) emphasize the importance of the nature and organization of the political system in determining the level and quality of participation. A CSO should be equipped with the expertise and resources to initiate a program to improve government effectiveness through various transparency and accountability mechanisms. Its efforts will not yield significant benefits, however, if the poli- tical system is rooted in the politics of identity, personality, and patronage. When issues of public policy get more play in voter preferences, politicians have less leeway to perpetuate behaviors that invite voter dissatisfaction.

In order to bring about change (or prevent deterioration of services), initiatives need to convey to state actors the implicit threat of "public accountability discomfort." The more vibrant a country's democratic governance and the more real the contest for political power, the more options there are for effective civil society participation. Electoral volatility and the degree to which the contest for political power is policy based are also enabling factors. Initiatives that work on the policy and allocation side of the budget process will find it much harder to deliver results in environments in which politics are not rooted in citizens' preferences for public goods and services. In such environments, initiatives that focus first on the implementation and service delivery side may have a greater chance of stirring voter dissatisfaction and therefore a higher chance of impact. An example is Bangladesh, where local government elections draw large voter turnouts and are hotly contested but local governments remain weak and unequal to the task of delivering effective services efficiently.

Of the four cases presented below, the participative auditing and score card methodologies deliver the most tangible results: redress and improved implementation of services and projects. Tangible impact is much harder to achieve in initiatives that focus on influencing the allocation of funds against priorities. Of course, the voices of citizens and citizen groups compete with many others in policy and resource allocation processes. Even if citizens' voices are heard in policy decisions, many linkages must occur through the budgeting and spending cycle for citizens' preferences to effect changes in spending. While analyses that expose such gaps may pressure officials, accountability is much harder to establish, particularly in an intergovernmental fiscal environment, and it occurs only over a long time. Moreover, governments (and citizens) are more likely to recognize citizens' right to hold government to account in implementing projects or programs than they are to allow them to have a say in policy and budgeting processes. That said, the dynamics of "accountability discomfort" should not be disregarded when trying to understand differences in effectiveness across locations in different political environments.

The Development Initiative for Social and Human Action (DISHA) in Gujarat State, India

The Development Initiative for Social and Human Action (DISHA) is a local voluntary organization. Founded in 1985 as a trade union and a tribal welfare organization, DISHA aims to improve the living conditions of the large tribal populations in Gujarat. It created a unit, Pathey, to undertake budgetary analysis and advocacy work as a complement to its more activist campaigns. The strong membership base of Pathey's parent organization lends weight to its engagement with public officials and elected representatives. Pathey also has access to outside economic and financial specialists.

Pathey analyzes issues in the state budget of special relevance to poor tribal people. Comprehensive analysis is kept to a minimum and used to frame specific analyses, including analysis of budget allocations to the most relevant sectors (health, education) and the tracking of specific schemes that affect local people. Pathey also tracks expenditures on programs of high relevance to its client population, through records in the field and interviews with beneficiaries. For example, Pathey tracks expenditures on critical programs through district budgets in order to determine whether specific purpose grants are used as required.

Pathey distributes its findings simultaneously to legislators and target population groups. At the outset, Pathey realized that ordinary people were not equipped to understand or use its rather technical analyses. It therefore built a network of nongovernmental groups, including trade unions, to create a coalition for dialogue with the government. DISHA/Pathey also launched campaigns to inform and educate state legislators and officials on budget findings. Disseminating findings to the media helps reinforce DISHA/Pathey's voice in the legislature and with officials. Pathey uses its district analyses to motivate local citizen groups and NGOs to meet with local authorities.

Surveys conducted by Pathey to measure its impact show that the target audiences welcome the organization's work. In fact, a third of the people who receive material about the budget undertake follow-up action. Many of Pathey's nongovernmental partners use the analysis to draw the government's attention to specific issues. They see long-term value in the information. Members of the state legislature, political parties, and senior public servants make significant use of Pathey's findings and suggestions (Paul 2005a; Wagle and Shah 2003).

Mazdoor Kisan Shakti Sangathan (MKSS) in Rajasthan, India

Mazdoor Kisan Shakti Sangathan (MKSS), a union of peasants and workers in the Indian state of Rajasthan, uses another approach to stimulate citizen participation in budget processes. MKSS holds public hearings—or "social audits"—at which citizens discuss government expenditures on development in their communities. Citizens then hold public officials accountable for these funding decisions.

Typically, a social audit public hearing includes five stages. In the first stage, MKSS gathers all public agency documents, including cash books, wage rolls, and expenditure voucher files; project engineers' measurement books; and utilization certificates on development projects. Some of these documents are used to verify expenditures.

In the second stage, the information is organized into matrices that present technical information in terms that villagers are familiar with. (For example, volumes are expressed in terms of camel or bullock cartloads rather than tons.)

In the third stage, project staff members go house to house, distributing the information to villagers. Residents who have worked on sites provide feedback on whether the records appear accurate. In some cases, workers may identify discrepancies between information provided on wage rolls and what they actually earned. Villagers notice when wage rolls are inflated with the names of fictitious or deceased people. This process can take as little as one week or as long as a few months.

The fourth stage of the process is the public hearing itself. Anticipation runs high. Public officials, local elected representatives, local media, and citizens attend the hearing, which is held in an open area in the village.

A panel of respected citizens oversees the proceedings, which are facilitated by MKSS project team members. Citizens are called to give testimony that may point to inefficient spending, poor planning, or corruption. The public officials responsible are given a chance to defend the projects. In some cases officials have admitted wrongdoing and paid back illegally obtained funds on the spot (Ramkumar and Krafchik 2005). In the last stage, MKSS prepares an official report, which is circulated to senior state officials, the media, and other civil society groups.

The initiative has had a significant impact. At the most basic level, it has mitigated corruption. But the full impact has been broader: the state government now requires that a social audit be held in every village every year. As part of the audit, all village residents must be given an opportunity to vote on a resolution verifying that the projects in their village were successfully completed. The state has passed a law on access to information. While this process has limitations, it represents a radical change in the institutional space provided to citizens to audit public funds (Ramkumar and Krafchik 2005).

Public Record of Operations and Finance (PROOF) in Bangalore, India

Public Record of Operations and Finance (PROOF) is a local civil society coalition initiative to improve civic participation in budgetary processes at the city level in Bangalore, a city of 6 million people and a hub of India's high-tech industries. PROOF aims to demystify the budget process and make budgets more accessible to citizens. It conducts periodic dialogues between the government and citizens on budget allocations, priorities, and performance.

The PROOF initiative occurred against the background of the modernization of Bangalore's municipal financial management system, which resulted in reformed budget formats and timely reports on revenues and expenditures. The availability of timely budget information was a major factor that stimulated the promoters of PROOF to launch their campaign. Partners in the PROOF campaign brought complementary skills to the table: budget analysis, civic organization, capacity to establish state-civil society dialogues and communication, and community awareness building.

PROOF created a public forum for discussing the city budget on a quarterly basis, preceded and followed by more detailed investigations into specific aspects of the budget. Preparation for the first forum began with an information campaign to educate citizens about budgets in general. This exercise was necessary to encourage ordinary citizens to attend the public meeting. In the effort to increase citizens' economic literacy, PROOF held training seminars for citizens by qualified accountants and financial analysts.

The initial focus of PROOF's interventions was on the budget as a whole; this focus later narrowed to specific expenditure or revenue issues. It also moved from an analysis of input and expenditure trends to looking at what is achieved with funds. PROOF is now in the process of developing performance indicators.

In addition, it uses the citizen report card surveys conducted by the Public Affairs Centre, a founding member, to inform its dialogue. These report cards use public opinion surveying techniques to generate robust information about citizens' satisfaction with core government services, such as provision of electricity. The cards thus represent an assessment of the city's public services from the perspective of its citizens. They provide useful feedback on the quality, efficiency, and adequacy of the services and problems citizens face in their interactions with service providers. Where multiple service providers exist, it is possible to compare their ratings across services. The cards also collect information about private expenses incurred as a result of poor services and analyze the economic costs to households and the city of inefficient public services. The report cards have had a real impact on the level, quality, and efficiency of public services.

With this analytical background, attendance at the quarterly PROOF meetings has grown over the three years since the initiative began, and citizens' awareness and understanding of local budgetary issues have increased. The city is more open to sharing budgetary information, and initial tensions between the city and civil society groups have eased, allowing a sense of partnership to develop. The mayor, the municipal commissioner, and senior officials participate in the meetings and respond to the PROOF analysis and citizens' questions.

Despite attempts to make participation more broad based, PROOF has been criticized as being dominated by professionals. Critics charge that the concerns raised in the public forum are elitist and that meetings have failed to address certain key issues, such as corruption. Another frequent criticism is that the budget discussions are so technical that ordinary citizens can follow only up to a point. Some critics believe the process would be more worthwhile if ward-level budgets were examined (Paul 2005b; Vijayalakshmi 2004).

Concerned Citizens of Abra for Good Governance (CCAGG) in the Philippines

The Concerned Citizens of Abra for Good Governance (CCAGG) was founded in 1986, when new opportunities were created for NGOs to participate in development programs in the Philippines. CCAGG members signed a memorandum of understanding with the National Economic Development Authority and received training from the agency in project monitoring.

When the Ministry of Public Works and Highways falsely declared in a public advertisement that it had successfully completed 27 projects in Abra province, CCAGG members decided to take action. CCAGG gathered evidence of the actual state of the projects, including photographs and statements by residents in the project areas, which it submitted to the national government. An official audit followed, and several officials were charged with corruption. When there was danger that punishment would be minimal, with officials receiving mere reprimands, CCAGG mobilized public opinion. As a result, the officials were suspended.

Since then CCAGG members have developed a unique technique for monitoring road construction projects. Investigations look for a variety of types of corruption. The method is straightforward. Volunteers—primarily housewives, students, and other young people—observe work sites and report findings to specialist colleagues, such as engineers and accountants, who conduct detailed investigations on the project sites.

Common malfeasance includes the use of substandard materials (cement mixtures), substandard construction techniques, and fraudulent contracting procedures (rigged contracts). In one project CCAGG members found that contractors had embezzled project funds. In response to CCAGG's findings, the government forced the contractor to pay for a road expansion. A sign of the group's effectiveness is that the supreme audit institution of the Philippines has entered into a partnership with CCAGG to provide audit information on projects in the Abra region (Ramkumar and Krafchik 2005).

Initiatives that Involve Citizens in Consultation and Joint Decision Making

Paul (2005a) argues that programmatic shifts in budget allocations are far less likely to result from arm's length participation than they are from direct citizen involvement in funding decisions. The next set of case studies investigates what happens when civil society—both organized civil society and citizens at large—steps into what was traditionally the state's action space to join hands with government in making public resource decisions.

Indirect participation in the budgeting process

Citizens are indirectly involved in the budgeting processes in three cases, where participation is limited to consultation. The local government decides if and when consultation will take place, sets the agenda for consultation, and, to a degree, determines who will be consulted. It is unclear from these case studies that any of the benefits expected from participation—improved policy decisiveness and public accountability, better quality democracy, social consensus and trust in government—are better served through public consultation than through civil society–led activities aimed at improving transparency and accountability. In fact, several risks attach to consultation of this nature, particularly if initiated and controlled by the state. In particular, citizens may be consulted only on "safe" public policy issues that are not sensitive or resource consuming.

The demarcation of the public policy participatory space in the three case studies is simultaneously too vague and too precise to be meaningful. Consultation may actually be divisive: governments may use it as a way to manage the government–civil society interface. Reuben (2003) describes such strategies as developing harmonious relationships with some civil society groups and organizations while confronting others, thereby creating factions in civil society. Participation may also be elitist: citizens selected to participate may be people who are already influential and well resourced. Participation may be meaningless and therefore shunned by citizens, as it was in Rayong City, Thailand, where the participatory commissions operated outside of policy and budget processes and soon were dormant. Overall, consultation may detract from civil society's ability to be critical of the state and hold it to account, without much benefit in terms of policy appropriateness or increased trust in government.

This is not to say that consultation is always an ineffective participatory mechanism. Whether it is effective depends largely on the intention of the local government and the institutional arrangements—the rules, structures, processes, and information management—of the consultative process. Local governments that are sincere about soliciting citizens' views can form focus groups and pay attention to the views that participants express. This type of consultation can enhance the quality of democracy, improve policy decisiveness, and build trust in government.

Allowing citizens the right to initiate consultation—as they can in some Eastern European countries, where citizens can call meetings or initiate referendums on public policy issues of their choice—would mitigate the risk of empty processes. The provision by the local government of good, accessible information in a timely manner also enhances citizen participation. Transparent and impartial selection of participants helps ensure good representation. If citizens' groups must be accredited by the government before they can participate, as is the case in Naga City, or the government selects participants, the risk of co-option, patronage, and elitism is high.

LEGAL PROVISIONS FOR PARTICIPATION IN NAGA CITY, THE PHILIPPINES. Local government officials in Naga City, the Philippines, complemented national enabling legislation with specific legal provisions for participation at the local level. Its 1995 Empowerment Ordinance attempts to translate the participatory spirit of national legislation into a concrete reality. The ordinance states that the city government of Naga should recognize that "the will of the people shall always reign supreme" and that the primary duty of the government is to ensure that this will is carried out. The people should therefore organize themselves to address common or sectoral concerns. Recognizing that governance is best carried out when responsibilities are shared with the people, the ordinance proposes a partnership between the local government and citizens such that sovereignty effectively resides with the people. The ordinance proposes a partnership with NGOs and people's organizations for the conception, implementation, and evaluation of all government activities and functions.

In addition to having local civil society and citizen representation on several city bodies (as required by national legislation), Naga City introduced two specific mechanisms to create an enabling environment for participation of citizens and NGOs in local decision making. First, the city created the Naga City People's Council, made up of businesspeople, citizens, and NGOs. Members of the council have to be accredited by the city. The People's Council has representation on other bodies, such as the local legislation council and the local decision board. It also has the right to observe, vote, and participate in local planning; propose legislation; and act as the people's representative on governance issues, such as access to official records and documents.

Second, the city conducts multilevel consultations on priorities for development and holds citywide referendums on local issues. These issues have included concerns about the development of a golf course, the creation of a shelter program, the establishment of a bus terminal, and the color coding of three-wheel vehicles (Brillantes 2005; McGee 2003).

FOCUS GROUPS AND TOWN HALL MEETINGS IN KHON KAN CITY, THAILAND. Khon Kan City, with a population of 130,000, is the rapidly growing, dynamic center of northeastern Thailand. The municipality provides city infrastructure, primary education, community health and sanitation, social welfare, law and order, and disaster management and prevention services.

Local demand for civic participation grew out of the active participation of local residents in the constitution-drafting process in the late 1990s. The city first contracted the local university to conduct a series of focus groups at the community level; the sessions provided valuable information concerning problems, needs, and priorities. The activity also generated suggestions for policy directions and strategic projects for development planning. Thirty-eight new development programs were put into the city development plan as a result of the meetings. The city has now extended the focus group meeting program to include specific meetings to discuss education, health and sanitation, income promotion, social welfare, and other important concerns. More than 50 meetings were held in 2003.

In 1998, a year after the focus group meetings began, the city introduced town hall meetings, which are held every three months, with additional special purpose meetings held as necessary. A new practice evolved: town hall meetings, with full discussion, are now required whenever a policy issue has potential significance for the general public. Public consent is needed before any such policy can be implemented. Local experts are invited to make presentations, after which the mayor, officials, the general public, and the experts debate the policy. In 2003 more than 140 civic organizations and as many as 150 public participants were active in these meetings.

Before a meeting is held, the event is widely announced. The city sets the meeting agenda. Town hall meetings are conducted in the evenings to allow most citizens to attend. The chair is an experienced person, such as the governor of the province. The mayor's leadership was a major factor in making the meetings successful. Surveys show that citizens are satisfied with the civic participation measures (Suwanmala 2004).

CIVIC COMMISSIONS AND FOCUS GROUPS IN RAYONG CITY, THAILAND. Rayong is a metropolitan municipality in Rayong Province, in eastern Thailand. Its population of more than 60,000 is growing due to high migration into the area.

The city identified increased tax collection efficiency as a priority. To counter negative feelings about the tax collection program, it introduced citizen participation in budgetary processes. In initial efforts Rayong City twinned with the city of Portland, Oregon, and used international expertise to develop a program centered on establishing civic commissions, one for development planning and another for fiscal policy. The commissions included representatives of civic organizations, business leaders, and trade leaders. The city also conducted focus groups to monitor project implementation.

Of the two interventions, only the project-level focus groups were successful, with citizens providing input into the design and feedback on the implementation of a city park. The civic commissions were never fully functional: only the fiscal policy commission ever produced policy proposals. Both commissions stopped meeting in 2003. Rayong City then fine-tuned focus group mechanisms, tested earlier with the construction of the city park, to develop its local development plan. A local NGO was contracted to manage the consultation process. At the time of this writing, the project was under way, and the first round had been completed (Suwanmala 2004).

Direct participation in the budgeting process

Citizens are directly involved in the budget process in Bangladesh and Thailand, where initiatives have achieved significant success. Local development projects are better aligned with citizen preferences; accountability has been enhanced through oversight of implementation; infrastructure development is more sustainable, with citizens taking an interest in maintaining village assets; trust in government has been enhanced; revenue collection is up; and villagers have a direct say in local development expenditure.

CAPACITY BUILDING OF UNION PARISHADS IN SRAJ-GANJ DISTRICT, BANGLADESH. In 2000 the government of Bangladesh, the United Nations Development Programme (UNDP), and the United Nations Capital Development Fund (UNCDF) jointly initiated the Srajganj local government development project, aimed at developing capacity for participatory processes at the lowest tier of local government, the union *parishads*. The project consists of two interventions: provision of annual block grants of about $6,000 to each union for allocation to projects in wards and the institutionalization of open budget sessions to establish citizen engagement with the local budget.

For the block grants, each union forms development committees at the ward and union levels. Scheme supervision committees oversee the implementation of projects. The ward development committees conduct participatory planning sessions. One of their critical responsibilities is to ensure broad participation in the planning sessions. Sessions are chaired by the ward union parishad member and facilitated by the union facilitation team.

At the outset a tour of the ward is undertaken to identify problems. The ward-level process that follows can take up to three days and involve up to 500 people. Participants are divided into groups; separate women's groups prioritize gender-sensitive schemes. After the participatory process, members of the ward development committee visit proposed schemes to assess feasibility and make preliminary cost estimates.

Deciding between competing projects ultimately rests with the union development committee. In the final stages of selection, the committee uses a screening matrix to assess criteria such as poverty alleviation, environmental impact, and gender impact. The union development committee then recommends which projects should be implemented. However, the ultimate decision rests with the union parishad.

The scheme supervision committees monitor the pace and quality of work during project implementation. They hold the power to stop payments to contractors. Communities are highly involved in project implementation, often providing additional resources, such as labor and money.

The second project intervention seeks to establish open budget sessions aimed at improving budget literacy at the ward level. The union budget proposal is posted on a notice board before the session. During the session, participants review the budget against the investment plan that was produced from the ward-level participatory exercises. Community representatives ask for clarification of revenues and expenditure, and they provide comments for inclusion in the final document. After these discussions, changes may be made to the budget proposals before the entire budget is approved by the union parishad. The final budget is made public when it is posted on the notice board.

According to Rahman, Kabir, and Razzaque (2004), the open sessions create an opportunity for real needs to be addressed. The sessions also create scope for the union parishads to raise resources, as citizens are motivated to pay their local taxes. The sessions tend to encourage more local support for implementing projects.

The quality of participation remains a challenge. Despite several design interventions (colored cards to identify women's issues, women-only groups in planning meetings, and women's representation on committees), the voices of women are still not being heard, and men dominate most meetings.

Another weakness is the quality of deliberation in the open budget sessions, which is determined by the local government leaders' relationships to the ruling party. If local leaders are in opposition, the meetings tend to be highly critical of proposals in the budget. If the local leader is from the ruling party, the session is overly supportive of the budget (Rahman, Kabir, and Razzaque 2004).

CIVIC FORUMS AND EFFORTS TO IMPROVE TAXATION IN HUAI-KAPI TAO, THAILAND. Huai-Kapi is a mixed urban/rural subdistrict in Chonburee Province, Thailand, with more than 11,000 residents. In 1999 the subdistrict level, called tambon administrative organization (TAO), initiated an overhaul of its public finance management systems (including budgeting, taxation, and financial management) with the introduction of participatory budgeting. The change followed the introduction of legislation supporting participatory budgeting by the Ministry of the Interior. Huai-Kapi created civic forums at the village level, culminating in a subdistrict forum.

The civic forum process in Huai-Kapi is supported by annual household surveys, aimed at improving the quality of information on citizen needs and preferences. The surveys include general questions about households (size, age structure, access to services), as well as questions on urgent household needs and the prioritization of community problems and needs. The survey results are fed into the civic forums.

Huai-Kapi also adopted three measures to use citizen participation to improve local tax collection—creating a civic tax committee, providing civic tax education, and improving the tax collection process. The civic tax committee includes TAO officials, village heads, and local business representatives. It is tasked with conducting a field survey, meeting with taxpayers, and recommending measures to improve tax collection. Tax committee members also play a significant role in finding, bargaining with, and bringing new taxpayers into the tax system.

The Huai-Kapi program improved both expenditure quality and tax collection. Survey results reveal that citizen satisfaction with the local development plan, with the allocation of funds, and with services has grown. Local tax revenues increased by 48 percent in the three years following the introduction of the tax committee (Suwanmala 2004).

CIVIC FORUMS IN SUAN MON TAO, THAILAND. Suan Mon TAO, Thailand, comprises 14 villages, with a total population of 7,881 citizens. The majority of taxpayers are poor farmers, which means that the TAO depends on transfers from the central government.

The TAO has a long history of civic activism. Inability under the old system to resolve conflicts between interest groups and between villages led to a budget that was "pork-barreled": more and more projects were loaded onto the budget, and prioritization was weak. In 1998 the Ministry of the Interior's regulation on participation at local levels created the opportunity for the TAO to establish civic forums (made up of local leaders, interest groups, and government officials) in all villages. Their purpose was to identify local problems, suggest remedies, and provide a prioritized list of projects to the subdistrict or TAO civic forum committee.

The TAO-level civic forum committee includes 100 members, including representatives of the village forums. Its task is to make tradeoffs between the projects that villages propose and submit its recommendations to the chair of the Suan Mon TAO. The TAO provides a standardized planning framework and formats to all village civic forum committees. Meetings are held in the evening, so that most villagers can attend. The villages' civic culture facilitates the quality of deliberation (Suwanmala 2004).

The regular budget preparation process starts after the civic forum processes: the civic forum's proposals are included in the local annual budget plan and adopted unchanged by the TAO council. The final budget and development plan is then sent back to the village civic forum committees so that they can monitor project implementation.

In the first years, the TAO undertook capacity-building programs in the 14 villages. It took some time for villages to learn to trust one another and allow tradeoffs to be made between villages. This effort was supported by the TAO chief officer, who played a key mediating role and kept promises to roll over priorities to subsequent years.

In addition to solving the long-term negative impact of pork-barreled budgeting and increasing participation in a meaningful way, the revised budget process has had a positive impact on own revenues, as village leaders now take an active interest in tax collection, finding defaulters and convincing them to pay taxes in order to increase revenue available for projects. Village leaders and citizens also take an active interest in project implementation, making the TAO more accountable (Suwanmala 2004).

Initiatives that Give Local Communities Control over Funds

In Indonesia local communities have established village councils and development forums that exercise full control over the allocation and use of the block grant to the village. The Kecamatan Development Program (KDP) targets the poorest *kecamatans* (subdistricts) in Indonesia. It aims to foster more democratic and participatory forms of local governance by strengthening kecamatan and village capacities and improving community participation in development projects. The project covers 30 percent of villages at this level, touching the lives of 10 million people. It is supported by facilitators and consultants at both the village and national levels who provide technical support and training.

In many respects, KDP operates like a social fund. However, rather than a central fund for which communities compete through project proposals, the project allocates block grants of about $43,000–$125,000 a year directly to all participating kecamatans and villages. Through village councils and development forums, villagers determine how the funds are aligned with their priorities. The "open menu" approach is a critical part of ensuring that decisions are truly community driven and that communities have full ownership over them. Under the project, funds flow directly from a central project account to a joint village account at a local subdistrict bank. Although a branch office of the national Treasury processes transfers, at no stage do funds pass through a government ministry.

An impressive feature of the KDP is its rapid rollout. In the first year of implementation, the program reached 501 kecamatans; it added 271 kecamatans in the second year and 257 in the third year. Key to success was a four-to-six-month-long facilitation process in each village leading to project selection. After this process was completed, funds were transferred to the village accounts. Edstrom (2002, p. 5) argues that this "ready-aim-fire" approach of rapid implementation "avoided the pitfalls inherent in 'boutique' operations, with their heavy, often expatriate, technical assistance, their unrealistic cost structure, and their rarefied implementation environment." Rapid rollout is important to test a project's replicability within a country, to retain simplicity, and to gain the credibility and enthusiasm necessary to garner villagers' confidence.

The KDP project cycle has several stages: information dissemination, planning, proposal preparation and verification, decision making, implementation, and follow-up. A high degree of community participation and transparency is sought throughout the process (Edstrom 2002).

Lessons from the Asian Experience

The case studies provide an array of examples of citizen and citizen group participation in local-level public decision making. Several lessons can be drawn from these experiences.

Outcomes of Participation Initiatives

At the outset of this chapter, four possible benefits from participation were identified: improved policy decisiveness, improved accountability, better quality democracy through direct and broader participation, and improved trust in government. This section evaluates how well participatory initiatives in Asia succeeded in achieving these objectives.

Improved policy decisiveness

There is some evidence that participation can improve local responsiveness to citizen preferences. This is the critical assumption behind promoting participatory exercises and decentralization as a route to improved state effectiveness. The case study evidence suggests that mechanisms that deliver on meaningful joint decision making and citizen initiation and control offer the greatest benefit. In Thailand village residents determine the array of projects for implementation through the local public budget; citizen development forums at the district level make the final decisions. In Bangladesh and Indonesia, citizens have full control over spending a development grant provided to each village. Assuming that the deliberation process is functionally democratic and not dominated by elite interests, these processes will yield the selection of projects that are aligned with citizen needs and preferences.

None of the cases shows how such participation could be extended to cover broader public policies or the delivery of public services. How, for example, can citizens have an effective say in the type of education their children receive, in their public health care modalities and facilities, in measures for public safety and security? Public consultation exercises and policy advocacy efforts by civil society offer more possibilities in this regard. However, it is not clear from the case studies that consultation exercises can be as effective at improving policy responsiveness. Moreover, the risks of ineffective, meaningless, divisive, and co-opted consultation and continuing systems of patronage are significant.

Citizen-initiated public advocacy exercises can be effective in bringing citizens' concerns about spending priorities to the attention of local officials, office holders, and representatives. The work of DISHA/Pathey in Gujarat State, India, has "substantially enhanced the quality of debate on the budget, both inside the (state) assembly and outside, serving as an effective channel of feedback to the government" (Wagle and Shah 2003, p. 2). However, the impact of such initiatives depends on the degree to which policies drive local politics and the CSO can combine "people power" with rigorous analyses that have immediate validity in public debates.

Increased accountability of public officials and elected representatives

The most powerful examples of how participation can improve vertical accountability are the citizen report cards in Bangalore, India; the MKSS social audits in Rajasthan, India; and the CCAGG initiative in the Abra region of the Philippines. All these initiatives operate on the execution and audit side of the budget process. These initiatives yield much more decisive results than initiatives aimed at improving government accountability for policies and budget decisions, and they achieve results more quickly. In the MKSS and CCAGG cases, the support that such improved vertical accountability provides to the quality of horizontal accountability is clear: in both cases oversight institutions have forged partnerships with citizen organizations to improve accountability. Improved accountability of public structures also results in cases where joint decision making in development planning is backed by the oversight of citizen committees during implementation.

It is not clear from the case study material that consultation increases public accountability. In fact, if consultation divides civil society and co-opts scarce civil society capacity, it may actually reduce citizens' ability to hold public structures to account.

Better democracy

The demands of democracy are complex. In addition to voting and respect for election results, democracy also requires the protection of liberties and freedoms, respect for legal entitlements, and the guarantee of free discussion and uncensored distribution of new and fair comment. Democracy is "a demanding system, and not just a mechanical condition (like majority rule) taken in isolation" (Sen 1999, p. 9).

Insofar as their activities provide increased opportunities for citizens to engage their representatives directly in the public arena, not only at the ballot box, all of the initiatives described in this chapter can contribute to making democracy substantive. However, if McGee's caution that access should be broad based and the resulting deliberation meaningful is valid, increased participation alone is not sufficient.

Several obstacles prevent participation from being broad based and meaningful. Efforts by NGOs to engage the state in a public dialogue run the risk of being elitist, as do government-initiated exercises of consultation and joint decision making. The level of dialogue easily deteriorates when there is a lack of incentives—when citizens do not believe the consultation is likely to achieve results or the political environment places little value on issues of policy and service delivery as political currency.

These obstacles can be overcome. NGOs that are successful in making budgets relevant to local communities are more effective in building broad-based democratic practice. Government-initiated participatory exercises can offer broad-based, meaningful opportunities for engagement. The quality of deliberation depends on the "rules of the game." Meaningful deliberation is an outcome of citizens' capacity to learn how to deliberate and to trust the process. This is illustrated well in the Suan Mon TAO case, where positive outcomes from district civic forums took some time to emerge, as participants learned to trust one another and the local government. However, it is clear from both the Bangladeshi and Indonesian cases that ensuring meaningful participation by marginalized groups in such exercises is not a quick-win exercise. Despite mechanisms to ensure that their voices are heard, women are still dominated by men in village decision-making forums.

Greater trust in government

Building trust in government through participation is a double-edged sword. In Thailand trust in government was sufficiently strong to improve tax collection. Where participation was initiated in the right circumstances and in the right way, state effectiveness increased, social cohesion rose, and democracy was strengthened.

Participation alone does not yield benefits, however. If participation fails to deliver real benefits, trust in government can decline. If participation represents mere process without substance, it can entrench poor governance practice and deteriorate the citizen-state relationship.

Success Factors

How do the context and nature of participation affect the effectiveness of initiatives? Two sets of factors play a role. The first belong to the environment in which the participation initiative is launched. The second concern how the initiative is designed and implemented.

The environment in which the participation initiative is launched

Several factors in the environment surrounding a participatory exercise have a decisive impact on outcomes. The unwillingness of state actors to listen is a "kill factor" for consultation and joint decision-making initiatives. The unclear division of roles and responsibilities and the lack of policy or fiscal autonomy at the local level render civil society initiatives meaningless in influencing policy making and budgeting. An array of factors in the environment may be more or less disabling, but a successful participation initiative can create its own reinforcing enabling conditions over time.

FACTOR 1: THE NATURE OF THE FORMAL AND INFORMAL POLITICAL SYSTEM. What drives politics in a country is an important enabling/disabling factor in determining the scope for civil society–driven policy and budget initiatives. If policy issues have little currency, initiatives that focus on influencing policy and resource allocation decisions may have less scope than initiatives that track expenditures and service delivery quality.

If the political system is based on patronage and the politics of identity, the risk of government-based participation systems becoming instruments within that system is great. If politics are more closely related to policy issues, there is a greater likelihood the state will be interested in genuine participation.

FACTOR 2: THE WILLINGNESS OF STATE AND LOCAL GOVERNMENT OFFICIALS TO LISTEN. If state actors are willing to listen to citizens' needs and preferences and to take their opinions about service delivery seriously, the scope for meaningful civil society initiatives that operate outside of government is much larger. If state actors are unwilling to listen, initiatives that focus on policy and budget decisions ex ante may be less effective than initiatives that highlight delivery inefficiency and wastage.

In government-initiated participatory exercises, the intention of state actors is critical. If they are truly willing to engage with citizens, as in the Thai case studies, tangible results can emerge. If their willingness is unclear or absent, efforts may not only be futile but counterproductive.

FACTOR 3: LEGAL, INSTITUTIONAL, AND POLICY FRAMEWORKS FOR PARTICIPATION. If the national constitutional context or formal legal and policy frameworks encourage citizens' voice, civil society–initiated exercises are more able to find effective access to public institutions. The absence of these legal and policy conditions does not disable initiatives, however. The two audit-type examples show that successful civil society initiatives can lead to a more conducive policy framework.

Establishing national legal and policy frameworks for participatory measures can stimulate successful practice at the local level, as illustrated by the case studies from the Philippines and from Thailand, all of which emerged from a national policy directive. Local participation can still occur if the national framework is weak, however, as it did in Bangladesh and Indonesia. In both cases, however, participation was predicated on grants that bypassed local government structures and budgets. Access to funds is therefore an enabling factor. The lack of legal and policy frameworks is likely to be disabling only if the local government is dependent on nationally generated or collected revenues.

FACTOR 4: CLEAR AND FUNCTIONAL DECENTRALIZA-
TION FRAMEWORK. Lack of clarity of the government's roles and
responsibilities and lack of policy and fiscal autonomy are limiting factors:
there is little point in holding subnational governments to account for
service delivery if they do not have the fiscal capacity to provide adequate
services. Lack of clarity and autonomy could therefore be seen as a kill factor
for policy advocacy initiatives but not necessarily for initiatives that focus on
accountability for delivery.

If subnational governments have little policy or fiscal autonomy,
participation initiatives are unlikely to take hold unless the government has
access to external sources of funding (as in Bangladesh and Indonesia) or
uses the participatory mechanism to generate more of their own resources
for greater autonomy (as in Thailand). Lack of clarity and autonomy is
therefore an enabling/disabling factor but not necessarily a kill factor.

FACTOR 5: THE BUDGETING ENVIRONMENT, INCLUDING
LINKAGES BETWEEN PLANNING AND BUDGETING. Citizen
involvement in the budget process often involves identifying priorities rather
than allocating resources to those priorities; budgeting is still the domain of
government officials. Where strong mechanisms link planning and budgeting,
this is of little consequence. Where planning and budgeting are separated,
however, the impact of citizen participation is much less evident.

In the Philippines, for example, planning and budgeting at the local level
are still separated. This may mean that the impact of participation mechanisms on entrenched systems of patronage and on corruption and abuse of
power is limited, because it is through the budget process that these factors
come into play (Brillantes 2005). In contrast, in Thailand deliberative civic
forums, coupled with commitment by local officials and elected office holders to the outcomes of the participative process, have narrowed the gap
between planning and budgeting. The budgeting environment is therefore
an enabling/disabling factor for both initiatives that effect change through
activities outside the state and those that increase civil society participation
in the public action space. In Bangalore the city financial management
improvement program provided an enabling information environment for
the activities of PROOF.

FACTOR 6: THE CIVIC CULTURE AND CIVIC CAPACITY
FOR PARTICIPATION. While the presence of a civic culture and
capacity for participation are enabling factors for quicker results, a successful
process provides incentives for the development of such capacity, as the Suan

Mon TAO case study illustrates. The DISHA and MKSS cases provide convincing evidence that, if other enabling factors are present, the technical nature of policy making and budgeting need not be a barrier to participation. The civic culture and civic capacity for participation are therefore enabling/disabling factors for both initiatives that effect change through activities outside the state and those that increase civil society participation in the public action space.

The design and implementation of participatory initiatives

Several factors affect how participatory initiatives can best capitalize on enabling environments or overcome disabling ones. These include the quality of leadership and the level of facilitation skills employed in public forums; the extent to which the initiative balances between including traditional community leaders and ensuring broad-based participation; the application of universal rules of good budgeting to participatory processes; the use of multiple mechanisms; and the provision of accessible, relevant, and timely information to citizens.

Suwanmala (2005) singles out the quality of mayoral leadership as a significant factor in ensuring that participatory practices are embedded in local budgetary practice. Leadership of civic forums in Thailand and of social audit hearings in India was critical in ensuring that participatory mechanisms led to substantive outcomes. Mechanisms for reconciling different interests also depend on the level and quality of facilitation. In Bangladesh, India, and Thailand, external facilitation has made civic development forums and development committees functional.

The Thai case studies demonstrate the tension between including traditional community leaders and ensuring broad-based participation. Village-level civic development committees were functional from an early stage in the Huai-Kapi and Suan Mon TAOs because the project design incorporated traditional local leaders into the structures. Doing so created cohesive local support for the initiative. When inclusion of traditional leaders is not counterbalanced with mechanisms to ensure broad-based participation, however, such an arrangement can perpetuate the power base of local elites. Mechanisms to ensure broad support include holding meetings in the evenings so that most people can attend, inviting new groups onto civic committees, and putting in place process rules that favor marginalized groups.

The civil society initiative in Gujarat, India, illustrates how the balance between expert (and perhaps more elite) inputs and broad-based participation can be facilitated by careful translation of information so that ordinary citizens can access and identify with the campaigns. However, broad-based participation can remain elusive and should be a constant monitoring point for project managers.

The Indonesian case points to the importance of building the necessary capacity for participation in civil society before deciding on which projects will be undertaken within the grant envelope. In India, DISHA/Pathey devoted much attention to building the capacity of state legislators and local client groups to engage with the Pathey analysis and to understand the local budgeting system. MKSS project staff members put considerable effort into building local capacity by engaging citizens in discussion and information-gathering. In contrast, in Thailand less time was spent on preparation and capacity building, possibly because a platform for civic participation already existed.

Participatory initiatives that follow the basic principles of good budgeting are more effective in producing desired outcomes. In the Suan Mon TAO in Thailand, for example, village civic forums, development committees, and district committees operated within a financial constraint; the processes were predictable; and clear rules were established and enforced regarding when decisions are made. This approach facilitated the development of trust between citizens and the state and among different interest groups and villages. Such trust is essential if the ubiquitous budgeting problems of weak prioritization, pork barreling in the face of competing interests, uneven access to information, and counterproductive conflict are to be avoided.

In contrast, initiatives that operate outside of the budgeting system without a clear process and decision-rule framework flounder easily. An example is the civic policy commissions in Rayong City, Thailand.

Participatory projects will fail to achieve broad-based, meaningful participation unless they ensure that ordinary citizens have timely access to information in formats that make the issues relevant and understandable. Both the MKSS project and the DISHA/Pathey initiative were mindful of the necessity to translate information into forms citizens could understand.

The impact of civic participation is enhanced if NGOs and state actors deploy an array of mechanisms that reduce the risk of participation failing and enhance the quality of the measures. DISHA deploys analysis of budget allocations together with tracking expenditures and surveying beneficiaries. The TAO of Huai-Kapi uses household surveys to improve the quality of discussion and decision making in civic forums. Naga City uses several mechanisms, including referendums, committees, consultations, and information provision to enhance participation.

Conclusions

The Asian case studies suggest that civic participation mechanisms can improve development outcomes while improving the quality of the citizen-state relationship. Whether initiatives are successful depends both on factors in the environment in which an initiative develops and on the design and implementation of the initiative itself. The maturity of the political system and the nature of the political culture in a country or local area are a determining environmental factor for the type of participation initiative that is likely to be effective.

In settings where public actors are willing to listen to citizen voice and the local political culture is driven by public policy issues, well-designed mechanisms that allow civil society direct access to and participation in public decision making have the greatest impact on policy decisiveness, accountability, democratic practice, and trust in government. The case studies of Suan Mon and Huai-Kapi TAOs in Thailand belong in this category. Program initiators have more scope for selecting the type and level of participation than initiators who face different conditions.

Conditions of greatest risk in terms of participation occur where initiatives draw citizens into the state action space when the political culture is not policy based and local officials and office holders have no real interest or incentive to align policy and spending with citizen preferences. In these contexts such types of participation can be counterproductive. The Bangladeshi and Indonesian case studies operate in this area. They manage these risks by providing external funding and bypassing state structures where it matters—in managing the money. Village-level participation structures in both cases have authority over project funds. While this may yield short-term benefits, the sustainability of such initiatives is not certain. Effective long-term engagement can occur only if sufficient local taste and capacity for participation are built to change the overall environment so that the political and governance context forces state actors to engage substantively.

Citizens' own initiatives to improve public transparency and the accountability of state actors can yield successful results, even in environments in which citizens may not have immediate effect. The MKSS, CCAGG, and DISHA/Pathey case studies illustrate how citizens who are thoroughly prepared and work through coalitions can push their way into the public space and demand a hearing. Such initiatives can also transform the participatory environment from one in which state actors are unwilling to engage with citizens to one in which they have little choice but to do so. Success depends largely on selecting the correct entry point and carefully designing and implementing projects in order to maximize citizen participation.

Notes

1. Participatory budgeting in the broad sense refers to citizens' engagement with public budgets, including such mechanisms as civil society analysis of spending policies (as an input into public debate) and public audits. A narrower use of the term denotes instances in which citizens have direct input into decisions about public resource use, usually at the local level of government.
2. Reuben (2003) refers to this dimension of governance—the ability of governments to fulfill citizen expectations—as decisiveness.
3. In Reuben's (2003) model of governance, this dimension of improved conditions is referred to as accountability.

References

Azfar, Omar, Satu Kähkönen, and Patrick Meagher. 2001. "Conditions for Effective Decentralized Governance: A Synthesis of Research Findings." IRIS Center, University of Maryland, College Park.

Brillantes, Alex. 2005. "Civic Participation in Local Governance in the Philippines: Focus on Subnational Budgeting and Planning." World Bank Institute, Washington, DC.

Dongier, Phillipe, Jenny Litvack, Keith Mclean, and Anirudh Krishna. 2002. "Forging Partnerships between Elected Local Governments and Community-Based Organizations." World Bank, Environmentally and Socially Sustainable Development Network, Washington, DC.

Edstrom, Judith. 2002. "Indonesia's Kecamatan Development Project: Is It Replicable?" World Bank, Washington, DC.

Goetz, Annemarie, and John Gaventa. 2001. "Bringing Citizen Voice and Client Focus into Service Delivery." IDS Working Paper 128, Institute for Development Studies, University of Sussex, Brighton, United Kingdom.

Malena, Carmen, Reiner Forster, and Janmejay Singh. 2004. "Social Accountability: An Introduction to the Concept and Emerging Practice." Social Development Paper 76, World Bank, Washington, DC.

McGee, Rosemary. 2003. "Legal Frameworks for Citizen Participation: Synthesis Report." LogoLink report, Institute for Development Studies, University of Sussex, Brighton, United Kingdom.

Paul, Samuel. 2005a. "Auditing for Social Change: Learning from Civil Society Initiatives." Paper presented at the Sixth Global Forum on Reinventing Government, Seoul, May 24–27.

———. 2005b. "Citizen Report Cards in Bangalore: A Case Study in Accountability." Public Affairs Centre, Bangalore.

Rahman, Atiur, Mahfuz Kabir, and Abdur Razzaque. 2004. "Civic Participation in Subnational Budgeting in Bangladesh." Paper prepared for the World Bank Institute, World Bank, Washington, DC.

Ramkumar, Vivek, and Warren Krafchik. 2005. "The Role of Civil Society Organizations in Auditing and Public Finance Management." International Budget Project, Washington, DC.

Reuben, William. 2003. "The Role of Civic Engagement and Social Accountability in the Governance Equation." Social Development Note 75, World Bank, Washington, DC.

Russell-Einhorn, Malcolm. Forthcoming. "Legal and Institutional Frameworks Supporting Public Sector Accountability to Citizens for Service Delivery Performance: Opportunities and Limitations." In *Performance Accountability and Combating Corruption*, ed. Anwar Shah. Washington, DC: World Bank.

Sen, Amartya. 1999. "Democracy as a Universal Value." Keynote address given at the Conference on Building a Worldwide Movement for Democracy, National Endowment for Democracy, Centre for Policy Research, New Delhi.

Suwanmala, Charas. 2005. "Civic Participation in Subnational Governments in Thailand." Paper presented at the International Conference on Engaging Communities, Brisbane, Queensland, Australia, Aug. 14–17.

Vijayalakshmi, V. 2004. "Fiscal Performance Audit: Public Record of Operations and Finance (PROOF) and Citizens' Participation." Paper prepared for LogoLink study on Resources, Citizens' Engagements, and Democratic Local Governance (ReCitE), Institute for Development Studies, University of Sussex, Brighton, United Kingdom.

Wagle, Swarnim, and Parmesh Shah. 2003. "Case Study 3: Gujarat, India: Participatory Approaches in Budgeting and Public Expenditure Management." Social Development Note 72, World Bank, Washington, DC.

6

Sub-Saharan Africa's Experience with Participatory Budgeting

ADRIENNE SHALL

This chapter reviews the experience of participatory budgeting by subnational governments in Kenya, Mozambique, South Africa, Tanzania, Uganda, Zambia, and Zimbabwe.[1] It is based on a series of case studies commissioned by the World Bank Institute on the experience of participatory budgeting in each of these countries.

The focus is on subnational governments because they are best able to reach communities. These governments are diverse, each facing a unique context in terms of settlement patterns, service needs, revenue access, and capacities. Every local authority must approach community participation in its own way, taking into account the cultural backgrounds, capacities, and needs of its citizens.

The starting point for any participatory process is the legal framework within which it is situated. The ability of subnational governments to determine their own fiscal arrangements within the legal framework also plays an important role in identifying how civic participation is organized. Specific mechanisms have been identified for encouraging participation in the budget process, and in theory each country has allowed for participation that is accommodated in the budget cycle. In practice, the impact of participation on planning, budgeting, and implementing projects and programs has not always been as great as intended.

The first section of this chapter describes the legal and fiscal framework for civic participation in policy making and budgeting at the subnational level in each country. It outlines the mechanisms available for participation in each country and how they operate in practice, examines how civic participation is handled in the budget process, and assesses the impact participation has had on policies and budgets in terms of meeting community needs. The second section describes the challenges countries face in implementing participatory budgeting and the lessons learned during this process. The chapter concludes with recommendations relevant for Africa.

Legal Framework, Mechanisms for Participation, and Impact of Participatory Budgeting

Every country examined in this chapter uses some form of citizen participation in the budgetary process. This section describes the different approaches they have adopted and examines the impact participatory processes are having on increasing the allocation of scarce resources where they are needed most.

Legal Framework for Civic Participation in Policy-Making and Budgeting Decisions

Specific legislation governs subnational governments in all of the countries reviewed in this chapter. Except in Kenya and Zimbabwe, the constitution recognizes local government and in some cases prescribes the need for civic participation in local matters.

Kenya

Local authorities in Kenya are not enshrined in the current constitution. The new draft constitution—which addresses the current constitution's shortcomings and allows for a more democratic and transparent state—sets out the need to give powers of self-governance to the people at all levels and to enhance public participation in the exercise of the powers of the state.

The Local Government Act sets out the requirements for the composition of local authorities, which consist of elected and appointed councillors. There are three types of local authorities: municipal councils, county councils, and town councils. Each council exercises legal powers and duties; the mayor plays a largely ceremonial role, with no executive powers. Most council business is carried out through committees established under the Local Government Act. However, the full council must approve all recommendations made by committees.

The Local Authorities Transfer Fund Act, implemented in 1999, provides the mechanism for transferring funds from the central government to local authorities. The act provides some certainty about the level of funding, enhancing the predictability of intergovernmental fiscal transfers.

Mozambique

The Constitution of Mozambique defines the legal framework for decentralization and the ways in which municipalities are set up. It enshrines civic participation as one of the national values for local development.

The legal and institutional framework for local authorities is set out in the Municipal Law. According to this law, municipal assemblies are to establish civic participation, promote accountability, and improve coordination between the central and local governments. The participatory development approach is not mandatory.

South Africa

Local government in South Africa is to a large extent governed by the Constitution of South Africa and four national acts related to local government. The constitution promotes the idea of developmental local government, with each municipality giving priority to the basic needs of the community and promoting its socioeconomic development. It encourages the involvement of communities and community organizations in local government.

The Municipal Structures Act of 1998 entrenches community participation by stating that the executive committee must report on the involvement of communities in municipal affairs, ensure public participation and consultation, and report the effects of such participation and consultation on decisions made by local councils. Chapter IV of the Municipal Systems Act of 2000 deals with community participation. Municipalities are required to develop a culture of municipal governance that complements formal representative government with a system of participatory governance. Community participation is required in the integrated development planning process, the performance management system, the budget process, and strategic decisions around service delivery.

Tanzania

The Constitution of Tanzania establishes local authorities in every region, district, urban area, and village of the country. It states that the purpose of these local authorities is to transfer authority to the people, and it gives local authorities the power to involve citizens in the planning and implementation of development programs within their areas. Local Government Acts 7 and 8 require local authorities to foster cooperation with civil society, promoting and ensuring democratic participation and control of decision making by the people. Local authorities are required to consult with local communities as part of their planning processes.

Uganda

The Ugandan Constitution and the Local Government Act of 1997 outline the principles, structures, and functions of the local government system. Local government in Uganda consists of a five-tier hierarchical structure, with specific legislative, financial, and administrative roles assigned to each tier. The constitution guarantees civic participation in the budget process by requiring government to take the necessary steps to involve citizens in formulating and implementing development plans and programs that affect them. The Local Government Act also provides for popular participation as a policy objective. The act requires district councils to prepare comprehensive and integrated development plans that incorporate the plans of lower-level local governments for submission to the National Planning Authority. It also requires lower-level local governments to prepare plans that incorporate the plans of lower-level councils in their areas of jurisdiction. Although local authorities can formulate bylaws, they appear reluctant to do so, especially with regard to civic participation.

Zambia

The Local Government Act of 1991 establishes local authorities in Zambia and sets out their functions and responsibilities. The mayor of a local authority has no executive powers; all decisions are made by the full council, unless such authority is delegated to a committee. The Local Government Act allows local governments to formulate their own bylaws as long as they adhere to certain prerequisites set out by the central government.

The act contains some provisions that promote civic participation and others that deny participation. It states, for example, that all council meetings shall be open to the public, but the council may, by resolution, exclude the public from a meeting whenever confidential matters are to be discussed and publicity may be prejudicial to the matter. A copy of any bylaw must be deposited at the offices of the council and be open to inspection. The fact that anyone may lodge a written objection to the bylaw allows for a degree of community participation in decision making. In practice, however, participation is limited, as viewing the bylaw requires citizens to travel to the council offices, which is costly and in some cases unaffordable.

Zimbabwe

Local government in Zimbabwe is governed by the Rural District Councils Act and the Urban Council Act. In addition to carrying out the functions and powers detailed in these acts, local authorities can make policy through bylaws, regulations, and resolutions dealing with local planning and development. Bylaws of councils cannot, however, become law unless the minister of local government approves them.

The Constitution of Zimbabwe does not recognize local government. The enabling legislation in Zimbabwe advocates for consultation rather than participation. Citizens are not included in the decision-making process but are permitted to make public objections after decisions have been made.

The Subnational Government Fiscal Framework

In all seven countries, local government has the power to manage its own fiscal revenues and expenditures, subject to national framework conditions. In Mozambique and South Africa, specific acts spell out how local finances are organized. In the other countries, financial arrangements form part of the general local government legislation.

Kenya

The financial arrangements for local authorities in Kenya are specified in the Local Government Act. These include the need to prepare annual budgets, raise revenues, and incur expenditures according to the approved estimates. The budget is produced under the guidance of the minister of local government. Revenue sources include user fees and charges, income from trading activities, rents, permits, and property taxes. Local authorities may also borrow and issue bonds or stock, subject to conditions laid out by the minister of local government. Local authorities also receive grants from the central government.

Mozambique

The Municipal Finance Act specifies how local finances are organized in Mozambique. Subnational governments are expected to prepare, approve, and control their own budgets, observing the general rules and principles of the national budgeting system. Revenue sources include taxes, levies, user charges, and transfers from the central government. Transfers from central government are calculated according to a formula based on population size, area, revenues collected by the local authority from the community, and level of development. These transfers are unconditional. The Municipal Finance Act allows subnational governments to borrow from banks and other financial institutions to finance capital expenditure. In practice this has not happened; instead the central government has borrowed on behalf of local governments.

South Africa

The Municipal Finance Management Act of 2003 determines the management of fiscal and financial affairs of municipalities and municipal entities in South Africa. The act extends community participation by requiring that the accounting officer of the municipality make public the budget and all supporting documentation and invite the local community to submit comments on the budget. The municipal council is obliged to consider the views of the local community regarding the budget.

Municipalities have the ability to raise their own revenue through taxes and user charges. The Municipal Property Rates Act of 2004 regulates the power of a municipality to set rates on property. The act has a direct impact on communities and allows for community participation. Funds are allocated to local governments from both the national and provincial governments through three major funding sources: an unconditional equitable share, conditional grants, and grants-in-kind. Municipalities may also raise debt, within strict guidelines set out in the Municipal Finance Management Act.

Tanzania

The Local Government Finance Act defines financial arrangements for local authorities in Tanzania. It allows local authorities to incur expenditures necessary for functioning and gives authorities the power to raise their own revenue by imposing taxes. Other revenue sources include conditional central government transfers for education, health, water, roads, and agriculture.

The current allocation system is inefficient, cumbersome, and nontransparent. Allocations are not based on objective criteria or formulae but on the lobbying ability of local authorities. The system thus perpetuates existing inequalities and inhibits civil society from participating in the prioritization, planning, and budgeting processes.

Uganda

Local authorities in Uganda have three sources of revenue: government grants, locally generated revenue, and donor funds. The vast majority of grants from the central government are conditional grants earmarked for primary service delivery. These grants account for as much as 80 percent of local revenue. Other grants include unconditional or block grants, mainly to fund administrative costs, and equalization grants for local authorities whose service delivery is below the national average standard for particular services. A Local Government Finance Commission recommends the amounts for the various grants to be allocated to each local authority. It also advises local government on appropriate tax levels.

Zambia

The Local Government Act gives local authorities in Zambia the power to define, collect, and manage their own fiscal revenue from own local sources and spend it in the best possible manner. Revenue comes from local taxes, including property taxes, personal tax (levies), and licenses; fees and charges, including fees for meat inspections, permits, and building plans; and specific and general grants from the central government. Local governments may also borrow from the central government or from private sector institutions.

Zimbabwe

Local governments in Zimbabwe determine their own operating and capital budgets. They also have the power to raise revenue by means of property taxes, permits, levies, license fees, and user charges. Local authorities may also borrow, subject to certain conditions. Long-term borrowing is permitted only for capital expenditure or for eliminating outstanding long-term debt. A ministerial directive requires that local authorities prove that residents were consulted in the formulation of annual budgets.

Mechanisms for Participation

In all countries except Mozambique and Zambia, participation is mandatory and the mechanisms for participation are spelled out in national legislation governing the local sphere. Most countries use a participatory planning process to prioritize community needs and feed those needs into the budget process.

Although each country has its own mechanisms for participation, all divide the local authority into wards. Each ward has a ward committee, consisting of an elected councillor and community representatives.

Kenya

Under the Local Government Act, citizens in Kenya cannot attend council committee meetings at which important issues are discussed; they are permitted to attend only full council meetings, where proceedings are largely a formality. Citizens can participate in local government decision making only if the mayor calls a public meeting of the residents of an area to solicit their input—something that few mayors have done.

The Local Authority Transfer Fund (LATF) provides funds and incentives to local authorities to improve service delivery and strengthen financial management. One of the conditions for receiving funding is that local authorities submit a Local Authority Service Delivery Action Plan (LASDAP) documenting that the local authority conducted a participatory planning process and identified a three-year rolling program of projects and activities linked to the budget. Before the LASDAP process was established, no forum existed for citizens to voice their demands. The LASDAP affords citizens the opportunity to make proposals on the basis of their local priorities. All stakeholders—including formal and informal community-based groups, religious, women's, nongovernmental organizations (NGOs), citizens, and any other groups registered for participating in the process—are encouraged to participate in the process by identifying their priority needs and participating in implementing and monitoring the projects. As part of the LASDAP process, ward representatives are elected to follow up on project matters on behalf of all stakeholders. Evidence from the case studies suggests that citizen participation has been more extensive than originally expected and has come from a wide cross-section of society.

Ministerial circulars from the Ministry of Local Government describe elaborate procedures for convening LASDAP consultative meetings. In Nairobi consultative meetings are first held in each of the city's eight constituencies. At these meetings ward representatives are invited to make presentations. All people attending the meetings together decide on priorities. The priorities from all constituencies are then harmonized in a citywide consultative forum attended by three representatives from each ward, the ward councillor, and city officials. The citywide meeting is not always harmonious, with disagreements sometimes arising between the ward representatives and the ward councillors.

The resource envelope for the capital budget (which constitutes 10–15 percent of the entire budget) must be publicized before the meeting. The LATF also prescribes strict criteria for disseminating information, including legal notices, newspaper advertisements, and government circulars detailing the allocation of funds and criteria for these allocations. Citizens are encouraged to demand regular process reports from councils to determine and monitor the use of funding.

Other participation mechanisms in Kenya include *barazas* and *harambee* meetings. *Barazas* are public meetings called by traditional chiefs to educate citizens about government policies and mobilize them for development. Ward councillors use these meetings to reach out to constituents. *Harambee* committees are self-help groups that identify priority projects and then raise funds to finance them through personal and well-wishers' contributions.

Mozambique

Participatory budgeting is not mandatory in Mozambique, although local authorities are free to embrace this approach if they wish. Dynamic mayors who appreciate the value of citizen participation have done so; others have not.

Community participation in Mozambique originates through *bairro* (ward) development committees made up of residents from each ward. The committee convenes meetings to discuss communal needs, forwarding a list of needs to the municipality. The bairro development committees agree on a program and its budget, which are then incorporated into the local authority's plans. The local authority then budgets for the community financial shortfall.

In Dondo municipality the local authority mobilizes the community through civic groups. Working together, municipal officials and civic groups identify areas of need and agree on the interventions required. The local authority calls the civic groups to meetings and determines the agenda. Together the authority and civic groups then determine the budget requirements and find funding, which is usually external if it is for capital projects.

The local authority begins the civic participation program by conducting research and consulting communities on demographic and infrastructural issues. It also administers a survey on civil society organizations (CSOs). With the assistance of the municipality, the bairro development committee identifies three priority projects. A two-day participatory workshop attended by community representatives is then held, at which participants agree on the top three priority projects, which are subsequently integrated into the municipal budget.

In Manhica municipality the community did not understand the role of the newly formed municipal council or their role in community participation. To increase their capacity, civic awareness meetings were established for 100 people from each bairro. The meetings covered the role of municipalities in local development, civic participation in municipal issues, democracy, and the effect of floods (the major problem in the area) on the community. The municipality provided a transport allowance and snacks for meeting participants as well as technical input. Twenty meetings were held, covering 29 bairros, with a 90 percent turnout of invitees. One of the main outputs of this process was a shared vision of how the municipality should cooperate with its community.

South Africa

Civic participation in South Africa takes place mainly through a ward committee system or a subcouncil participatory system for large cities. Ward committees consist of a ward councillor and 10 members elected by the community. Participation of ward committee members is voluntary, and they receive no remuneration. Ward committees remain largely advisory committees, making recommendations on any matter affecting the ward to the ward councillor, who takes them to the council. Subcouncils consist of councillors representing each ward as well as other councillors, to ensure that each political party is represented according to the proportion of votes received in a ward. Other mechanisms for enhancing community participation include public meetings, public hearings, consultative sessions, report-back meetings, advisory committees, focus or interest groups, announcements in the newspaper, community radio, and e-government.

In Mangaung municipality the major mechanism for participation in policy-making and budgetary processes is the ward committee system. The ward committees use a community-based planning approach that aims to empower local communities to play a role in the planning process. This approach allows the ward committee to identify and meet with different social groups separately. Each group identifies its priority outcomes and main vulnerabilities.

Ward committees focus on "on the ground" participation. In contrast, the Integrated Development Planning Representative Forum allows broader participation in the discussion of municipal issues.[2] The Forum includes government, civil society, the private sector, and academic institutions. In 2004 a budget conference was held for the first time in order to deepen democracy by involving stakeholders in the process of defining the development priorities, programs, and projects of the municipality and aligning Integrated Development Planning priorities with the budget.

The Ekurhuleni municipality uses the ward committee system as well as other participation mechanisms. These include:

- an Integrated Development Planning campaign targeting the broader community in order to strengthen participation in the Integrated Development Planning process. Mass meetings have been held using theatrical performances explaining the planning process and describing the various actors and their responsibilities;
- a "Budget Tips" campaign encouraging the public to provide feedback and suggestions on priorities for the budget by means of e-mail, notes deposited in boxes at libraries, and letters to the mayor;
- a mayoral road show at which the mayor and members of the mayoral committee travel to the three regions, inviting citizens to attend meetings where questions from the community are answered;

■ the Mayoral Business Initiative, which invites selected groups, such as labor movements, the business community, and the mining sector, to ask questions and contribute to discussions;

■ a monthly newsletter produced by the municipality, which is distributed to the community.

Tanzania

The Local Government Reform Project was initiated to build the capacity of local authorities, increase their financial autonomy and decision-making authority, foster good governance, and improve access to and the quality of service delivery. One of the objectives of the project is to ensure democratic and participatory decision making, transparency, and accountability. The reform manual that guides local authorities in the implementation of the project mandates stakeholder consultations at various stages of the reform process. All local authorities have formed council reform teams, consisting of councillors, management staff, and civil society, to supervise the reform process and advise the local authority on various issues.

Consultation is required for the annual budget and development planning processes. Guidelines have been issued that require local government authorities to use the Obstacles and Opportunities to Development planning tool for participatory budgeting. The tool is a simplified model for a SWOT (identifying Strengths, Weaknesses, Opportunities, and Threats) analysis that identifies ways in which a community can overcome major constraints to local development in service delivery, infrastructure, or economic development deficiencies. Using the tool, communities prioritize their problems for budget allocation by the local authority and identify resources that can contribute to the solutions. Only a few local authorities have fully implemented these consultations, as the guidelines have only recently been issued.

In the Singida District Council, many institutions—including community-based organizations at the ward and village levels, theme- and sector-based CSOs, political parties, and the private sector—play important roles in the participatory development process. These institutions help create public awareness, mobilize citizens, develop training in participatory and technical skills for planning and budgeting, and provide administrative and financial support to the process. The annual participatory planning and budgeting process involves direct participation of citizens in grassroots meetings of the village assembly. Communities rank and prioritize their problems and submit project proposals for discussion and approval of the ward development committee. The proposals are forwarded to the Singida District Council, which consolidates them into the district annual budget and development plan.

Medium-term decisions at the district level are developed from two stakeholder consultations. Participants to these consultations are carefully selected from the institutions mentioned above. Medium-term decisions at the village level are reached through participatory rural appraisal processes that allow all residents to participate directly in approving village plans and budgets.

The Ilala Municipal Council developed a tailored training program on urban participatory planning and budgeting, in collaboration with the Institute of Regional Development Planning. In 2002 residential and field training sessions were conducted for council staff, ward councillors, and representatives of NGOs and community-based organizations (CBOs) from each ward. The training focused on planning, budgeting, advocacy skills, and roles and responsibilities of all stakeholders. In 2003 the Ilala Municipal Council established 22 community-level planning and budgeting support teams in each ward to empower communities with participatory planning and budgeting skills. Each team consists of 10 members. An effort was made to ensure that teams were apolitical, gender balanced, and inclusive of vulnerable groups. Team members were trained in participatory mechanisms, technical planning, and budgeting, skills that they could then pass on to communities.

Uganda

Several mechanisms are in place to involve citizens in the budgetary process in Uganda. The budget conference allows key stakeholders to reach consensus. According to Ministry of Local Government guidelines on participatory planning by lower councils, annual planning and budget conferences to review performance and agree on priorities should be held by November 15. A wide spectrum of stakeholders agrees on local government priorities at these conferences. Citizens submit their needs and priorities through elected councillors. Citizens and representatives of CSOs may also attend the budget conference.

Community needs are raised at village- and ward-level planning meetings in Soroti municipality. In Entebbe municipality the council has run outreach programs to educate and inform citizens about budget processes (although some citizens complain that the dates for the budget conference are not communicated in time). Once the draft budget has been finalized, citizens may obtain copies from the council, although their inputs are rarely considered at this stage.

Another mechanism for participation is the Participatory Poverty Assessment Project, established in Uganda in 1997. A Participatory Poverty Assessment aims to solicit the views of poor people and incorporate them into policy planning and the allocation of resources. The information derived from the project has been incorporated into the Poverty Eradication Action Plan, the framework for Uganda's budgetary policy formulation. Budget reference groups were established in 2000, with the mandate to simplify the language of budget documents and demystify budget figures in order to make them more accessible to the general public.

The media play an important role in enhancing civic participation in the planning and budgeting processes in Soroti municipality. Announcements to attend the budgetary conference are made on the radio and in the newspaper, creating awareness and educating citizens on municipal affairs. Local radio stations host phone-in talk shows where citizens may ask questions and comment on municipal procedures. The council also maintains a database of all registered NGOs and CBOs based in its jurisdiction. The leaders of these organizations play an influential role during the budget conference, as they represent the needs of their community.

In contrast, the media do not play an important role in the participatory process in Entebbe municipality. As a result, communication between the council and citizens is not very effective. To improve communication, in 2000 the mayor, his technical team, and civic leaders launched an outreach program, during which members of the community were informed of and educated about the budget process and consulted on their priorities. The program gave councillors and council officials an opportunity to become acquainted with the situation on the ground. It also gave citizens the opportunity to question councillors and officials about various aspects of the council's functions. Although the outreach program was successful, it was very expensive and could not be repeated.

Zambia

Zambia has no formalized participation mechanisms, no local structures for raising awareness and educating citizens about council business, and no mechanisms for sharing information or building consensus. Councillors do not appear to consult members of their constituency, and members of the public are not aware of their rights to attend council meetings or to inspect council accounts or proposed bylaws. As a result there is no civic participation in policy and budget decision-making processes.

On its own initiative, the Kabwe Municipal Council has embarked on a program to involve its residents in decision making, planning, and implementation of developmental projects to improve living conditions. It created subdistrict structures called residents development committees, made up of a group of residents living in an area or ward. Through the committees, citizens have the opportunity to provide input regarding desirable improvements, set and prioritize goals, evaluate work done by the local authority, redefine needs, and lobby and negotiate with the council and the Ministry of Local Government. Recommendations from the committees are passed on to the ward councillor and the council's departmental heads, who together present them to the full council. To establish a link between the council, the residents development committees, and other stakeholders, the Kabwe Municipal Council created a Settlement Improvement Unit in the Public Health and Social Service Department, charged with promoting civic participation. The local Chamber of Commerce is supportive of increasing civic participation and is campaigning for a more formalized participatory process. The Municipal Development Partnership for Eastern and Southern Africa together with the Kabwe Municipal Council initiated a pilot project to strengthen civic participation in municipal governance by mainstreaming civic input into the strategic planning process in Kabwe.

Zimbabwe

Subnational governments in Zimbabwe use a variety of instruments for public consultation. They include the government gazette; notices calling for objections in more than one issue of the newspaper; public notices at the subnational government office; ministerial commissions; ministerial investigations; consultation with the local authority; councillor input; ward development committees; the right of the community to attend council meetings; the right of citizens to make copies of bylaws, budgets, resolutions, and voter rolls; and council subcommittees. These mechanisms assume a high degree of literacy and interest in civic matters and are consistent with a top-down approach. Although Zimbabwe has a high literacy rate, it appears that these mechanisms are not as widely used as initially envisaged.

With the introduction of the 1984 Rural District Act, a more grassroots approach to civic participation emerged. Participation is now based on a bottom-up approach, beginning with development committees at the village, ward, district, and provincial levels. Each ward development committee is chaired by the ward councillor and consists of chairs and secretaries of village development committees, neighborhood development committees, or both. The main function of the ward development committees is to prepare and submit an annual ward development plan to the district development committees, which then recommend to the council matters to be included in annual and long-term development plans.

In the city of Gweru, civic participation occurs through ward committees. Partisan cells (political structures) and village committees contribute issues to the ward development committee meeting agenda, setting out and prioritizing needs. Councillors bring the minutes of these meetings to the town clerk, who puts the issues raised on the council agenda for discussion. The ward development committee meeting is also used by councillors to give feedback to ward members. Through representative attendance in budget formulation workshops, civic groups in Gweru have played a role in identifying needs, participating in strategic planning, and formulating budgets. They have also helped determine tariff levels and capital expenditure priorities through budget formulating committees.

The Mutoko Rural District Council encourages civic participation through workshops, ward meetings, village development committee meetings, joint meetings with traditional leaders, and meetings with political bodies in the community. Civic society organizations hold workshops every quarter at which they review the local authority budget performance and agree on modifications and actions required to keep plans on course. After these quarterly reviews, feedback meetings are organized at the ward and village levels to disseminate information and generate debate.

Civic Participation and the Budget Process

In theory all countries provide for some form of consultation or participation during the budget process. This occurs mainly at the beginning of the process. In only a few countries is public input solicited after the final budget is put together.

Although the budget process allows for participation, it is not always clear that input from citizens is taken seriously. In many cases the budget still appears to be driven by officials and to a lesser extent councillors.

Kenya

Participation in the budget process started with the preparation of the 2001/02 budget. Local authorities are required to prepare a Local Authority

TABLE 6.1 Budget Cycle for Subnational Governments in Kenya

Month	Activity
September	Ministerial circular is issued explaining procedures for preparing the budget for the LASDP.
December	Appointed council representatives analyze performance of current budget.
January	Appointed council representatives prepare the LASDP envelop, based on previous performance plus 10 percent.
	Information is published in local newspapers and posted on local notice boards in all wards.
	Stakeholders are invited to attend ward-level participatory budget meetings at which capital projects are prioritized.
	Stakeholders suggest projects and agree on priority lists.
February	Citywide consultative meeting is held at city hall. Wards negotiate on projects with cross-border implications and agree on citywide projects.
	Council meets to adopt recommendations from citywide meeting.
	Budget is submitted to Ministry of Local Government and Finance Ministry.
March	Appointed council representatives prepare departmental budgets (capital and recurrent).
April	Departmental budgets are submitted to relevant committees for discussion and recommendations.
May	Finance Committee considers consolidated budget (LASDP and departmental budgets).
June	Special full council adopts budget submitted by Finance Committee.
	Council submits budget to Ministry of Local Government, with copy sent to Finance Ministry for approval.

Source: Adapted from Wamwangi 2004c.
Note: LASDP = Local Authority Service Delivery Plan.

Service Delivery Plan using a participatory process that includes local residents and stakeholder groups (table 6.1).

Although citizens participate in the process, the budget is still driven by municipal officials. Citizens participate only in the prioritization of capital projects; they have no opportunity to provide input once the consolidated budget is produced. Furthermore, the consolidated budget presented to the council is a technical document that councillors find difficult to understand. Councillors' intervention is thus limited and generally occurs only in cases where they may derive personal benefits or political mileage.

Mozambique

Participation in the budget process occurs at the bairro level in Mozambique, where citizens are given an opportunity to prioritize needs within their communities. Preparatory research into community needs is done through a participatory planning approach. Councillors then meet with bairro development committees to set priorities. Stakeholder meetings are held to set global priorities. Community priorities are incorporated into council budgets and plans and approved by the council before the budget is sent to the Ministry of State Administration for approval. The budget is then implemented and monitored. It is not clear from the case studies whether citizens have the opportunity to provide input into both the capital and recurrent budgets.

South Africa

Mayors in South Africa are responsible for coordinating the processes for preparing the budget and for reviewing the municipality's integrated development plan and budget-related policies. At least 10 months before the start of the financial year, the mayor must table in council a time schedule outlining key deadlines, including deadlines for consultative or participatory processes. Immediately after the annual budget is tabled at a municipal council meeting (at least 90 days before the start of the financial year), the municipality must make public the annual budget together with any supporting documentation and invite submissions to the council on the budget from the community. The council must then consider any views put forward by community representatives or any other organs of state and, if necessary, revise the budget and table amendments for consideration by the council. Each municipality may prepare its own budget process within this framework. The budget preparation process for Mangaung municipality is typical (table 6.2).

For the 2004/05 budget cycle in Mangaung, communities were asked to comment and provide input only on the capital budget. The city manager has acknowledged the need to strengthen participation and expressed his intention to solicit input on the operational as well as the capital budget. He has also agreed to provide the clusters with more information on project backlogs, service levels in different areas, trends and patterns of expenditure, and growth projections.

Tanzania

Tanzania's annual planning and budgeting process involves direct participation of citizens in grassroots meetings of subward and village governing councils (table 6.3). Communities rank their problems and submit project proposals to the ward development committee for discussion and approval.

TABLE 6.2 Budget Process in Mangaung, South Africa

Stage	Activity
1: External and internal environment consultation	Budget parameters are established to make revenue projections.
	Municipality is divided into clusters of wards. Wards are notified of the dates of cluster meetings well in advance of the meetings.
	Cluster meetings are held, at which development priorities and projects are discussed and prioritized for each cluster.
	Refined community proposals are presented to the broader stakeholder forum to solicit additional input.
2: Screening of projects and programs	All submissions from the clusters and stakeholder forums are submitted to the mayor, the mayoral committee, and the executive management team, which discusses them and prepares the budget bill.
	Budget bill is publicized, so that stakeholders and the public can prepare for the budget conference, which provides another opportunity to provide input into the budget.
	After the budget conference, the draft budget is submited to the National Treasury for input and comments.
	Budget committee finalizes the budget.
3: Approval and reporting	Final budget is tabled and approved by the council.
	Final budget is submitted to the auditor-general and the national and provincial governments.
	Stakeholders are informed of the budget cycle for the forthcoming budget year.

Source: Adapted from Mangaung Local Municipality 2004.

Uganda

The budgetary process for local authorities in Uganda consists of seven steps (table 6.4).

Citizen participation is limited to identifying needs and priorities for submission to the budget conference. Citizens may obtain copies of the draft budget once it has been finalized, but at this stage it is too late to consider any changes that citizens may suggest.

Zambia

Citizen participation is not mandatory in Zambia, but some municipalities, such as Kabwe, have nevertheless accommodated it in the budget cycle

TABLE 6.3 Budget Process for Subnational Governments
in Tanzania

Stage	Activity
1: Preparation of budget guidelines	The President's Office, the regional administration, and the local government issue budget policies, guidelines, and ceilings. The regional secretariat advises the municipal council on policy, guidelines, and instructions. The municipal council prepares local guidelines and policies for wards.
2: Public consultation and identification of priorities	Ward extension staff are trained, and the ward development committees issue guidelines to community-level planning and budgeting support teams. Community-level planning and budgeting support teams conduct participatory poverty assessment budgeting. Public meetings are held to rank priorities. Ward development committees approve priorities.
3: Compilation of draft budget	The council management team compiles and synthesizes budget proposals. The council management team consults with CSOs. The council management team compiles the final draft budget, which is then discussed by council committees.
4: Approval and adoption of budget	The full council approves and adopts the budget. Citizens have the opportunity to provide input both during the initial discussion of priorities and after the draft budget has been put together.

Source: Adapted from Lubuva 2004b.

(table 6.5). Citizens in Kabwe participate through ward-level residents development committees.

Recommendations by the committees are passed on to the ward councillor and to council department heads. Participation occurs only in the first stage of the process and is limited to identifying needs and priorities.

Zimbabwe

Formal budget cycle processes in Zimbabwe are established by law and by informal processes adopted by local authorities that build on experience developed from wider participatory practices. An example is the budget

TABLE 6.4 Budget Process for Subnational Governments in Uganda

Stage	Activity
1: Budget conference held (January–February)	Citizens' needs and priorities are raised at village- and ward-level planning meetings. Needs and priorities are submitted through elected councillors to the budget conference. During the conference, which citizens and representatives of CSOs can attend, the council agrees on a list of priorities and on guidelines for sectoral allocation.
2: Sectoral priorities identified (March–April)	The chief executive as well as members of the standing committees (including heads of departments) set sectoral policy guidelines and agree on costed sectoral priorities. Citizens are not directly involved in this stage, but the needs they raised at the budget conference are considered.
3: Costed sectoral priorities reviewed (April–May)	Members of the standing committee for finance, together with heads of department, review the proposals made and try to establish sectoral linkages. The output of this stage is a draft budget proposal for the council.
4: Final draft budget considered (May)	The standing committee for finance, the technical planning committee, and the chairs of the standing committees meet to consider the draft budget. The financial allocations and prioritization are reviewed and the draft is taken to the local council executive.
5: Draft budget finalized (June)	The executive meets to consider the draft budget as well as comments from the previous stage. He or she makes final changes and approves the final draft. Citizens may obtain copies of the final budget from the council, but their input at this stage is rarely considered.
6: Council hearing held (by June15)	The chief executive, through the secretary for finance, tables the budget and seeks council approval.
7: Budget implemented and monitored	The chief executive, cabinet, standing committees, and heads of departments develop detailed implementation plans and performance reports. Monitoring is done by council officials, councillors, and civil society representatives.

Source: Adapted from Kundishora 2004d.

cycle in Gweru City, which includes both formal and informal approaches (see table 6.6).

TABLE 6.5 Budget Process in Kabwe, Zambia

Stage	Activity
1: Consultation with residents	Consultation with residents through residents development committees. Field teams, consisting of representatives of the four departmental heads, meet with residents to solicit suggestions, ideas, and opinions and learn of problems and needs. Residents development committees, with the assistance of field teams, list and prioritize their needs and draw up annual work plans based on an agreed set of priorities. The field teams then prepare their annual departmental budget estimates and submit them to the council.
2: Preparation of departmental budgets	Departmental budgets are prepared and consolidated. Each departmental budget estimate should be able to fund priority activities for the coming year.
3: Consolidation of the budget	Departmental budget estimates are submitted to standing committees for debate and necessary changes. The finance department then consolidates the departmental budgets into the council's annual budget.
4: Submission of the budget to the council for adoption	The director of finance submits the proposed annual budget to the council for adoption. During this meeting councillors and other interested parties, including department heads, can bring in more project proposals and resident needs, which may be incorporated into the budget if they are deemed important and resources are available.
5: Final approval	Once the full council meeting approves the consolidated annual budget, it is submitted to the Ministry of Local Government and Housing for final approval.
6: Budget implementation	The budget is implemented, and prioritized projects are monitored and evaluated.

Source: Adapted from Mumvuma 2004.

Stakeholder participation occurs informally at three stages in the process. First, citizens are involved in identifying needs and priorities, which feed into the strategic development plan. Second, consultations with stakeholders are held to discuss the implications of their input on the budget and to vote on the preferred scenarios. Third, citizens are involved in monitoring and evaluating implementation of the budget.

TABLE 6.6 Budget Process in Gweru, Zimbabwe

Stage	Formal activity	Informal participation
1: Identification of needs and priorities	Five-year strategic development plan with annual priorities used to determine and adjust year's priorities. National guidelines received and incorporated into local budget. Executive committee issues budget guidelines for Council adoption.	Stakeholders review guidelines with SNG and agree on impacts to be incorporated into SNG budget.
2: Costing and determination of global funding requirements	Manpower committee negotiates with labor unions on level of wages and salaries. Finance committee meetings held to determine global funding requirements and set level of charges as well as capital programs and their financing.	Broad stakeholder committee delegates detailed budgeting to a stakeholder budget committee it elects. Committee works closely with treasurer and finance committee.
3: Budget finalization	Council meeting adopts recommendations of finance committee, advertises budget in two issues of the newspaper in order to allow for public objections. Council considers objections before finalizing budget. Budget sent to Ministry of Local Government for approval of high-density area charges (poor areas).	
4: Budget implementation	Budget is implemented, monitored, and evaluated.	Councillors hold regular ward meetings to consult on budget with stakeholder budget committee.

Source: Adapted from Mika 2004.
Note: SNG = subnational government.

The Impact of Participation

Participation in budgetary processes is still relatively new in most of the countries reviewed here. Already, however, it has increased the number of projects that directly benefit communities and correspond to the priorities identified through the participation process. Relationships between citizens and local authorities have improved, and citizens have a more positive attitude toward and better understanding of the local authority.

Kenya

Citizens have participated in the budget process in Nairobi since 2003. The result has been a large increase in the number of projects suggested and implemented. Project ideas originate with residents, based on their perceived needs. As a result of resident involvement, there is a strong sense of ownership. Through improved dialogue, good rapport has developed between the council and residents, which did not exist in the past. The Local Authority Service Delivery Action Plan process provides a good opportunity for meaningful dialogue and the identification of service delivery activities that respond directly to the needs of local residents. Of 154 projects identified in 2002/03, 106 were shortlisted for funding and implementation. Council staff have also made themselves more accessible to all stakeholders.

Mozambique

Civic participation is still in its infancy in Mozambique. However, in both Manhica and Dondo municipalities, interaction between the local authority and civic groups has increased and relations have improved. The local authorities have a better idea of the composition of society. Community members now participate jointly with the local authority in planning, programming, implementing, and monitoring and evaluating local projects. In Manhica a multistakeholder management committee was established in 2000 that raises funds and deals with a local flooding problem. Civic awareness meetings were held in 29 bairros, resulting in cleaning and reconstruction campaigns and the building of two boats to overcome flooding problems. Village committees in Dondo are active in local economic development, with local women maintaining community facilities such as water pumps and refuse removal.

South Africa

In Mangaung municipality the use of community-based planning in ward committees has seen the focus of budget funding shift from infrastructure development to local economic development, a higher priority for citizens.

The community also perceives the municipality as being more transparent. More people are informed about what is happening in the municipality and can now demand accountability by regularly asking questions regarding issues raised at meetings. There is constant participation through the ward committees, which provide the municipality with regular feedback and input. Submissions received from the budget conference on various budgetary issues are seriously considered and taken into account when finalizing the budget.

In Ekurhuleni municipality the major impact from the participation process has been a change in funding priorities rather than an increase in spending. Through the participation process, the municipality has taken a closer look at the lives of pensioners and increased the concessions given to them. There has also been an influence on the indigent policy and the allocation to free basic services. Policies have been modified in ways that benefit the poor, and budget allocations to free basic services have increased.

Tanzania

Civic participation has had a positive impact on the structure and effectiveness of budget and development plans in Tanzania. Staff of the Singida District Council solicited community participation in preparing and approving village budgets for 2004/05. The logical framework approach was applied to medium-term plans and budgets in four villages for the rehabilitation of the water scheme, the rehabilitation and construction of shallow wells, and the construction of a cattle dam.[3] The Ilala Municipal Council now directly involves citizens in meetings to discuss and prioritize community problems and propose projects for budgetary resource allocation. In both councils the number of projects implemented jointly by the council and communities has increased. Participation has fostered a more positive attitude among citizens, resulting in greater acceptability of cost-sharing, user charges, and other cost-recovery mechanisms. The effectiveness of budgets and development plans in addressing community concerns has improved. Equity and transparency in the allocation of resources across communities have increased, especially with regard to resources allocated to the previously neglected inner city and periphery. Relations between the council and citizens have improved, as has the ability to analyze and prioritize problems and issues. The level of community involvement in designing, executing, and monitoring and evaluating projects has increased. Official recognition of private and public contributions from the center to community projects, which are now incorporated into plans and budgets, has encouraged nonpublic contributions and given hope to citizens for improved service delivery.

Uganda

Through the participatory process, citizens in Entebbe municipality are now involved in drafting the city's three-year strategic plan, which guides development activities in the municipality. An attempt has been made to establish a good working relationship between councillors, officials, and citizens. The council has a list of all registered civic organizations and invites at least some of their leaders to attend its meetings.

Civic organizations and NGOs in Soroti municipality have a positive attitude toward attending council meetings, where they present the priorities and interests of the community. Through the participatory process, a network of NGOs and civic groups has been formed to ensure that the interests of citizens are articulated before the council. Civic groups have learned and internalized the procedures of the council in preparing the budget. The resource base of the municipality has increased as people who previously refused to pay taxes now do so, because they have a better understanding of the use to which council resources are put.

Zambia

Thirty-six residents development committees have been established in Kabwe municipality. Three health centers have been established, and piped water has been provided for two of the centers. New markets have been constructed and improvements made to existing markets.

To ensure that cross-cutting issues are mainstreamed in community projects, members of residents development committees have been trained to deal with problems of HIV/AIDS, gender mainstreaming, the environment, and infrastructure maintenance. District officials, residents development committees, and neighborhood committees formed a task force to deal with these issues. As a result, funding was allocated to a home-based care project in Chowa; a project for the care of terminally ill people with HIV/AIDS; expansion of the Ngungu health center, which cares for the chronically ill; and expansion of a school, the clearing of its storm drains, and the planting of trees around the school.

Zimbabwe

Civic participation in the Mutoko Rural District Council has given residents there a new sense of belonging and ownership. Linkages have been strengthened between the local authority and stakeholders, and cooperation between government departments, traditional leaders, and civic society organizations has increased. A common and shared vision has developed to guide future community development and annual budgets.

The result has been less conflict and more eagerness to use dialogue to solve differences. Marches have not occurred protesting local budgets (as they did in the past), suggesting that citizens now accept and feel ownership of funding. This has allowed speedier approval of the budget and more timely implementation. Citizens have a better appreciation of what the council does and how services are costed. As a result, they are more willing to pay for services.

In Gweru participatory processes have resulted in a more simplified budget format that is easier for citizens to understand. Citizens have been involved in developing a strategic plan that shapes the city's future and guides the budget process. There is also an increased sense of ownership and belonging regarding the budget process and a reduction in suspicions of abuse of funds and lack of transparency. As citizens are more involved, budgets are produced more quickly and implemented on time.

Challenges and Lessons Learned

Participatory budgeting has already met with successes in Africa, but challenges remain. Important lessons have been learned as subnational governments try to deal with these challenges.

Challenges

Many of the countries reviewed face similar challenges, including a lack of capacity, a limited understanding of the roles and responsibilities of all actors, the limited scope of participation, legislative constraints, inadequate monitoring and evaluation systems, a lack of transparency and trust, a breakdown in communication, insufficient resources, and political and social differences. Not all the countries reviewed have experienced all of these challenges, but many are common to all.

Every country reviewed cited the lack of capacity of councillors, municipal officials, and citizens as the most serious impediment to civic participation in planning and budgetary processes. Citizens are often not aware of their right to participate, and they lack an understanding and awareness of policy-making and budgetary processes. The low level of literacy hampers participation. Citizens with very low levels of education tend to participate less, because they lack access to information and do not understand municipal procedures. As a result, the budget-making process involves mainly the elite. The language used in discussing policy and budgets is often technical and introduces unfamiliar concepts. The discussion is therefore beyond the comprehension of both councillors and the people they represent. This means that residents and councillors are often excluded from participating effectively in the policy and budgetary decision-making processes. In some countries, residents in a given area may speak different languages, making it difficult for them to fully participate in discussions.

Some councillors, especially those from rural areas, have not had adequate training and are therefore unable to impart the relevant information and inform their constituents on council activities. This makes it difficulty for them to articulate the problems and needs of their constituencies during council debates. Municipal officials themselves may lack the necessary technical capacity.

In most of the countries under review, the roles and responsibilities of the different actors were not clearly understood. This resulted in certain actors assuming responsibilities that were inappropriate. In particular, the distinction between the roles of officials and the roles of councillors was not always clearly defined. In some instances, officials made decisions that should have been made by the political body. In doing so, they manipulated the budgeting and planning processes, using councillors as rubber stamps. Some countries also experienced misunderstandings over state departments' role in the budgeting process.

In some countries citizens participate in decision making only with regard to the capital budget, which represents a small part of the entire budget. They are not included in discussions of revenue sources or the setting of rates and tariffs.

The monitoring and evaluation of projects is weak, and the process does not involve citizen participation. Improving the monitoring and evaluation process would enhance the accountability of councillors and the administration to the community.

In Mozambique, Uganda, Zambia, and Zimbabwe, legislative constraints limit civic participation. There are no specific provisions for direct public participation in decision making at the municipal level. Instead, it is assumed that participation will happen indirectly.

Civic participation is also hampered by a lack of transparency in the use of public funds. In Uganda, for example, provisions in the law ensure transparent and accountable use of financial resources at the local level, but many of these provisions have not been acted on because of lack of capacity. Subnational governments lack the capacity to prepare the necessary books of accounts and enforce strict financial discipline; central government institutions lack the capacity to follow up on audit recommendations in a timely and comprehensive manner.

In Zambia fiscal transfers from the central government are unpredictable. Councils do not have information about funding policies, the amounts available for distribution from various sources, the criteria or formula adopted in disbursing grants, or the reasons for delays in releasing funds. This uncertainty makes it difficult if not impossible to plan for and use resources effectively.

Lack of resources, both financial and physical, has had a negative impact on citizen participation. In some instances, dependence on donor funding to run participatory processes makes the participation process tenuous. The large size of the population in some towns and cities puts pressure on the resources available for participatory activities, as more meetings need to be held and more people require transport. In rural areas, where large distances must be covered, the council has to pay transport and subsistence costs in order to make it possible for citizens to attend meetings and participate in decision making.

Councillors often lack institutional and resource bases to meaningfully consult with the people they represent. They lack the physical infrastructure, such as information management systems, as well as the human resource capacity necessary for encouraging participation among their constituencies.

Participation is still viewed with suspicion in some of the countries under review, sometimes with reason. Some councillors have ignored what has come up through the participatory process, instead putting forward issues that suit them. Issues raised by individuals or groups have sometimes been lost in the communication process from village to ward to municipal council.

In Uganda the relationship between the council and citizens has improved greatly, but suspicion between the two still exists. Invitation letters are reportedly sent to some civic groups after meetings have been held. Some councils still deliberately exclude civic groups from council meetings. In Zambia even where citizens are aware of their right to attend council meetings and are informed about the schedules of these meetings, most will not attend, mainly because they have lost confidence in local authorities. In Zimbabwe elected officials view civic groups with suspicion.

In all the countries reviewed, ineffective communication between the subnational government and citizens has a negative impact on civic participation. In South Africa communication among councillors, ward committees, and departments within the administration is not as good as it should be. There is also a lack of communication between the representatives of organizations who attend the major stakeholder meetings and their constituencies. Members of the community often complain that their representatives do not provide feedback from the meetings they attend. In Uganda logistical and financial limitations hamper council efforts to inform citizens about procedures and policies. Most poor people also lack resources to buy newspapers and radios, which provide information about council procedures.

In many countries the budgetary participation process does not start early enough, limiting the amount of time available for consultation. In some cases people feel that meetings are merely informational rather than participatory. Often these meetings are held at times when people are at work or at venues that require them to travel long distances.

Political and social differences also affect participation. Political differences in Tanzania diminished the solidarity and cohesiveness of communities, reducing the level of participation in planning and budgeting or stalling the process in affected areas. In the Kabwe Municipal Council in Zambia, inclusion of political appointees in the form of a deputy minister and permanent secretary in the governance structure of the council reduced the level of civic participation. Local stakeholders pull in different directions due to conflicting instructions from the provincial political leadership on the one hand and the principal officers of the council on the other hand.

In South Africa social and cultural differences between areas that were once all white and areas that were once all black remain. The participation process must be able to meet the needs of the diverse communities that municipalities in South Africa serve. In Zimbabwe populations in cities tend to be more diverse. Reconciling different cultures poses tremendous challenges, because different needs surface as priorities.

Lessons Learned

Important lessons have been learned in implementing participatory mechanisms. The main lessons learned from the experiences of the countries reviewed are described below.

Garner political will and create an appropriate legislative framework

Successful civic participation requires the political will to engage with citizens: in countries in which participatory processes have been successful, political support for civic involvement has been consistent. Such support creates an atmosphere of trust and allows citizens to feel that they are playing a role in determining how local government structures spend their resources and how such spending will affect their lives.

The constitution as well as all legislation relating to local government should recognize autonomous local government and enshrine the value of participation. Countries in which participatory budgeting has been successful have put in place an institutional and regulatory environment that allows for local autonomy and direct participation of citizens in decision making that has an impact on local communities.

Build the capacity of local actors

Extensive and continuous capacity building of councillors, officials, and citizens is key to successful budgetary participation. In every country reviewed, empowering communities with knowledge of the budget process and technical skills to analyze budgets enabled more direct participation. Capacity building increases understanding of the municipal planning and budget cycle and how resource allocation occurs, allowing communities to provide more meaningful input into the process. Experience shows that councillors and local officials who have received training are better able to engage with citizens and encourage them to participate in planning and budgeting processes.

Continuing civic education and capacity building is a top priority in dealing with the challenges of participatory budgeting. Communities that have provided ongoing training workshops have seen significant improvement in the quality and quantity of the input received by citizens. For example, in Ilala municipality, Tanzania, where training was provided to all stakeholders, the participatory budget became more realistic and priorities were much more clearly identified. In Singida district municipality, Tanzania, extensive and continuous awareness building and public education improved the effectiveness of participation, allowing specific problems to be addressed through the budget process.

Training of officials and councillors also improves interaction and understanding among all actors. The training workshops should have a strong practical component and cover issues such as the following:

- Why do tradeoffs need to be made in using scarce resources to address unlimited needs?
- How do local authorities function?
- What is the relationship between strategic planning and budgeting?
- What is the difference between a capital and an operating budget? Is the proportion of capital to current spending appropriate? Within current spending, is the proportion of salaries to maintenance spending appropriate?

Where communication between the local authority and citizens is an issue, it is also important to include the development of a communication strategy in any capacity-building program. It may also be useful to form learning networks so that groups can learn from the experiences of others. These networks could include local authorities within a country or local authorities from different countries.

Ensure commitment by local authorities

Commitment by both elected and appointed officials of the local authority is vital to the success of participatory practices. In countries in which both councillors and officials are committed to involving all stakeholders in the decision-making processes of the local authority (Mozambique, Tanzania, and Uganda), citizen participation in municipal governance issues has been enhanced and the participation process is more sustainable and meaningful. Traditional leaders, as custodians of community values, also need to be taken on board and factored into participatory processes.

Central government support for participatory approaches is also necessary, as it lends legitimacy to the process. Its support is manifested in legal provisions for participation, government policies, and facilita-tive institutions.

Include all stakeholders and accommodate diversity

Careful identification of all key stakeholders to ensure broad-based representation of all segments of society, including disadvantaged and vulnerable groups, is essential in facilitating the participatory process. Countries that have adopted a systematic approach that includes all sectors of the community have enhanced ownership of the process by the community. The community must be part of driving the process if it is to be sustainable. In order to accommodate diversity, it may be necessary to adopt different strategies for the various groupings so that each may participate in the way that is most appropriate.

Give citizens plenty of time to prepare

Consultation with civil society must occur well in advance of meetings, so that citizens have the opportunity to discuss their needs and priorities. Citizens need time to be able to provide meaningful input into the budget.

Citizens need to be notified of meetings well in advance, so that they have plenty of time to make their travel plans. Meetings should be scheduled at times that are convenient for people who work during the day.

Conclusions

In all the countries reviewed here, local government is recognized as a sphere of government in its own right, with powers to manage its own fiscal revenues and expenditures. Each country has legislation governing the local sphere. Some have made civic participation mandatory, requiring local authorities to cooperate with citizens and give them the opportunity to be part of decision-making processes.

Even in countries that have not legislated participatory processes, participation is recognized as an important tool for improving service delivery to communities. Countries have therefore put in place mechanisms to allow for more inclusiveness in the planning and budgetary processes. These mechanisms include ward committee structures, participatory planning processes, public meetings, budget conferences, consultative sessions, budget campaigns, monthly newsletters, a participatory poverty assessment project, and various forms of media intervention.

In each country the budget preparation process includes a stage that allows for civic participation in identifying needs and priorities. In some cases participation occurs only at the beginning of the process; in others citizens are given another opportunity to provide input regarding the allocation of resources once the draft budget is finalized.

Citizens have opportunities to provide input, but in many instances their input is limited and the allocation of resources is still determined largely by local officials and councillors. In many cases citizens are not given adequate time to analyze and discuss their input. Moreover, citizen input is solicited only with regard to the capital budget, which represents only a small proportion of the total budget.

Despite these problems, civic participation has increased the number and range of projects implemented by local authorities that have a direct impact on communities involved in the participation process. Participation has also improved relations between citizens and local authorities, as citizens feel that local authorities have become more transparent and trustworthy.

Notes

1. *Subnational government, local government, local authority,* and *municipality* are used interchangeably in this chapter. All refer to governance at the local level.
2. Integrated Development Planning is the planning methodology that identifies priorities and plans.
3. The logical framework approach is a management tool used mainly in the design, monitoring, and evaluation of development projects.

References

Kundishora, P. 2004a. "Capacity Building Needs to Support Civic Participation in Subnational Budgeting in Uganda." World Bank Institute, Washington, DC.

———. 2004b. "Civic Participation in Subnational Budgeting: The Case of Entebbe Municipality, Uganda." World Bank Institute, Washington, DC.

———. 2004c. "Civic Participation in Subnational Budgeting: The Case of Soroti Municipality, Uganda." World Bank Institute, Washington, DC.

————. 2004d. "Civic Participation in Subnational Budgeting: Ugandan National Framework Condition." World Bank Institute, Washington, DC.

Lubuva, J. 2004a. "Capacity Building Needs to Support Civic Participation in Subnational Budgeting in Tanzania." World Bank Institute, Washington, DC.

————. 2004b. "Civic Participation in Subnational Budgeting: The Case of Ilala Municipal Council in Dar Es Salaam, Tanzania." World Bank Institute, Washington, DC.

————. 2004c. "Civic Participation in Subnational Budgeting: The Case of Singida District Council, Tanzania." World Bank Institute, Washington, DC.

————. 2004d. "Civic Participation in Subnational Budgeting: Tanzanian National Framework Condition." World Bank Institute, Washington, DC.

Mangaung Local Municipality. 2004. "Mangaung Budget Cycle 2004/05." Mangaung, South Africa.

Mika, J. 2004. "Civic Participation in Subnational Budgeting: The Case of the City of Gweru, Zimbabwe." World Bank Institute, Washington, DC.

Mumvuma, T. 2004. "Civic Participation in Subnational Budgeting: The Case of Kabwe Municipality, Zambia." World Bank Institute, Washington, DC.

Shall, A. 2004. "Civic Participation in Subnational Budgeting in South Africa." World Bank Institute, Washington, DC.

Wamwangi, K. 2004a. "Capacity Building Needs to Support Civic Participation in Subnational Budgeting in Kenya." World Bank Institute, Washington, DC.

————. 2004b. "Civic Participation in Subnational Budgeting: Kenyan National Framework Conditions." World Bank Institute, Washington, DC.

————. 2004c. "Civic Participation in Subnational Budgeting: The Nairobi Case Study, Kenya." World Bank Institute, Washington, DC.

7

Participatory Budgeting in the Middle East and North Africa

ALTA FÖLSCHER

Participatory budgeting does not occur in a vacuum: environmental and design factors facilitate citizen engagement in public affairs. This chapter discusses necessary and enabling factors that help participatory mechanisms take root, assesses whether they are present in the Middle East and North Africa, and examines whether participatory mechanisms can catalyze or contribute to societal changes in terms of governance, development, and democracy in the region. It also explores whether participatory processes are consistent with Islamic rules and values.

Potential for Participatory Budgeting

An extensive body of literature associates participatory budgeting with good governance outcomes (McGee 2003; Reuben 2003; Wampler 2000). Civic engagement in public affairs is seen as instrumental to state effectiveness. It also leads to better public decisions by increasing vertical, or social, accountability. When citizens are engaged in processes of planning, funding, delivering, and monitoring public goods and services, the incentives of public officials and office holders change.

In addition to improving state effectiveness, participatory approaches promise two additional benefits that are relevant to the Middle East and North Africa. First, institutions supporting wider citizen involvement are instrumental to human development—the continuous expansion of human capabilities, opportunities, and freedoms. Second, participation offers opportunities for meaningful participation, an end (or a human right) in itself.

Recent work by the United Nations Economic and Social Commission for Western Asia (ESCWA) (Fawaz 2002), the World Bank (2003), and the United Nations Development Programme (2005) has identified poor governance as a significant contributing factor to poor growth and underdevelopment in the Middle East and North Africa. Could partipatory processes help improve governance in the region?

The political, governance, and social conditions in the region appear to limit the scope for participatory budgeting initiatives. The 2004 *Arab Human Development Report* (UNDP 2005, p. 9) notes that despite several recent regional and country-specific reform initiatives, reforms have been "embryonic and fragmentary." Although the gains are "undoubtedly real and promising . . . they do not add up to a serious effort to dispel the prevailing environment of oppression." The report identifies the prevalence of autocratic regimes combined with traditionalism and tribalism as major impediments to such political and civil liberties as the right to information, participation, growth, and human development. Other reports, including Abootalebi (1999), Al-Masmoudi (2004), Fawaz (2002), Gilbraith (1996), and World Bank (2003), mirror these findings.

Citizen Budget Initiatives

State exercise of power in the region does not bode well for the successful implementation of citizen budget initiatives. Autocratic rule combined with restrictions on freedom of speech, media, and association and political practices that pay little heed to principles of contestability, equality, and accountability may impede the robust growth of such initiatives. A World Bank review of governance and development in the region (World Bank 2003, p. 4) noted that "nepotism, tribal affinity, patronage, or money determines who gets public services and who does not."

Contestability and representivity are largely absent in the region. Even when the formal system of government includes procedural democracy, these features are lacking in the informal system. Instead, without the majority of people behind them, most regimes have resorted to other sources of legitimacy, including religion, tribal affiliation, and an emphasis on the authority of powerful elites—often family based—to rule (Abootalebi 1999, 2004; UNDP 2005; World Bank 2003). The survival of these regimes "has become more dependent on control and propaganda; on marginalizing the elites through scare-and-promise tactics, on striking bargains with dominant global or regional powers; and on mutually supportive regional blocs" (UNDP 2005, p. 16).

This lack of contestability in the political culture—a problematic environment for citizen budget initiatives—manifests itself at many levels in the formal system. Within the region, only Algeria, Egypt, the Palestinian Authority, Sudan, and Yemen elect their president through direct elections in which more than one candidate runs. Presidential term limits are not imposed (UNDP 2005). While totally or partially elected parliaments now exist in all countries in the region except Saudi Arabia and the United Arab Emirates, political participation through parliamentary representation is often little more than a ritual: parliaments are largely without power, and elections have not taken power out of the hands of ruling elites (UNDP 2005). In fact, elections are often designed or executed to limit parliamentary power. In Iran, for example, where the election of a reformist president brought hope for further democratic reforms, reformist-minded candidates were disqualified from standing for the February 2004 parliamentary elections, leaving power in the hands of the ruling elite (Abootalebi 2004). According to a World Bank report on governance in the region, "the independence of . . . parliaments is generally limited, as is their constitutional or actual power to hold the typically strong executive accountable" (2003, p. 46). In most countries in the region, parliaments lack oversight over the head of state and cannot initiate or control legislation or the budget.

Several authors point to a long-term trend of democratization (Abootalebi 2004; Ibrahim 2004) that reflects both pressure from within countries in the region and gradual social, economic, and political liberalization. There are also significant signs of recent reform. In May 2004 an Arab summit issued a Declaration on the Process of Reform and Modernization, calling for the continuation and intensification of political, economic, social, and educational change initiatives that reflect the will and aspirations of Arabs. It called for a deepening of the foundations of democracy and consultation and a broadening of participation in political life and decision making, in tandem with the rule of law, equality among citizens, and freedom of expression (UNDP 2005). The elections in Iraq and the Palestinian Authority, domestic political mobilization in Lebanon, municipal elections in Saudi Arabia, and presidential election reforms in Egypt are all recent indicators of a shift in response to mounting internal pressure for more freedoms and increased democracy.

Abootalebi (1999) does not view these changes as indicative of a fundamental move toward democracy by state or society. Greater space for and growth of political parties may be signs of a minimum adjustment to pressure from reformist groups rather than a genuine political groundshift. He argues that political parties in the region play a largely ceremonial role that serves to legitimate the state and its policies. "Although the formalities of a democratic state are in place (for example, elections and debates), the people remain politically and economically without much functional power." The real basis of state power in Middle Eastern countries is largely informal, not institutional, for it is personal, family, and group ties that help sustain the executive power of the ruling elites.

This is not equally true for all countries in the region; the extent of the ruling elites' autocratic power varies. Kuwait and the Persian Gulf sheikdoms, along with Oman and Saudi Arabia, are highly autocratic. In other countries, such as Egypt, Lebanon, and Morocco, there are stronger grounds for arguing that a shift in the balance of state-society relations in favor of society is occurring.

In some countries, the slow gains achieved in the 20th century were rolled back in the aftermath of September 11, 2001. Early in 2003, Arab interior ministers agreed to an antiterrorism strategy that led to further restrictions on personal freedoms. Unprecedented numbers of arrests have occurred, according to UNDP (2005), and legal safeguards against mistreatment in prisons, camps, and detention centers have been violated. Citizens in some Arab countries live under threat of having their citizenship withdrawn on the basis of administrative decisions by lower-level government officials. Journalists, political activists, and human rights advocates often face prosecution or outright attack (UNDP 2005). Freedom of opinion and expression is curtailed through official censorship.

Basic civil and political liberties, such as freedom of thought, peaceful association, belief, and opinion, are guaranteed by national constitutions. However, under the banner of national security, either the constitutions themselves or lower-order legislation restricts these freedoms, particularly freedom of association (UNDP 2005). Political parties are permitted in 14 Arab countries; they are banned in Libya and the Gulf states. However, in many countries where constitutions allow the formation of political parties, legislative restrictions limit this right (by, for example, requiring prior authorization from committees with heavy government representation, restricting party activities, or assigning the right to dissolve a party to the state). Other examples of restrictions on the right to associate include provisions prohibiting or restricting the right to strike, demonstrate, hold mass gatherings, or assemble peacefully.

Most countries in the region place restrictions on the formation of civil society organizations (CSOs), whose activities are highly constrained (exceptions are Lebanon and Morocco). In some countries, organizations are dissolved if found to be too critical of the state. Most restrictions have been directed against grassroots human rights organizations (UNDP 2005), typically those calling for higher levels of participation and transparency within a human rights framework.

Despite the barriers, organized civil society is not absent from the region. There are many voluntary organizations, trade unions, human rights groups, women's associations, minority rights groups, and various other social movements (Gilbraith 1996). Despite constraints on the media, independent views are heard from growing numbers of independent research organizations and think tanks. However, across the region civil society remains constrained by the state; in some countries it is totally oppressed or co-opted. In Egypt, for example, where civil society is relatively free and vibrant, a 1964 law requires that CSOs refrain from "political" activity and empowers the state to replace the governing councils of CSOs if they do.

Ibrahim (2004) provides evidence of how think tanks in Egypt and elsewhere have succeeded in broadening the political, social, and economic reform agenda in the Arab world despite these constraints.[1] He emphasizes their ability to provide timely information and change the way in which leaders and intellectuals conceive of politics and policy making. These groups have been particularly successful in introducing a new "discourse that is more concerned with gathering facts and research than just with abstract concepts of ideology, law and philosophy. This new discourse is largely in line with the policy and financial analysis provided by successful budget (or public policy and finance) nongovernmental organizations elsewhere in the world" (Ibrahim 2004, p. 5).

The Al-Ahram Centre for Political and Strategic Studies in Egypt was the first Arab-state think tank to be established. It "opened the door for individuals and groups to create new foundations for promoting democracy, fighting illiteracy and poverty, projecting civil society advancements, and empowering women" (p. 1). Its establishment, supported by gradual economic, political, and social liberalization, led to a boom in think tanks (box 7.1).

A major impediment to broad-based participation initiatives is the high level of illiteracy throughout the region. The ability of CSOs to get "people power" behind their analyses and the potential for direct participation in decisions about resource allocation and use may be circumscribed by citizens' capacity to engage with technical issues. About one-third of Arab men and half of Arab women are illiterate. Although there have been significant

BOX 7.1 Think Tanks in the Arab World

The first think tank in an Arab country was established in Cairo in 1967. The Al-Ahram Center, which was linked to the government, was designed to provide Egypt and the rest of the Arab world with information about Israel. Today the center is the largest and most influential research institution in Egypt, focusing on international politics and the political, economic, and social aspects of Arab and Egyptian society. The center disseminates its analysis through an array of publications, including a strategic report, weekly articles, and discussion papers. The development of the center served as a blueprint that has since been duplicated by many other institutions in the country.

Egypt's Ibn Khaldun Centre can be viewed as the first truly independent think tank. Founded in 1988, this center has a more directly public policy–oriented agenda: it applies contemporary social science research methodologies to serve the developmental goals of Egypt and the Arab world. It was founded with private resources. In June 2000 the Egyptian government closed down the center, arresting its founder and 27 center associates. Since then the center has reopened, and its founder has been released. The center publishes and organizes seminars on a wide range of political and socioeconomic issues, including religion and politics, history, civil society, and democratic transformation and development.

Egypt's first independent nonprofit economic-oriented research institute, the Egyptian Centre for Economic Studies (ECES), was established in 1992. It conducts economic research in support of an open market system and a larger role for the private sector. The center was initially funded by Egypt's private sector and the U.S. Agency for International Development (USAID), together with other development partners. It conducts research on topics such as trade liberalization, the role of the state, and deregulation.

Since its founding, several other think tanks have been established. Ibrahim (2004) identifies two trends. First, think tanks make increasing use of information and communication technology to disseminate their own information. Some are virtual research centers only, with no brick and mortar infrastructure. Second, many think tanks are affiliated with universities. Many of the university-based centers are staffed with scholars who have studied abroad. Cairo University and the American University in Cairo recruit talented young scholars who use their expertise to develop Western-style research centers. These trends are reflected elsewhere in the region.

Three constraints face think tanks. The first is their control by the state. Regimes often frame think tank agendas or define the institutions from their founding. In Egypt, Jordan, Lebanon, and Morocco, conditions are more hospitable for establishing semi- or fully independent research centers, although their agenda is still influenced by their relationship with the government. Other countries, such as Libya, Syria, and many of the Gulf states, provide very little opportunity for the creation of independent think tanks.

(*Box continues on the following page.*)

The second challenge is the lack of financial and human resources. The "overall weak state of the social sciences in the Arab world has hindered the development of qualified indigenous researchers to staff the region's think tanks" (Ibrahim 2004, p. 11). According to Ibrahim, just 5,000 Arab researchers are working on social and political trends in the Middle East. This shortage is exacerbated by a severe lack of funding; most funding for CSOs in the region goes to radical organizations. The largest financial support come from Western (or Northern) development partners.

The third challenge is the lack of credibility. Liberal-oriented think tanks face enormous difficulties in translating their messages in such a way that the wider—often illiterate—public can connect to them. Think tanks are often discredited for their "foreign style, outside connections and lack of authenticity" (Ibrahim 2004, p. 12).

Despite these limitations and challenges, Ibrahim points to the success of think tanks in introducing new ideas into public debates and introducing new, more rational, forms of research on policy issues. He cautions against overemphasizing the role of Arab civil society as a force for change, however: the role of traditional forces and the dismissal of independent think tanks as puppets of the West, together with the co-opting of other institutions by power structures, hamper their capacity to take this role forward.

Source: Ibrahim 2004.

recent gains in access to education across the region, the quality of education remains low (UNDP 2005).

Low literacy levels in themselves do not necessarily impede participation. The peasant- and worker-based initiatives of the Development Initiative for Social and Human Action (DISHA) and Mazdoor Kisan Shakti Sangathan in India illustrate how ordinary and often illiterate citizens make significant contributions to public resource management once public budgets and public service delivery are made relevant to their lives (see chapter 5 in this volume). However, in both cases, as in almost all initiatives in Eastern Europe (see chapter 4 in this volume), popular citizen participation in the programs was predicated on educating citizens about their rights. These activities have occurred in environments in which threats against rights-based activities and activists did not exist or were far less pronounced than they are in the Middle East and North Africa, however.

Low levels of knowledge about citizen-state relationships also impede active participation by citizens. Like citizens in Eastern Europe, citizens in this region perceive themselves as passive recipients of government services, as fortunate beneficiaries of resources that belong to the state. The large contribution of oil revenues to public coffers and the relatively low levels of taxation contribute to this perception. Citizens are unlikely to perceive themselves as clients of government or as the principal holders of power in the relationship.

Citizens' lack of knowledge of their rights and their perception of the state as all powerful may limit the likelihood that participatory budgeting will take root in the Middle East and North Africa in the short to medium term. Given the political, social, and cultural norms in the region, more limited forms of citizen participation—by think tanks, for example—may be more plausible. Of course, this type of participation would be open to the criticism that participation continues to involve the elite rather than a broader group of citizens. Such a criticism is particularly relevant in this region, where poverty levels in some countries are high despite high per capita income rates and women and minority groups are excluded from political processes.

Even initiatives aimed at influencing the intellectual and policy-making elite remain dependent on a free media to disseminate their findings. According to the World Bank governance study (2003), countries in the region have "limited and reluctant" transparency. In no country is the right to information guaranteed. In Egypt, despite a vibrant civil society, the budget is not published outside of parliament, limiting public discussion of it. In contrast, in Iran the national budget is published and parliamentary debates are televised. In Algeria, Iran, and Lebanon the media participate in public debates on government.

Kadhim (2004) believes that traditional or nontraditional social forces block transparency. There is a "deliberate absence of knowledge and an attempt to intervene in the details of knowledge." The lack of access to information and communication technology is the most obvious example. It "stems from a fear of the spread of knowledge and of the raising of awareness" (Kadhim, 2004, p. 1). Regulations in 11 countries in the region allow ex ante or ex post (after printing) censorship of the press, severely truncating press freedom. Laws are also in place that require publishers to have a license, leaving the media under constant threat and leading to self-censorship. Only five countries—Algeria, Egypt, Jordan, Sudan, and Yemen—ensure journalists the legal right to obtain information (UNDP 2005).

Despite these restrictions, media freedom has made its appearance in the Arab world through satellite television and the Internet. Governments still impose their control on written media (books, textbooks, newspapers, and magazines), however (Al-Masmoudi 2004). In some countries—notably

Algeria, Egypt, Lebanon, and Morocco—journalists have freedom on paper. However, "even in these countries, the media know that there are 'red lines' that they cannot cross" (p. 3). In particular, they cannot explore corruption, transparency, nepotism, or favoritism.

The overall picture of an enabling environment for civil society budget initiatives in the region is mixed, but on balance it is not encouraging. On the positive side, there are signs that societies in the region are undergoing systemic change—albeit uneven and halting—toward an underlying political culture that is more conducive to participation. This change often triggers backlashes that close down political space for participation. The outcome of this process is thus not at all certain.

Participation in Resource Decisions

Many countries in the region have committed themselves to decentralizing power and empowering local authorities. Some have also put on the agenda partnerships with CSOs and the private sector at the local level as a means of empowering local governance. In Iran, Jordan, Lebanon, and Syria, local elections have taken place, local authority legislation has been reviewed, or new regulations have been adopted. In some cases central governments have also invested in strengthening local government capacity, in terms of both human resources and technical systems. These steps have not been accompanied by the devolution of real decision-making power, however, or the decentralization of resources. According to Fawaz (2002, p. 3), Arab states are going through a "mixed de-concentration/delegation process in which most administrative, financial and political decisions still happen at the top." Overall, while responsibilities have often been shifted downward, the shift has not been accompanied by the necessary changes in power. This has caused municipalities to be overwhelmed by their daily responsibilities without the necessary capacity or resources to act on them (Fawaz 2002).

Fawaz (2002) is skeptical that local governments will be able to change the underlying power structures prevalent in many of the countries. She notes that municipal boards of elected local governments have rallied constituencies largely on a sectarian, tribal, regional, or religious basis, and they have depended on their political and social networks to survive. The ability of local authorities to enable better representation, participation, and empowerment is therefore contentious. The World Bank governance study (2003) contends that local elections have improved local governance and created a proving ground for future national political leaders, but it concedes that power in the region is still highly centralized, not only toward the central level of government but also within the executive. This weakens checks and balances and limits the opportunities for participation.

Sarrouh (2003) identifies the "militarization of administrative functions" at the local level (the appointment of former military personnel to decision-making and leadership positions) as a challenge to effective local government. This practice deters public participation, delegation of authorities to local actors, and responsiveness to local needs. Resistance to change or devolution of powers is a serious challenge. Without the support of top leadership and the involvement of elected members, reforms will not occur.

Inequality between individuals and groups is great in the Middle East and North Africa. Given that trust seems to act as an enabler of meaningful and broad-based direct participation in decision making, this is likely to act as a silent barrier to such participation. Experience elsewhere where deep divisions exist—in Bangladesh, for example, where women's issues remained excluded from a community-driven development program despite specific design interventions—shows that an uneven distribution of power is very difficult to overcome.

Alvi (2005) draws attention to the urgency of addressing the barriers faced by women, particularly given trends of "regressive social transformation." She notes two reinforcing factors that contribute to these trends. The first is the strengthening of attitudes and social policies in some countries that deny women their fundamental rights and freedoms. The second is weaker social indicators—such as educational level and social status—which make it difficult for women to challenge these attitudes. If local governments are not operating on principles of inclusivity and equality, it is unlikely that mechanisms allowing direct participation by citizens will overcome the governance gap affecting women.

Despite these challenges, some communities have participated successfully in decision-making processes that have had a real impact on their lives. Fawaz (2002) points out that local government initiatives often succeed in states that are in or have recently emerged from conflict, citing several examples that are included in the UN-Habitat good practice database. According to her, the weakening of the central state that occurs in these conditions allows space for local governments to assume their mandates. Participation has also occurred in states where the balance of power has shifted away from totalitarian regimes toward society. External funders have played an important role in some countries in the region, as they have in Eastern Europe (see chapter 4).

Rehabilitating and upgrading the Manshiet Nasser informal settlement in Cairo

In 1997 more than 500,000 inhabitants of an informal settlement in Cairo, Egypt, were relocated to a nearby planned settlement equipped with all services (UN-Habitat 2001). The new settlement is equipped with piped water and sanitation, a road network, open space, training and health care centers, libraries, schools, telecommunications, and artisan workshops. In short, it has the infrastructure to be a human settlement rather than a housing project. The site of the old slum was redeveloped and renewed.

Infrastructure is necessary but not sufficient for turning housing projects into human settlements. The participation of those affected is required, too. The project was therefore based on a participatory socioeconomic survey and supported by mechanisms of transparent dialogue. The poor were provided with affordable housing options, financed by soft loans to the inhabitants of the new housing units. The project empowered civic engagement at the early stages of decision making, reducing the scope for conflict and aiding the mobilization of citizens' own resources for effective implementation. The success of this project suggests that coordination among government agencies, CSOs, and development partners, though challenging, is necessary for effective and sustainable urban development.

Effecting change through quartier associations in Tunisia

Quartier (neighborhood) associations and committees—local nongovernmental groups that can mobilize the population in support of particular issues, such as combating environmental degradation—are a relatively new feature of decentralization in Tunisia (Ben Salem and Vengroff 1992). The associations operate at the lowest level of government, that of the municipal councils. These unelected councils are charged with certain key functions, mainly in the area of service delivery, especially at the municipal level. They also levy and collect a variety of local taxes. The mayor (the president of the council) is selected by members of the council from among themselves. Decision making in the municipal councils is relatively open. Committee hearings and council meetings are open to the public. The potential for access by nongovernmental organizations (NGOs) and association groups is relatively high. The quartier associations are especially important in this regard.

A typical quartier association is structured around a 10-member bureau, which has a diverse, highly motivated, and potentially very powerful set of members. The leaders are relatively mature in age and are drawn from the upper economic class of society. Their function is similar to that of local interest groups that build and create alliances with other groups, such as the local mosque, political party cells, local officials, and environmental groups. Members also use their connections at the central level to gain some advantages. In some cases, quartiers mobilize modest amounts of resources to support local projects and engage in neighborhood clean-up and self-help programs.

The quartiers concentrate mainly on environmental and community issues. Their status as local and community-based organizations is key for attracting popular support and participation. If these groups prove to be successful, it is likely that their impact will expand to the municipal, regional, and even central levels. Despite limitations, the quartier associations increase opportunities for citizens to provide input into policy-making processes at the municipal and regional levels.

Rehabilitating a neighborhood in Baghdad

The Neighborhood Rehabilitation Project was initiated in 1999 in response to the appalling living conditions of families in areas where public services had collapsed, leading to sewage overflows, disruption of health services, inadequate garbage collection, and scarcity of drinking water (UN-Habitat 2006a). The project was implemented with the participation of the beneficiary low-income families. For the first time in Iraq, a community-based approach to public management was used to ensure that the services would be sustainable. The project was first piloted in two neighborhoods and then extended in 2000 to two more areas. It was implemented by UN-Habitat, in partnership with the municipality of Baghdad, NGOs, and other UN agencies. In 2002 the project was selected as an example of best practice by the Dubai International Awards for Best Practices in Improving the Environment. The lessons from this program are being applied in the postwar UN-Habitat Urban Development and Housing Programme, where large-scale rehabilitation of urban areas is being undertaken with a commitment to participation.

Reducing urban poverty in Lebanon

In 1998 the city of Ghobeiri, Lebanon (population 200,000), held its first local elections in 35 years (UN-Habitat 2006b). Most of the elected council members had backgrounds in the private or nonprofit sector. Managing the city was subsequently undertaken through partnership with all actors—citizen groups, NGOs, the private sector, the central government, and international agencies.

The Ghobeiri municipal council coordinates directly with 16 social NGOs and community-based organizations and indirectly with another 10.

The city has connected 18,000 households to the sewerage system, put up lights and signs on all city streets, and planted more than 4,000 trees. It has expanded a social service network, offering vocational training to more than 100 children and social assistance to more than 30,000 orphans, widows, people with disabilities, and other vulnerable groups through local NGOs. It also offers literacy and skill training to vulnerable women. The municipality receives support from the United Nations Development Programme's LIFE (Local Initiative Facility for Urban Environment) Programme and from UNICEF.

Participatory Budgeting as an Entry Point for Better Governance

Citizens' ability and willingness to engage with the state are predicated on a number of factors, including knowledge and capacity, freedom from fear of prosecution, political space for open debate on public decisions, and the ability to access a free media. Most of these factors are largely absent in the region. However, one of the hopes for participatory budgeting initiatives is that with careful design and targeted support, the initiatives would be able to start the process of effecting positive change in the political and governance environment, particularly by whetting citizens' appetite for contestable government and positive, empowered engagement with the state.

Even successful initiatives face a challenge overcoming the systemic barriers identified and supporting a regional shift toward better governance. Participatory processes will be able to do so only if the underlying social, cultural, and religious norms in the region are compatible with notions of representivity, consultation, and democracy. There should be acceptance of the idea that political and civil rights, including participation, are not contingent on social and cultural norms but are something that any person should be able to recognize as his or her own. If either of these situations is the case, tailored participatory budgeting initiatives should be able to develop and grow in principle.

Democracy and Islamic Rules and Values

Are notions of democracy compatible with Muslim norms?[2] According to Al-Masmoudi, president of the Center of the Study of Islam and Democracy in Washington, D.C., the *sharia* is designed to protect the individual and society (Al-Masmoudi 2004). A well-established process known as *ijtihad* is used to deal with changing needs of Muslim societies over time.[3] For example, in 2000 the Council of Muslim Clerics in Europe and the United States issued a *fatwa* (religious ruling) permitting Muslims residing in the West to purchase homes by taking out mortgages and paying interest. This practice clearly contradicts the Koran's prohibition on interest. Ijtihad "allowed Muslims and Muslim societies to adapt and evolve with changing circumstances and new discoveries" (Al Masmoudi 2004, p. 8). Al-Masmoudi (2004), Abootalebi (2004), and others argue that current regimes and fundamentalist movements force a choice between Islam and modernity or between Islam and democracy but that no choice actually needs to be made; many principles in Islam, including freedom, equality, and justice, are compatible with the values that drive democracy.

One such value is that of *al-shura*, or consultation. According to Al Ansari (2004), in many modern Muslim states this principle has been reduced to a narrow, traditional notion that consultation is good for the ruler if he wishes to adopt it but that otherwise he is free to do as he pleases. This notion contributed to the formation in many Muslim countries of consultative councils without full legislative and supervisory authority over the head of state. Al Ansari argues that Qatar's constitution and Oman's experience point toward political developments in the Gulf countries that are challenging the narrow interpretation. The Islamic notion of consultation is synonymous with democracy in many aspects, including the right of people to govern themselves and the right of individuals to select representatives. The only point of difference "lies in the extent of society's authority to legislate" (Al Ansari 2004, p. 3). Democracy grants society extensive power. The Islamic understanding of consultation, by contrast, "confines society's authority to legislate within the fixed teachings of the Qu'ran and the Sunna"(Al Ansari 2004, p. 3).[4]

Are individual citizens in Muslim countries in the region likely to respond to the idea that as citizens they have the right to elect their representatives and hold them to account for their use of public resources? The *Arab Human Development Report* (UNDP 2005) asserts that the failure of democracy in several countries in the region is not cultural in origin. "It lies in the convergence of political, social and economic structures that have suppressed or eliminated organized social and political actors capable of turning the crisis of authoritarian and totalitarian regimes to their advantage" (UNDP 2005, p. 11). Abootalebi (2004) raises similar arguments with respect to Iran, where the regime deliberately confuses the issue of secularization with popular sovereignty and political democracy by tagging reformists as threats to the survival of Islamic religious values.

Two attitudinal surveys conducted in the region suggest that citizens value governance, democracy, and certain freedoms. The first, conducted in five countries in late 2003 for the *Arab Human Development Report*, found that freedom from foreign occupation, freedom of thought and expression, independent media, and freedom of movement are critical to respondents. Some 89 percent believed that their choice of central and local government leaders through free and fair elections was critical for good governance.

A second survey, the World Values Survey (conducted between 2000 and 2002), found that respondents in Arab countries topped the list of those agreeing that democracy is better than any other form of governance. A high percentage of respondents also rejected authoritarian rule, defined as rule by a strong ruler who disregards parliament or elections (Pettersson 2003).

Some citizen groups advocating human rights and political freedom in the region have been successful in bringing about change. Human rights and political organizations in Morocco persuaded the government to acknowledge violations of human rights and to pass a new family law that met the demands of the women's movement to safeguard women's rights. CSOs in Syria asked for the state of emergency to be lifted and freedoms expanded. In Saudi Arabia documents and petitions on minority rights, religious freedom, civil rights, equality, and political openness were submitted to the crown prince. One petition went as far as to call for constitutional reform, including guaranteeing fundamental political freedoms and democratic reforms, including elections and popular control through representative institutions of public funds (UNDP 2005).

Religious debate and political dialogue in the region are promising for improving governance and development outcomes in the long run. Abootalebi (2004) argues, however, that democratic elections in the region will not succeed without addressing the underlying problem of uneven distribution of socioeconomic and political resources. Meaningfully engaging with issues of public resources allocations could be valuable in initiating such a redistribution of resources. However, countries in the region will not easily—and, as Fawaz (2002) argues, perhaps should not—adopt governance systems and mechanisms that parrot models from the secular world.

None of the factors identified in this chapter as critical to participatory processes—enabling political systems, including mature political parties; fundamental freedoms; civil society capacity; citizen knowledge and capacity; enabling legal frameworks; local government capacity; availability of information—is present in the Middle East and North Africa. Given the political and sociocultural environment in the region, citizen budgeting initiatives are unlikely to succeed, unless they are launched in locales where the leadership is open to citizen input or the initiative is supported by external development partner funding.

Notes

1. Israel has the largest number of think tanks and think-tank activities in the region, followed by Turkey (Ibrahim 2004).
2. The evidence presented in this section may be biased by the fact that it is restricted to literature published in English. A review that includes texts written in Arabic might yield different conclusions.
3. *Ijtihad* is an independent and authoritative interpretation of Islamic law. The process was once practiced by legal scholars to deduce secondary divine laws for regulating human life from their sources and to explain and articulate the law of God in a given situation based on expertise in jurisprudence. Ijtihad was abandoned centuries ago in Sunni practice (Al Masmoudi 2004).
4. The *Sunna* are the statements and actions of the Prophet, later established as legally binding precedents in addition to the law established by the Koran (Al Ansari 2004).

References

Abootalebi, Ali. 1999. "Islam, Islamists and Democracy." *Meria* 3 (1). http://meria.idc.ac.il.
———. 2004. "Iran's Struggle for Democracy Continues." *Meria* 8 (2). http://meria.idc.ac.il.
Al Ansari, Abid-al-Hamid. 2004. "The Possibility of Islamic Groups' Participation in Democratic Systems: Positions and Fears." Paper presented at the Islamic Reform Conference, Brookings Institution, Washington, DC, October.
Al-Masmoudi, Radwan. 2004. "Democracy and Ijtihad: The Twin Pillars of Reform in the Islamic World." Paper presented at the Islamic Reform Conference, Brookings Institution, Washington, DC, October.
Alvi, Hayat. 2005. "The Human Rights of Women and Social Transformation in the Arab Middle East." *Meria* 9 (2). http://meria.idc.ac.il.
Ben Salem, Hatem, and Richard Vengroff. 1992. "Assessing the Impact of Decentralization on Governance: A Comparative Methodological Approach and Application to Tunisia." *Public Administration and Development* 12: 473–92.
Fawaz, Mona. 2002. "Reflections on Best Practices in Governance in ESCWA Countries." Paper prepared for the Empowering Local Government Institutions in the Middle East and North Africa Region Workshop, Fourth Mediterranean Development Forum, Amman, October 6–9.
Gilbraith, M. 1996. "Civil Society in the Arab World." IBN Khaldun Centre, Cairo.
Ibrahim, Ezzat. 2004. "Arab and American Think Tanks: New Possibilities for Cooperation? New Engines for Reform?" Brookings Institution, Washington, DC.
Kadhim, Nadjah. 2004. "The Role of Moderate Islamic Groups in Easing the Severity of the Decline." Paper presented at the Islamic Reform Conference, Brookings Institution, Washington, DC, October.
McGee, Rosemary. 2003. *Legal Frameworks for Citizen Participation: A Synthesis Report.* LogoLink report, Institute for Development Studies, University of Sussex, Brighton, United Kingdom.
Pettersson, Thorleif. 2003. "Islam and Global Governance Orientations towards the United Nations and Human Rights among Four Islamic and Four Western Societies." Paper presented at the conference Explaining the Worldviews of the Islamic Publics Theoretical and Methodological Issues, Cairo, February 24–26.

Reuben, William. 2003. "The Role of Civic Engagement and Social Accountability in the Governance Equation." Social Development Note 75, World Bank, Washington, DC.

Sarrouh, Elissar. 2003. "Decentralised Governance for Development in the Arab States." Paper prepared for the Local Governance Forum in the Arab Region, United Nations Development Programme, Beirut.

Spahn, Bernd. 1998. "Issues of Governance in a Broad Context." Paper presented at the Mediterranean Development Forum, Marrakech, September.

UN-Habitat. 2001. *Implementing the Habitat Agenda*. Report on the Istanbul+5 Thematic Committee, presented at the 25th Special Session of the United Nations General Assembly, New York.

———. 2006a. *Baghdad Neighbourhood Rehabilitation Programme.* http://www.unhabitat. org/content.asp?cid=689&catid=203&typeid=13&subMenuId=0.

———. 2006b. *Municipal Practices for Urban Poverty Reduction.* http://www.bestpractices. org/bpbriefs/urban_governance.html.

UNDP (United Nations Development Programme). 2005. *Arab Human Development Report.* New York: United Nations Development Programme.

Wampler, Brian. 2000. *A Guide to Participatory Budgeting.* International Budget Project, Washington, DC.

World Bank. 2003. *Better Governance for Development in the Middle East and North Africa: MENA Development Report.* Washington, DC: World Bank.

Appendix
A Primer on Effective Participation

ALTA FÖLSCHER

Civic engagement in public affairs can increase state effectiveness. When citizens have the opportunity to make their needs known and hold public institutions to account, it is argued, public resources are likely to be used more efficiently and to deliver public goods and services that are better aligned with citizens' needs. Local communities have the best knowledge of their needs and preferences and of local conditions. Public policy and advocacy organizations outside of the state often give voice to needs and preferences that are not heard in closed budget processes. Citizen participation in decision making reduces the information gap between citizens and the state and makes it more likely that funds will be used to deliver the most-needed goods and services, improving government effectiveness.

Citizen Participation and State Effectiveness

Reuben (2003) refers to this dimension of governance—the ability of governments to fulfill citizen expectations—as *decisiveness*. Participatory systems have the potential to incorporate local knowledge at all levels of decision making: determination of citizen expectations, selection of public policy objectives, and the means of achieving

243

those objectives. Participation therefore results in better public policy and better public policy implementation. This is true for participatory budgeting mechanisms that involve citizens only indirectly (initiatives in which information on citizens' needs, interests, and opinions is put into the public domain), as well as for initiatives in which citizens participate directly in public resource decisions at the local level.

Participation also indirectly leads to better public decisions by increasing vertical, or social, accountability. When citizens are engaged in processes of planning, funding, delivering, and monitoring public goods and services, the incentives of public officials and office holders change. They become more accountable for the choices they make, reducing corruption and increasing effectiveness and efficiency. When supported by broader democratic political and social changes, citizens learn that not only are they the clients of government (rather than the recipients of government-granted goods and services), they are also the principals, with governments as their agents. This recognition inverts more autocratic systems of public power distribution, reinforcing citizen demand for accountable government. Reuben (2003) refers to this dimension of improved conditions for governance as *accountability* in holding public power under the control of those represented by the state.

The argument is that effective public participation in resource decisions builds social capital. Public participation increases the capacity of individuals and local communities for collective action, strengthening ties between individuals, households, and groups. This leads to more economic and social opportunities and to greater potential for improving the quality and coverage of developmental inputs such as public education, health, and social development services. Successful participatory mechanisms strengthen citizens' access to information by creating a framework that creates incentives for citizens to demand more and better information and puts pressure on state structures to provide information. Meaningful and effective citizen participation in public choices also improves trust in government and commitment to tradeoffs made. Together with improved budget transparency, participation can build social cohesion.

Insofar as democracy and participation are ends in themselves, participation in public decision making is a form of direct democracy that allows for a more meaningful democratic relationship between citizens and government than representative democracy (McGee 2003). It can also provide marginalized groups with access to policy makers.

This is in contrast to purely representative democracy, which presupposes absolute bureaucratic efficiency. However, effective participatory democracy is dependent on the quality of deliberation in the process. Deliberation emphasizes "eliciting broad public participation in a process which provides citizens an opportunity to consider the issues, weigh alternatives, and express a judgment about which policy or candidate is preferred. . . . It is distinguished from ordinary, thin modes of public involvement by the breadth and quality of participation" (Weeks 2000, cited in McGee 2003, p. 10). It is therefore not tokenistic. Participatory processes also presuppose decision-making processes that are dictated not by interest group politics but by rationality. If participative practices are to improve the quality of democratic governance, enabling conditions for quality deliberative processes should be in place. These include the incentives citizens face, their skill levels, and the quality of information available in the process.

The World Bank's 2003 MENA Development Report on governance puts forward a framework for good governance in the Middle East and North Africa that includes the aspects highlighted above (World Bank 2003). It is based on two core "universal" values of inclusiveness and accountability. If governance systems offer mechanisms to embody and protect these values, they support state effectiveness and human development.

The framework links inclusive governance to equality: inclusive governance means that all those who have a stake in governance processes and who want to participate in them have equal opportunities to do so. It contains mechanisms to define and protect all people's basic rights, and it provides remedies and recourse for those who are excluded, guaranteed by a rule of law. The need for accountability is legitimized in the notion of representation, which in governance terms means that those selected to act in the name of the people are answerable to the people for their successes and failures. Accountability in turn rests on knowledge and information—transparency—and on institutional arrangements that create incentives for public officials to act faithfully, efficiently, and honestly in carrying out the will of the people. The framework highlights contestability in the selection of public officials and the fostering of an ethic of public service as key ingredients in support of accountability.

Viewing participatory budgeting mechanisms against this framework illustrates significant conceptual congruence: successful participatory budgeting requires institutional arrangements that allow citizens to participate in public resource decisions on an equal platform and ensure the availability of good information. Selection of public officials should be contestable; if it is not, the incentives facing those in power work against meaningful public participation. Participatory budgeting (including mechanisms that facilitate horizontal accountability) fosters a system in which public officials are accountable and public policies become contestable. In short, participatory budgeting mechanisms operate at the core of a good governance system, embodying and reinforcing values that, it is argued, could help some regions of the world, including the Middle East and North Africa, narrow significant growth and human development gaps.

Types of Participation

Very different types and levels of citizen engagement with public resource decisions and service delivery are referred to as *participatory budgeting*. One can differentiate two broad types of citizen engagement, distinguished by the degree to which citizens enter the action space of the state in planning for, allocating, using, and monitoring the use of public resources. In the first set of participatory budgeting initiatives, citizens do not attempt to take over or partner with the state in the budget process but instead undertake activities in the broader public domain that are aimed primarily at improving the transparency of governments' actions and the accountability of state actors. This type of participation is within the boundaries of both representative democracy and more autocratic forms of government (provided that such activities are tolerated). Making public decisions is still the purview of government agencies and elected officeholders. However, citizens do not take the bureaucratic effectiveness of these institutions for granted but undertake activities to bolster transparency and accountability. These activities typically generate information on public policy and services outside of the state in order to influence what happens in the state. Activities in this broad category are usually initiated by CSOs. This type of participation relies on the quality of the information to persuade decision makers to change development and funding priorities or improve the quality of services.

Budget analysis and dissemination by skilled professionals are often aided by garnering the support of broad-based movements, by having "people power" behind it, as Paul (2005) argues. He emphasizes the need for coalitions of different types of CSOs. These coalitions need to use the media to reach citizens, forge ties with officials and members of oversight bodies, and be able to translate dry, technical material into information that ordinary people will understand and find relevant. These campaigns are strengthened if there is true representative democracy and citizens cast their votes on the basis of policy and service delivery issues. However, the success of such initiatives is not necessarily dependent on a democratic environment.

In the second set of initiatives, citizens engage or are engaged in the decision-making processes of public agencies. Examples of this participation, which can be seen as a form of direct democracy, can be found throughout the budget process. The mechanisms deployed represent different intensities of participation, because governments have discretion over the degree of access to traditional state-controlled action spaces they provide in setting up or taking over participatory mechanisms.

McGee (2003) distinguishes four types of participation:

- information sharing (the state puts budget and public policy information into the public domain);
- consultation (the state sets up mechanisms such as forums, councils, and referendums or surveys to gather information on citizen preferences);
- joint decision making (citizens not only provide information on their needs and preferences but are active in real decision making);
- initiation and control by stakeholders (citizens have direct control over the full process of developing, raising funds for, and implementing projects or policy, as in social fund and community-driven development projects).

As participatory practices move up this ladder, the argument goes, they become more effective instruments of participation: direct initiation and control by stakeholders is more powerful than joint decision making, which in turn is more effective than consultation and information sharing.

Preconditions and Enabling Factors for Citizen Engagement with Public Decisions

The capacity of citizens to engage the state on the allocation and use of public resources—and the likelihood of their actually doing so—depend on several factors. These include the openness and democratic depth of political and governance systems; the existence of enabling legal frameworks, including guarantees of basic freedoms; the capacity for participation both inside and outside of government; the existence of functional and free media institutions; and the willingness and capacity of the state to make budget information available.

Formal and Informal Political Systems

Paul (2005) contends that initiatives that encourage citizen participation in public decision making are more successful in societies that adhere to democratic governance, are open to public debate and criticism of those in authority, have relatively free media, and allow independent CSOs to take root. Goetz and Gaventa (2001) emphasize the importance of the nature and organization of the political system in determining the level and quality of participation. The argument is that even if a civil society group is well equipped with expertise and resources to initiate participation, its efforts will not yield significant benefits unless election to power is contestable. Contestability refers not only to the existence of real competition in the election of candidates but also to the requirement that the attractiveness of one candidate over another should be driven less by the politics of identity, personality, and patronage and more by issues of public policy. When issues of public policy and service delivery get more play in voter preferences, politicians have less leeway to ignore events or behave in ways that invite voter dissatisfaction.

Spahn (1998, p. 2) emphasizes that while good governance needs to be rooted in local norms and values, the legitimacy of governments remains an important element. Legitimate government "is essential to form consensus within a society and thus to foster political stability and social cohesion." Governments are legitimate when they are representative and their political and bureaucratic power is limited. A free media and effective opposition parties are important elements of a legitimate system of government.

Bringing a concept of legitimacy to good governance in the context of participatory budgeting is important in two ways. First, meaningful space for participation in government processes contributes to legitimacy and trust in government. Second, some degree of legitimacy is necessary before citizens will engage with government, particularly directly. Goetz and Gaventa (2001) emphasize the role of a mature political party system in legitimizing government and enabling participation.

Fawaz (2002, p. 11) refers to these aspects as an "environment of political pluralism and inclusiveness" and notes that notions of empowerment of local authorities, good governance, partnership, and accountable and transparent management carry implicit assumptions about the existence of media freedom, high levels of devolution of authority, equal power relations among actors, and civil society with sufficient capacity to participate. When these features are not in place, they act as "silent barriers" to change.

While participatory budgeting initiatives can build trust and social capital, they also depend on some already existing degree of trust (between citizens and the state as well as among citizens). Some of the most successful case studies in Asia have occurred in Thailand: within a nationally set policy and legal framework, several local area authorities have initiated sophisticated participatory budget processes in which hierarchies of civil committees make the tradeoffs between different interests within a community and between communities. The existence of trust that over time resources will be distributed equitably across interest groups has enabled the groups to agree on funding. The high level of trust may in part be supported by underlying social cohesiveness: Thai society is relatively homogeneous. Fawaz (2002) argues that the promotion of good governance based on notions of representivity, transparency, accountability, and participation often fails to take account of the reality of ethnic and religious divisions in some states.

The type of society, the type of political system, the legitimacy of the government, and attitudes toward governance also determine which types of participatory initiatives can be introduced successfully. The effectiveness of initiatives of all kinds depends on the likelihood of state actors experiencing "public accountability discomfort" when initiatives and their outcomes are ignored. The more vibrant a country's democratic governance and the more real the contest for political power, the more options are open for effective civil society participation. If the media are not free, access to information is repressed, societies do not allow public debate on issues of public interest, and freedom of association is constrained, civil society cannot conduct public policy and advocacy work.

The attitude of state actors to citizen voice is related in principle to systems of accountability, which in turn is related to contestability and representivity, as set out in the World Bank framework for governance discussed above. The importance of the relation between these issues correlates well with the case study evidence presented in this volume that participatory initiatives bringing citizens into the public sphere to make decisions about resource use are critically dependent on the willingness of local government representatives to pay attention to citizens' expressed preferences. This in turn is dependent on the nature of the political system. Where local civil society or third parties, such as development partners, initiate a direct participation initiative without having first secured real commitment from public officials, the impact remains questionable.

Figure A.1 provides a schematic representation of these relationships. The shaded area denotes instances of participatory mechanisms that are unlikely to yield results—mechanisms that bring citizens into the public sphere to make decisions within an environment in which local government officials have little interest in citizen participation and policy issues have low political currency. The risk of participation being counterproductive in such cases is real, because citizens soon learn that participation has no or very few real benefits, making them less interested in initiatives under more favorable conditions later.

Source: Author.

FIGURE A.1 State Attitude toward Citizen Voice and Effective Participation

One way of bypassing such constraints is to set up programs in which community-level participation structures have real authority over development funds that are not channeled through the state. While this may yield short-term benefits, the sustainability of such initiatives is not certain: this type of mechanism can lead to long-term effective engagement only if sufficient local taste and capacity ensue for participation and demand builds. In this case, the environment is transformed into one in which the political and governance context forces state actors to engage substantively.

Initiatives in the top right-hand corner have the greatest impact. Here, public actors are willing to listen to citizen voice (and are supported by a local political culture that is driven by issues of public policy), and well-designed mechanisms allow civil society direct access to and participation in public decision making. Program initiators operating in this type of environment have the most scope for selecting the type and level of participation.

On the left-hand side of figure A.1, citizens' own initiatives to improve public transparency and the accountability of state actors can yield successful results even in environments in which citizens' voice may not have immediate effect: in Africa, Asia, Eastern Europe, and Latin America, citizens have elbowed open space and demanded that their voices be heard. Doing so takes time, capacity, and careful strategizing, including coalition building. DISHA in India, the St. Petersburg Strategiya Centre in Russia, IDASA in South Africa, and CIDE (Centro de Investigacion y Docencia Economicas) in Mexico have succeeded in building credible voices on public resource matters (International Budget Project 2000). Initiatives like these can move the participatory environment from one in which state actors are unwilling to engage to one in which they have little choice but to engage with citizen voice, opening up the options for effective participation. To succeed, such initiatives must choose the correct entry point and carefully design and implement projects to maximize citizen participation. Perceptions of citizen-state relationships, power distribution, governance systems, and degrees of individual and press freedom, as well as perceptions of trust among citizens and between citizens and the state, are therefore important environmental determinants of whether and which types of participatory budgeting initiatives will bring benefits.

Supportive Legal and Policy Frameworks

A supportive legal framework is an enabling, even necessary, condition for citizens to participate in and contribute to processes in the public sphere. Legal frameworks regulate the terms of actors' engagement and the scope they have for influencing behavior in the arena of the other (McGee 2003), albeit the arena between central and subnational governments or between government and civil society actors. Such frameworks are never sufficient, however: government practices, the overall incentive framework, and action by citizens or the state are required to initiate and sustain participation.

For all types of citizen engagement, the most important feature of the legal framework is the guarantee of certain freedoms and human rights. If no provisions guarantee citizens' rights to freely associate, to express themselves, and to participate in a relationship with the state (or if provisions of the law limit these rights), the space for participatory initiatives is severely limited. CSOs or individual citizens who attempt to form associations to review public services and influence public resource decisions will have no legal basis for asserting their right to do so. If CSOs are to be able to put information in the public domain to influence what happens in the state, the legal framework must allow—or at least not prohibit or constrain—civic organization, freedom of speech, and access to information.

For direct citizen involvement in participatory budgeting, the legal framework requirements are greater. A review of community-driven development initiatives suggests that a higher level of decentralization of political, administrative, and fiscal competency to local levels of government is necessary for local communities to engage effectively in local resource decisions (ESCWA 2004). This makes sense: citizens will engage in local processes only if they believe that local governments have a real chance of determining which public goods and services will be delivered locally. This means that a legal framework for decentralization needs to be in place. Such a framework is not sufficient, however: attempts to decentralize, including the creation of a political apparatus, often occur at the administrative level but are not followed by sufficient fiscal autonomy for local governments, limiting the level of resources over which local governments have control and constraining participation.

An enabling framework for participation at the local level is also desirable, although it is arguably not necessary. A national enabling framework catalyzed the development of local level participatory practices in Thailand, where a national requirement for participation in local government practices prompted several local authorities to develop institutions to implement the requirement. Experience, particularly in Eastern Europe and the former Soviet republics, where participatory local governance is a standard feature of constitutional and national legal frameworks, has shown that national-level legislation may not be sufficient, however, particularly if it lack details on the institutions that may be deployed. One of the more succesful examples of community-driven development is Romania, where the legislative framework includes detailed provisions. Examples from elsewhere (such as Naga City in the Philippines) show that local-level development of national constitutional and legal frameworks institutionalizes participation.

Local Capacity and Knowledge

The assessment of community-driven development by the Economic and Social Commission for Western Asia (ESCWA 2004) singles out the need for continuous support to develop capacity for participatory practices if initiatives are to be successful. This finding echoes the results of other studies that point to the importance of local capacity for participatory success, including the capacity of local governments and local civil society and the capacity of third-party facilitating organizations.

The capacity of local governments—in terms of both human resources and systems—to plan, budget, and manage the delivery of public goods and services and participatory processes is critical. Transparency and an institutional environment conducive to citizen participation are also critical. This is particularly true for mechanisms that involve direct participation of citizens in decision making. Case study evidence points to the important role that clear, predictable, and enforced decision-making rules play in providing confidence to citizens that their participation will lead to direct results. More subtle incentives relate to good budgeting principles, such as having clear resource ceilings, so that real choices have to be made; avoiding wish-list planning, with the inevitable loss of trust in participation when proposed projects are not implemented, is critical. Strong local capacity also supports the development of civil society advocacy–type initiatives that do not involve direct participation in decision making. In India, for example, the development of a civil society advocacy network was possible only after financial management practices improved the level and quality of information available.

The existence of CSOs with capacity is also critical. Because of the technical nature of public budgets and public service delivery, significant depth of organization and some sophisticated capacity within organizations are required to engage with these issues. Putting good-quality information into the public domain requires expertise, the forming of coalitions (among CSOs and between CSOs and academic institutions), or both. The case study evidence indicates that coalition building among nongovernmental structures is important, both to bring on board needed skills and to build a wider front of support, making it more difficult for state actors to ignore campaigns. Civil society capacity is also required for successful citizen participation in local resource allocation decisions. In Eastern Europe, where societies emerged from a long period of limited citizen engagement, partnerships between local governments and key CSOs appear to have made an important contribution to making participation work.

In most of the mechanisms that allow citizens a direct say in local resource decisions, organizational, facilitation, and conflict-resolution skills are also required. Where development partners are involved in initiating and sustaining participatory budgeting initiatives, these skills are often provided by contracted third parties. In some municipalities, such as Porte Alegre, the quality of facilitation has been an important factor in widening participation.

Finally, the capacity of citizens themselves is important. Educational attainment is less important a determinant of participation than citizens' grasp of their right to engage in individual and collective action and to hold state actors to account.

Free Media Institutions

Strong local media institutions that can disseminate information to citizens— informing them of events on the budget calendar, discussing issues pertinent to the resource decisions, communicating the outcomes of processes—are critical to participatory programs that involve direct citizen involvement. This is particularly clear in the Eastern European case studies, where local media institutions have been important players linking local governments and citizens in processes allowing direct participation in public resource decisions.

For participatory budgeting initiatives that involve the introduction of budget information into the public domain, a free media is a precondition. Reaching as many citizens as possible is an essential part of ensuring the effectiveness of civil society analyses of public budgets and service delivery. Without free and functional media institutions, the reach of organizations will be limited to stakeholders whom CSOs can contact directly. A review of successful applied budget initiatives across the world reveals the importance of good relations with a free press. The Institute for Economic Affairs in Kenya; the Centre for Budget and Policy Priorities in Washington, D.C.; and IDASA in South Africa could not have been effective had they not been able to disseminate their findings widely through a free and responsive media.

Availability of Information

It is an axiom of participation that citizens need access to information to participate—this relationship is recognized in the international human rights framework (OHCHR 2004). The requirement of a minimum level of transparency about the allocation and use of public funds for citizen participation holds for both types of participatory budgeting initiatives. CSOs cannot engage with public resource decisions if they do not know what those decisions are. Similarly, citizens' ability to be involved directly with public decision-making processes in a meaningful way depends on what information they receive, when they receive it, and whether they are informed about the outcomes of the processes.

The availability of information on public funds is a function of governments' willingness and capacity. Fiscal transparency is not merely about the availability of information. Specific types of information must be provided regularly. The information must be provided in accessible formats in a timely manner. Legal frameworks that make provision for fiscal and budget transparency along these dimensions support participatory budgeting, as does legislation guaranteeing citizens' rights to access information. However, even if such legislation exists, providing full information requires sophisticated financial management capacity. Such capacity is often as much the result of demand for accountability—both internally and externally—as a prerequisite for it.

References

ESCWA (Economic and Social Commission for Western Asia). 2004. "Community-Driven Development as an Integrated Social Policy at the Local Level." United Nations, ESCWA, New York.

Fawaz, Mona. 2002. "Reflections on Best Practices in Governance in ESCWA Countries." Paper prepared for Empowering Local Government Institutions in the Middle East and North Africa Region Workshop, Fourth Mediterranean Development Forum, Amman, October 6–9.

Goetz, Annemarie, and John Gaventa. 2001. "Bringing Citizen Voice and Client Focus into Service Delivery." IDS Working Paper 128, Institute for Development Studies, University of Sussex, Brighton, United Kingdom.

International Budget Project. 2000. "A Taste of Success, Examples of the Budget Work of NGOs." Centre for Budget and Policy Priorities, Washington, DC.

McGee, R. 2003. *Legal Frameworks for Citizen Participation: A Synthesis Report.* LogoLink report, Institute for Development Studies, University of Sussex, Brighton, United Kingdom.

OHCHR (Office of the High Commissioner for Human Rights). 2004. *Human Rights and Poverty Reduction: A Conceptual Framework.* Geneva: United Nations.

Paul, Samuel. 2005. "Auditing for Social Change: Learning from Civil Society Initiatives." Paper presented at the Sixth Global Forum on Reinventing Government, Seoul, May 24–27.

Reuben, W. 2003. "The Role of Civic Engagement and Social Accountability in the Governance Equation." Social Development Note 75, World Bank, Washington, DC.

Spahn, B. 1998. "Issues of Governance in a Broad Context." Paper presented at the Mediterranean Development Forum, Marrakech, September.

Weeks, E. 2000. "The Practice of Deliberative Democracy: Results from Four Large-Scale Trials." *Public Administration Review* 60 (4): 360–72.

World Bank. 2003. *Better Governance for Development in the Middle East and North Africa: Enhancing Inclusiveness and Accountability.* (MENA Development Report). Washington, DC: World Bank.

Index

Boxes, figures, notes, and tables are indicated by b, f, n, and t, respectively. Entries found on the CD are indicated by that abbreviation.

Abers, Rebecca, 32

Abootalebi, Ali, 228, 238, 239

accountability. *See* transparency and accountability

administrative reform
bureaucracy, disillusionment with, 57–58
participatory budgeting leading to, 44–45, 52–53

advisory groups in Central and Eastern Europe, 138–40, 144

Africa. *See also* Middle East and North Africa, Sub-Saharan Africa, and specific countries
PRSP participation in, 64–65

Al-Ahram Centre for Political and Strategic Studies, Egypt, 229, 230*b*

Al Ansari, Abid-al-Hamid, 238

Al-Masmoudi, Radwan, 237–38

Albania, 7, 128, 130, 131, 139, 148*t*

Alemán, Arnoldo, 93, 108

Algeria, 227, 232, 233

Alvi, Hayat, 234

Andrews, Matthew, 64–65
approval of budget, 65–71, 67*f*

Armenia, 128, 130, 137–38, 148–49*t*

Arzú, Alvaro, 94

Asia, 9–10, 157–89. *See also* specific countries
capacity building in, 175–76
civic commissions, 174–75
civic forums, 177–78
civil society in, 163–64
consultation and joint decision making, projects involving, 171–78
decentralization in, 157, 160–61*t*, 161–63, 180
democratic practice in, 158–59, 181–82
developing countries' need for citizen participation, 158–59
focus groups, 173–75
impact of participatory budgeting in, 179–82
mechanisms of participation in, 168–69, 173–78
NGOs in, 163–64, 165–66, 173, 186
political, constitutional, and legislative context, 160–61*t*, 160–63
public meetings, 168–69, 173–74
stakeholder initiation and control of programs, 178–79
success factors in, 182–86

transparency and accountability, programs improving, 165–71, 180–81
types of participatory budgeting in, 164–65
auditing. *See* monitoring and evaluation
awareness of citizens. *See* citizenship education and knowledge

Baiocchi, Gianpaolo, 32
Bangladesh, 1–29*CD*, 9, 12–13, 157
  administrative autonomy at local level, lack of, 16*CD*
  budget procedures, 3*CD*, 6*CDf*
  capacity building, 18–22*CD*, 175–76
  civil society in, 163
  degree of participation, factors affecting, 10–12*CD*
  developing countries' need for citizen participation, 158
  effectiveness of program, 13–15*CD*
  empowerment and inclusiveness, 12–13*CD*
  fiscal framework, 11*CD*, 16–18*CD*, 24–26*CD*
  impact of programs, 12–18*CD*, 180
  local government institutions, 2*CD*, 6*CDf*, 16*CD*, 166
  marginalized groups, involvement of, 12*CD*
  mechanisms of participation, 9–12*CD*
  medium-term agenda, 23*CDt*
  monitoring and evaluation, 7–8*CD*
  open budget sessions, 7*CD*
  organization, 3–8*CD*
  parties involved in program, 8–9*CD*, 8*CDf*, 8*CDt*
  personnel issues, 16*CD*
  planning, 5–6*CD*, 12–13*CD*
  political, constitutional, and legislative context, 160*t*, 162
  PRSP, 1–2*CD*, 23*t*
  success factors in, 183, 184
  tax revenue increase due to, 15*CDf*
  training needs, 19–21*CD*, 20*CDt*
Banzer, Hugo, 104
Bartholdson, Örjan, 105

Bolivia, 5, 6
  decentralization in, 104
  historical background of participatory budgeting in, 93
  liberal approach to participatory budgeting in, 117
  local case studies, 112–14, 113*t*, 115*t*
  national program of participatory budgeting in, 101, 104–6
  PRSP participation in, 65
Brazil, 4, 5
  distribution of resources studied in, 36
  effects of participatory budgeting studied in, 33–36, 33*t*, 34*t*
  government attitudes towards citizen participation in, 79–80
  initiation of participatory budgeting in, 4, 6, 22, 23–24, 66, 91–94
  innovation and diffusion phases analyzed in, 32–33
  liberal approach to participatory budgeting in, 118
  as model, 63*CDb*
  national program of participatory budgeting in, 101–3
  resource allocation (budget preparation and approval), citizen participation in, 66–68, 67*f*
Brillantes, Alex B., Jr., xvii, 14, 49–66*CD*
Bulgaria, 7, 128
  impact of programs in, 149*t*
  local governments, legal framework for, 130, 131*b*
  public meetings for capital investment planning, 140–41, 144, 145
bureaucracy, disillusionment with, 57–58
business community, reasons for involvement of, 43–44

Cabannes, Yves, 100
Campbell, Tim, 96
capacity building
  in Asia, 175–76
  country case studies
    Bangladesh, 18–22*CD*
    India, 45–46*CD*

Philippines, 62–64*CD*
Russian Federation, 87–90*CD*
South Africa, 123*CD*
Thailand, 151*CD*
Ukraine, 170–75*CD*
in Sub-Saharan Africa, 220
CBOs (community-based organizations)
    in Central and Eastern Europe, 132
Central and Eastern Europe, 7–9, 127–56.
    See also specific countries
    advisory groups, 138–40, 144
    citizen participation and citizenship
        education, 132–33, 231
    citizenship education, 132–33, 231
    conditions common to participatory
        budgeting initiatives in, 129
    CSOs in, 7–8, 132–33, 146–47
    decentralization in, 128–29
    impact of programs in, 143–47,
        148–54*t*
    information generating programs, 134,
        135–37
    information sharing, consultation, and
        joint decision-making programs,
        137–42
    leadership, importance of, 147
    legal frameworks, 130–32, 131*b*
    local governments in, 130–32, 131*b*,
        146–47
    mechanisms of participation in,
        143–44, 146
    NGOs in, 7, 132, 136, 143, 147
    political context in, 133–34
    public meetings, 140–42, 144
    stakeholder initiation and control of
        programs, 142–43, 145
    typology of participatory budgeting
        in, 134–35
Chávez, Hugo, 117
citizen participation, 4–5, 55–87
    arguments in favor of, 55–60
    in budgeting process, 65–77
        audit and performance evaluation,
            75–77, 78*f*
        execution of budget, 71–75
        preparation and approval,
            65–71, 67*f*

bureaucracy, disillusionment with,
    57–58
in Central and Eastern Europe, 132–33
costs of, 80–83, 81*f*
democratic ideals and, 58
developing countries' need for, 58–60,
    158–59
difficulties in fostering, 62–63
factors involved in, 60–61
government attitudes towards, 4–5,
    78–83
importance of, 55–56
instrumental assessment of,
    80–83, 81*f*
motivations for, 41–42
NGOs' role in, 4, 63
postmodern discourse theory and,
    56–57
PRSPs, 56, 64–65, 79
typology of, 61, 62*t*, 246–47
citizenship education and knowledge
    availability of information, 254
    in Central and Eastern Europe,
        132–33, 231
    effective participation requiring,
        252–54
    free media
        effective participation requiring,
            253–54
        in Middle East and North Africa,
            232–33
    Middle East and North Africa lacking,
        229–33
    promoted by participatory budgeting,
        49–51, 60
    training concerns in country case
        studies
        Bangladesh, 19–21*CD*, 20*CDt*
        Thailand, 152–53*CD*
civic commissions, 141–42*CD*, 145*CD*,
    174–75
civic forums, 132*CD*, 134*CD*, 144–45*CD*,
    177–78
civil society organizations (CSOs)
    in Asia, 163–64
    in Central and Eastern Europe, 7–8,
        132–33, 146–47

effective participation and, 253
information generating programs in
   Central and Eastern Europe,
   134, 135
Middle East and North African
   restrictions on, 229
partnerships with local governments,
   146–47
reasons for involvement of, 3, 42
communication issues in South Africa,
   123*CD*
community-based organizations
   (CBOs) in Central and Eastern
   Europe, 132
consultation programs
   in Asia, 171–78
   in Central and Eastern Europe,
     137–42
   Islamic values and, 238
control of programs by stakeholders,
   142–43, 145, 178–79
costs of citizen participation,
   80–83, 81*f*
country case studies, 12–18. *See also*
   Bangladesh; India; Philippines;
   Russia; South Africa; Thailand;
   Ukraine
CSOs. *See* civil society organizations
cultural factors in Thailand, 147*CD*

decentralization
   in Asia, 157, 160–61*t*, 161–63, 180
   in Central and Eastern Europe,
     128–29
   as condition conducive to
     participatory budgeting, 98–99
   country case studies
     Philippines, 50*CD*, 51*CDf*
     Ukraine, 156–57*CD*
   in Latin America, 93, 100–101
   local case studies, 111–16
   in Middle East and North Africa,
     233, 235
democratic ideals and participatory
   budgeting, 58
   in Asia, 158–59, 181–82

free media
   effective participation requiring,
     253–54
   in Middle East and North Africa,
     232–33
   in Latin America, 94–96
   Middle East and North Africa, 226–29,
     238–39
   preconditions for effective
     participation, 247–51
   state effectiveness, 244–45
developing countries' need for citizen
   participation, 58–60, 158–59
development community's support
   for participatory budgeting, 96–97
discourse theory, postmodern, 56–57
distribution of resources, 36, 65–71, 67*f*
diversity and inclusiveness. *See also* women
   country case studies
     Bangladesh, 12–13*CD*
     South Africa, 123*CD*
   in Middle East and North Africa, 234
   Sub-Saharan Africa, in 221
Dutra, Olivio, 95–96

Eastern Europe. *See* Central and Eastern
   Europe
ECES (Egyptian Centre for Economic
   Studies), 230*b*
Edstrom, Judith, 158, 179
educating citizens. *See* citizenship
   education and knowledge
Egypt
   democratization in, 227, 228, 229
   Manshiet Nasser informal settlement,
     Cairo, 235
   think tanks in, 229, 230*b*
   transparency lacking in, 232
Egyptian Centre for Economic Studies
   (ECES), 230*b*
Europe, Central and Eastern. *See* Central
   and Eastern Europe
evaluation. *See* monitoring and
   evaluation
execution of budget, citizen participation
   in, 71–75

Fawaz, Mona, 233, 248
fiscal framework
  country case studies
    Bangladesh, 11*CD*, 16–18*CD*,
      24–26*CD*
    Russian Federation, 69–71*CD*,
      70*CDt*
    South Africa, 116–22*CD*, 121*CDt*
    Thailand, 128–29*CD*, 129*CDt*
    Ukraine, 158–63*CD*, 159*CDf*,
      160–62*CDt*
  in Sub-Saharan Africa, 195–97
focus groups, 138*CD*, 142–43*CD*,
  143–44*CD*, 173–75
Fölscher, Alta, xvii
  on Asia, 9–10, 157–89
  on Central and Eastern Europe, 7–9,
    127–56
  on effective participation, 82, 243–55
  on Middle East and North Africa,
    11–12, 225–41
Forner, Patricia, 65
free media
  effective participation requiring,
    253–54
  in Middle East and North Africa,
    232–33
Fujimori, Alberto, 109, 111

Gaventa, John, 133, 166, 248
Goetz, Annemarie, 133, 166, 248
Goldfrank, Benjamin, xvii, 5–6, 91–126
good governance
  association of participatory budgeting
    with, 225–26, 237, 245
  bureaucracy, disillusionment with,
    57–58
  importance of, xi–xii
  preconditions of effective participation
    and concept of, 248
government attitudes towards
  participatory budgeting, 4–5, 46
  citizen participation, 78–83
  effective participation, 249–51, 250*f*
  in Sub-Saharan Africa, 219, 221
Grazia, Grazia de, 32, 100

Guatemala, 5
  decentralization in, 106
  historical background of participatory
    budgeting in, 93–94
  local case studies, 113*t*, 114
  national program of participatory
    budgeting in, 101, 106–7

Habermas, Jurgen, 61
Habitat II Conference, Istanbul (United
  Nations), 93
Heavily Indebted Poor Countries (HIPC II)
  program, 94, 104, 106, 108
Heimans, Jeremy, 79
HIPC II (Heavily Indebted Poor
  Countries) program, 94, 104,
  106, 108
historical background of participatory
  budgeting, 22, 23–24, 92–94
Honduras, PRSP participation in, 65
Hughes, Alexandra, 63

Ibn Khaldun Centre, Egypt, 230*b*
Ibrahim, Ezzat, 229, 230–31*b*
ideological approaches to participatory
  budgeting
  Asian political context, 160–61*t*,
    160–63, 181–82
  Central and Eastern Europe, political
    context in, 133–34
  citizen participation, arguments in
    favor of, 55–60
  democratic ideals (*See* democratic
    ideals and participatory
    budgeting)
  in Latin America, 94–98, 117–18
  preconditions for effective
    participation, 247–51
  Thailand country case study of
    political context, 160, 161*t*, 163
illiteracy rates in Middle East and North
  Africa, 229–31
inclusiveness. *See* diversity and
  inclusiveness; women
independent budget analysis in Russian
  Federation, 74–78*CD*

India, 9, 13–14, 31–48*CD*, 157
  Bangalore report cards, 3*CD*, 14*CD*,
    39–40*CD*, 63*CDb*, 75–77, 78*f*,
    170, 180
  budget briefs, 47*CD*
  capacity building, 45–46*CD*
  civil society in, 163
  DISHA/Pathey project, 33–38*CD*,
    73–75, 167–68, 180, 185, 186, 187,
    231, 251
  dissemination of information,
    35–37*CD*
  execution of budget, citizen
    participation in, 73–75
  financial statements, issues
    concerning, 40–41*CD*
  gender issues in, 45*CDb*
  government structure, 32–33*CD*
  impact of programs, 37–38*CD*,
    42–43*CD*, 180–81
  lessons learned, 43–45*CD*
  MKSS (Mazdoor Kisan Shakti
    Sangathan), 168–69, 180–81, 185,
    186, 187, 231
  as model, 63*CDb*
  performance indicators, developing,
    41*CD*
  political, constitutional, and legislative
    context, 160*t*, 162
  PROOF project, 38–43*CD*, 169–70, 184
  public meetings, 168–69
  scope of budgetary analysis, 34–35*CD*,
    40*CD*
  success factors in, 184, 185–86, 187
Indonesia, 9, 157
  developing countries' need for citizen
    participation, 158
  impact of programs, 180
  KDP (Kecamatan Development
    Program), 178–79
  political, constitutional, and legislative
    context, 160, 161*t*, 162
  success factors in, 183, 184, 186
information generating programs, 134,
  135–37
information sharing programs, 137–42,
  247

initiation and control of programs by
  stakeholders, 142–43, 145, 178–79
innovation phase, 32
instrumental assessment of citizen
  participation, 80–83, 81*f*
Inter-American Development Bank, 96
Iran, 227, 232, 233, 238
Iraq, 227, 236
Islam, Roumeen, xiii
Islamic rules and values, 225, 237–39
Israel, 230*b*, 240n1

joint decision-making programs
  in Asia, 171–78
  in Central and Eastern Europe, 137–42
Jordan, 230*b*, 232, 233

Kabir, Mahfuz, xvii–xviii, 1–29*CD*,
  12, 176
Kadhim, Nadjah, 232
Kenya, 10, 191
  budget cycle in, 206*t*
  fiscal framework, 195
  free media, importance of, 254
  impact of participation in, 213
  legal framework, 192–93, 195
  local government, 195
  mechanisms of participation, 197–98
  methods of civic participation in
    budget process, 205–6
knowledge management networks in
  Thailand, 151–52*CD*
knowledge of citizens. *See* citizenship
  education and knowledge
Krafchik, Warren, 82
Krekeler, Jorge, 105–6
Krylova, Elena, xviii, 15–16, 18,
  67–90*CD*, 144
Kuwait, 228

Latin America, 5–6, 91–126. *See also*
  specific countries
  conditions conducive to participatory
    budgeting in, 99–100
  decentralization in, 93, 100–101
  historical background of participatory
    budgeting in, 92–94

ideological approaches to participatory budgeting in, 94–98
literature and research, gaps in, 100
local case studies, 111–16, 113*t*, 115*t*
national programs, 101–11, 116
NGO involvement, 112, 118
leadership issues, 146*CD*, 147
Léautier, Frannie A., xi–xii
Lebanon
  democratic practice in, 227, 228, 229
  Ghobieri urban poverty project, 236–37
  media freedom in, 233
  think tanks, 230*b*
  transparency in, 232
leftist politics, association of participatory budgeting with, 92–96
legal frameworks
  in Asia, 160–61*t*, 160–63
  in Central and Eastern Europe, 130–32, 131*b*
  country case studies
    South Africa, 93–96*CD*
    Thailand, 160, 161*t*, 163
  effective participation and, 251–52
  in Sub-Saharan Africa, 192–97, 219–20
Levene, Josh, 63
Libya, 228, 230*b*
local governments
  in Central and Eastern Europe, 130–32, 131*b*, 146–47
  country case studies
    Bangladesh, 2*CD*, 6*CDf*, 16*CD*
    Ukraine (*See under* Ukraine)
  effective participation and, 252–53
  in Latin America, 111–16, 113*t*, 115*t*
  in Middle East and North Africa, 233–34
  partnerships with CSOs, 146–47
  reasons for involvement of, 39–41
  in Sub-Saharan Africa, 195–97

Magdeburg Law, 167
Malawi, PRSP participation in, 65
Marcos, Ferdinand, 164

marginalized groups. *See* diversity and inclusiveness; women
"matrioshka" budgeting principles, 158*CD*
McGee, Rosemary, 63, 134, 181, 247
mechanisms of participation. *See also* specific mechanisms, e.g. public meetings
  in Asia, 168–69, 173–78
  in Central and Eastern Europe, 143–44, 146
  country case studies
    Bangladesh, 9–12*CD*
    budget procedures, 100–101*CD*
    Philippines, 61–62*CD*
    Russian Federation, 71–72*CD*, 74–81*CD*
    South Africa, 97–99*CD*, 101–6*CD*, 109–13*CD*
    Thailand (*See under* Thailand)
    Ukraine, 163–70*CD*
  single mechanisms *vs.* combinations, 146
  state effectiveness, 245–46
  in Sub-Saharan Africa, 197–205
  media freedom
    effective participation requiring, 253–54
    in Middle East and North Africa, 232–33
Mexico, 251
Middle East and North Africa, 11–12, 225–41. *See also* specific countries
  CSO restrictions in, 229
  decentralization, 233, 235
  democratic ideals, 226–29, 238–39
  diversity and inclusiveness, 234
  good governance and participatory budgeting, 225–26, 237, 245
  illiteracy and lack of public knowledge in, 229–33
  Islamic rules and values, 225, 237–39
  local governments, 233–34
  media freedom in, 232–33
  NGOs in, 235, 236, 237

potential benefits of participatory
    budgeting in, 225–26
think tanks in, 229, 230–31*b*
transparency, lack of, 232
women, 234
minorities. *See* diversity and
    inclusiveness; women
mobilization process, 28–31, 29*t*
Moldova, 7, 128, 130, 132–33
monitoring and evaluation
    citizen participation in
        audit and performance evaluation,
            75–77, 78*f*
        execution and tracking of budget,
            71–75
    country case studies
        Bangladesh, 7–8*CD*
        South Africa, 124*CD*
    report cards, 3*CD*, 14*CD*, 39–40*CD*,
        63*CDb*, 75–77, 78*f*, 170, 180
Morales, Evo, 105
Morocco, 228, 229, 230*b*, 233, 239
Moynihan, Donald P., xviii, 4–5, 55–87
Mozambique, 10, 191
    challenges faced in, 217
    fiscal framework, 195–96
    government attitudes, role of, 221
    impact of participation in, 213
    legal framework, 193
    local government, 195–96
    mechanisms of participation,
        197, 199
    methods of civic participation in
        budget process, 206–7
    PRSP participation in, 63

Near East. *See* Middle East and North
    Africa
Nicaragua, 5, 6
    decentralization in, 108
    historical background of participatory
        budgeting in, 93
    liberal approach to participatory
        budgeting in, 117
    local case studies, 112–14, 113*t*
    national program of participatory
        budgeting in, 101, 107–9

nongovernmental organizations (NGOs)
    in Asia, 163–64, 165–66, 173, 186
    in Central and Eastern Europe, 7, 132,
        136, 143, 147
    citizen participation and, 4, 63, 70–71
    in Latin America, 112, 118
    reasons for involvement of, 42–43
North Africa. *See* Middle East and
    North Africa

Oman, 228, 238
open meetings. *See* public meetings

PAC (Public Affairs Centre), 39–40*CD*,
        75–77
Painter, Genevieve, 79
Palestinian Authority, 227
participatory budgeting, xiii, 21–54.
        See also more specific topics,
        e.g. typologies of participatory
        budgeting
    administrative reform developing
        from, 44–45, 52–53
    advantages and disadvantages, 1–2,
        21–23
    annual cycle of, 29*f*
    chief actors and their motivations, 3,
        39–44
    as citizenship school, 49–51, 60
    conditions conducive to, 24–25, 47–49,
        99–100, 182–86, 247–54
    defined, 21, 92, 188n1
    desired outcomes *vs.* unintended
        consequences of, 27–28*t*
    diffusion phase, 32–33
    distribution of resources, 36
    good governance and, 225–26, 237, 245
    historical background, 22, 23–24,
        92–94
    impact of, 33–36, 33*t*, 34*t*, 49–53
    implementation of process, 31–32, 31*t*
    innovation phase, 32
    Islamic rules and values, 225, 237–39
    leftist politics, association with, 92–96
    limiting factors, 3–4, 45–47
    main elements of programs for, 2–3,
        25–32

mobilization process, 28–31, 29*t*
selection of projects, 29*t*, 30–31, 30*t*
social justice and, 51–53, 60, 158, 244
state effectiveness and, 243–46
trust, importance of, 182, 248–49
partnerships between CSOs and local
  governments, 146–47
Paul, Samuel, xviii, 13, 31–48*CD*, 75–77,
  165–66, 170, 247
performance evaluation. *See* monitoring
  and evaluation
Peru, 5, 6
  decentralization in, 109
  historical background of participatory
    budgeting in, 94
  liberal approach to participatory
    budgeting in, 117
  local case studies, 111–14, 113*t*, 115*t*
  national program of participatory
    budgeting in, 101–3, 109–11
Philippines, 9, 15, 49–66*CD*, 157
  budget procedures, 57–58*CD*
  capacity building, 62–64*CD*
  CCAG (Concerned Citizens of Abra
    for Good Governance), 170–71,
    181, 187
  civil society in, 164
  context of civil society involvement,
    50–53*CD*, 52*CDb*
  engaging participation, 56–57*CD*
  framework for participation,
    58–62*CD*, 59*CDf*
  impact of programs, 60–61*CD*, 180
  lessons learned, 57*CDb*
  mechanisms for participation,
    61–62*CD*
  Naga City project, 59–62*CD*, 172–73,
    186, 252
  planning, 53–55*CD*, 54–55*CDb*,
    54*CDf*
  political, constitutional, and legislative
    context, 160, 161*t*, 163
  real property tax system, streamlining,
    55*CDb*
  special bodies, 62*CDf*
  success factors in, 183, 184, 186, 187
Poland, 7, 128, 138, 146, 149*t*

political approaches to participatory
  budgeting. *See* ideological
  approaches to participatory
  budgeting
Portillo, Alvaro, 94
Porto Alegre. *See* Brazil
postmodern discourse theory, 56–57
poverty
  Lebanon, Ghobieri urban poverty
    project, 236–37
  participatory budgeting, effects of,
    116–17
Poverty Reduction Strategy Papers
  (PRSPs)
  in Africa, 64–65
  Bangladesh, 1–2*CD*
  citizen participation in, 56, 64–65, 79
  government attitudes regarding, 79
  preparation of budget, 65–71, 67*f*
PRSPs. *See* Poverty Reduction Strategy
  Papers
Public Affairs Centre (PAC), 39–40*CD*,
  75–77
public learning and knowledge. *See*
  citizenship education and
  knowledge
public meetings
  in Asia, 168–69, 173–74
  in Central and Eastern Europe,
    140–42, 144
  country case studies
    Bangladesh, 7*CD*
    Russian Federation, 78–79*CD*
    Thailand, 128–40*CD*, 145*CD*
    Ukraine, 163–70*CD*
public works programs, 36–38

Qatar, 238
quartier associations, Tunisia, 235–36
Quezada, David, 105–6
Quispe, Felipe, 105

radical democracy, 94–96
Rahman, Atiur, xviii, 1–29*CD*,
  12, 176
Razzaque, Mohammad A., xviii–xix,
  1–29*CD*, 12, 176

Rea, Oscar, 105–6
regional surveys, 5–12. *See also* Asia;
    Central and Eastern Europe; Latin
    America; Middle East and North
    Africa; Sub-Saharan Africa
report card surveys (Bangalore, India),
    3*CD*, 14*CD*, 39–40*CD*, 63*CDb*,
    75–77, 78*f*, 170, 180
resource allocation, 36, 65–71, 67*f*
Reuben, William, 172, 243, 244
Rios Montt, Efraìn, 107
Romania, 7, 128, 139–40, 150*t*, 252
Rudqvist, Anders, 105
Russell-Einhorn, Malcolm, 159
Russian Federation, 7, 15–16,
    67–90*CD*, 128
  advisory groups, 139
  capacity building, 87–90*CD*
  citizen participation in, 132–33
  concepts used in program, 74*CD*
  government and budget structure,
    67–69*CD*, 68*CDb*
  government attitudes, role of, 251
  impact of programs in, 81–87*CD*, 145,
    150–53*t*
  independent budget analysis, 74–78*CD*
  information generating programs
    in, 136
  local government autonomy and
    financing, 69–71*CD*, 70*CDt*
  local governments, 130
  "matrioshka" budgeting principles,
    158*CD*
  mechanisms for participation,
    71–72*CD*, 74–81*CD*
  organizations active in program,
    90*CD*
  public budget hearings, 78–79*CD*
  stakeholder initiation and control of
    programs, 142–43, 145
  transparent budgeting program,
    72–74*CD*
Rwanda, PRSP participation in, 65

Sánchez de Lozada, Gonzalo, 93, 104, 106
Sarrouh, Elissar, 234

Saudi Arabia, 227, 228, 239
Segura, Chirinos, 111
  selection of projects, 29*t*, 30–31, 30*t*
September 11, 2001 terrorist
    attacks, 228
Shah, Anwar, xix, 1–18
Shah, Parmesh, 77
Shall, Adrienne, xix, 16–17, 91–126*CD*,
    191–223
Shapiro, Isaac, 82
Silva, Luiz Inácio da, 118
social justice and participatory
    budgeting, 51–53, 60, 158, 244
South Africa, 10, 16–17, 91–126*CD*, 191
  budget conference, 105–6*CD*
  budget procedures, 103–5*CD*,
    111–12*CD*
  capacity building, 123*CD*
  challenges faced in, 218, 219
  communication issues, 123*CD*
  diversity of population, 123*CD*
  Ekurhuleni municipality project,
    109–14*CD*
  fiscal framework, 116–22*CD*,
    121*CDt*, 196
  government resistance to citizen
    participation in, 82
  government structure, 92*CD*,
    114–22*CD*
  IDASA, 70–71, 82, 251, 254
  impact of programs, 106–7*CD*,
    113*CD*, 213–14
  legal framework, 193
  legislative framework for participation,
    93–96*CD*
  lessons learned, 107–8*CD*, 113–14*CD*,
    122–24*CD*
  local government, 196
  Mangaung municipality project,
    101–8*CD*, 207, 208*t*
  mechanisms for participation,
    97–99*CD*, 101–6*CD*, 109–13*CD*,
    199–201
  methods of civic participation in
    budget process, 207, 208t
  monitoring and evaluation, 124*CD*

resource allocation (budget preparation and approval) in, 70–71
ward committees, 100*CDt*, 102*CDt*, 109–10*CD*, 123–24*CD*
South America. *See* Latin America
Spahn, B., 248
stakeholder initiation and control of programs, 142–43, 145, 178–79
state effectiveness and participatory budgeting, 243–46
Sub-Saharan Africa, 10–11, 191–223
    See also specific countries
    capacity building, 220
    challenges faced in, 216–19
    diversity and inclusiveness, 221
    government attitudes, role of, 219, 221
    impact of participation in, 213–16
    legal frameworks, 192–97, 219–20
    lessons learned, 219–21
    local government fiscal framework, 195–97
    local governments, 195–97
    mechanisms of participation in, 197–205
    methods of civic participation in budget process, 205–11
Sudan, 227, 232
surveys
    Bangalore (India) report cards, 3*CD*, 14*CD*, 39–40*CD*, 63*CDb*, 75–77, 78*f*, 170, 180
    in Thailand country case study, 135*CDbt*, 140*CDt*, 145–46*CD*
Suwanmala, Charas, xix, 17–18, 127–54*CD*, 185
Syria, 230*b*, 233, 239

Tanzania, 10, 191
    capacity building, 220
    challenges faced in, 219
    fiscal framework, 196
    government attitudes, role of, 221
    impact of programs, 214
    legal framework, 193–94
    local government, 196

mechanisms for participation, 201–2
methods of civic participation in budget process, 207, 209*t*
taxation in country case studies
    Bangladesh, tax revenue increases in, 15*CDf*
    Philippines real property tax system, streamlining, 55*CDb*
    Thailand, tax collection in, 133*CD*, 136–37*CD*, 136*CDf*, 137*CDt*
Thailand, 9, 17–18, 157
    agendas, 134*CDb*, 139*CDt*
    budget guides for citizens, 146*CD*
    budget procedures, 129–30*CD*
    capacity building, 151*CD*
    civic commissions, 141–42*CD*, 145*CD*, 174–75
    civic forums, 132*CD*, 134*CD*, 144–45*CD*, 177–78
    civil society in, 164
    factors affecting participation, 146–47*CD*
    fiscal framework, 128–29*CD*, 129*CDt*
    focus groups, 138*CD*, 142–43*CD*, 143–44*CD*, 173–74
    government structure and responsibilities, 128*CD*
    Huai-Kapi TAO, 133–37*CD*, 136*CDf*, 137*CDt*, 177, 185, 186, 187
    impact of programs, 133*CD*, 137*CD*, 141*CD*, 143*CD*, 150*CD*, 151*CDt*, 180
    Khon Kan City, 137–41*CD*, 173–74
    knowledge management network, need for, 151–52*CD*
    mechanisms for participation, 143–46*CD*, 146*CDt*
        Huai-Kapi TAO, 134–35*CD*
        Kohn Kan City, 138–40*CD*
        origins of, 147–48*CD*
        Rayong City, 141–43*CD*, 142*CDf*
        Suan Mon TAO, 132*CD*
    partnering organizations, 153*CD*
    planning, 131*CD*, 134*CD*, 138*CD*, 141–42*CD*

political, constitutional, and legislative
    context, 160, 161*t*, 163
Rayong City, 141–43*CD*, 172, 174–75,
    186
Suan Mon TAO, 130–33*CD*, 130*CDt*,
    177–78, 184–85, 186, 187
success factors in, 183, 184–85, 186, 187
summary diagnosis, 149*CDt*
surveys, 135*CDbt*, 140*CDt*, 145–46*CD*
town hall meetings, 128–40*CD*,
    145*CD*, 173–74
training needs, 152–53*CD*
trust, importance of, 248–49
thematic programs, 38–39
think tanks in Middle East and North
    Africa, 229, 230–31*b*
Thomas, John Clayton, 78–79
Toledo, Alejandro, 94
Torres Ribeiro, Ana Clara, 32, 100
town hall meetings. *See* public meetings
training concerns in country case studies
    Bangladesh, 19–21*CD*, 20*CDt*
    Thailand, 152–53*CD*
transparency and accountability
    Asian programs improving, 165–71,
        180–81
    citizen participation believed to
        encourage, 60
    Middle East and North African
        countries lacking, 232
    trust, importance of, 182, 248–49
Tunisia, 235–36
Turkey, 240n1
typologies of participatory budgeting
    in Asia, 164–65
    in Central and Eastern Europe, 134–35
    citizen participation levels, 61, 62*t*,
        246–47
    McGee's typology, 134–35, 247
    public works/thematics, 36–39

Uganda, 10, 191
    challenges faced in, 217, 218
    execution of budget, citizen
        participation in, 72–73
    fiscal framework, 196–97
    government attitudes, role of, 221

impact of programs, 215
    legal framework, 194
    local government, 196–97
    mechanisms for participation, 202–3
    methods of civic participation in
        budget process, 208, 210*t*
    as model, 63*CDb*
Ukraine, 7, 18, 128, 155–79*CD*
    budgeting principles, 158*CD*,
        159–60*CD*
    capacity building, 170–75*CD*
    chief actors involved in, 174–75*CD*
    decentralization in, 156–57*CD*
    factors influencing participation in,
        167*CD*
    government structure, 155–56*CD*,
        176–77*CDf*
    impact of programs in, 153–54*t*,
        168–69*CD*
    information generating programs in,
        136–37
    Kamyanets-Podilski town meetings,
        141–42, 164–69*CD*
    local government
        ambiguous legal frameworks, 130
        competence and autonomy,
            157–58*CD*
        fiscal framework, 131, 158–63*CD*,
            159*CDf*, 160–62*CDt*
        structure, 176–77*CDf*
    People's Voice Project, 136–37
    public hearings, 141–42, 144,
        163–70*CD*
    resource materials, 171–73*CD*
United Arab Emirates, 227
United Nations
    Habitat II Conference, Istanbul, 93
    participatory budgeting supported
        by, 96
United States
    Centre for Budget and Policy
        Priorities, 254
    citizen summits in Washington, DC,
        68–70
Uruguay, 93, 117
USAID (U.S. Agency for International
    Development), 109

Vázquez, Tabaré, 117
Venezuela, 93, 117

Wagle, Swarnim, 77
Wampler, Brian, xix, 2–4, 21–54, 61,
    65–66, 80
Weber, Max, 57
Widmark, Charlotta, 105
Williams, Anthony, 69
women
    country case studies
        Bangladesh, 12CD
        India, 45CDb
    in Middle East and North Africa,
        234

Yemen, 227, 232

Zambia, 10, 191
    challenges faced in, 217–18, 219
    fiscal framework, 197
    impact of programs, 215
    legal framework, 194
    local government, 197
    mechanisms for participation, 197,
        203–4
    methods of civic participation in
        budget process, 209–11, 211t
Zimbabwe, 10, 191
    challenges faced in, 217, 218
    fiscal framework, 197
    impact of programs, 215–16
    legal framework, 192, 195
    local government, 197
    mechanisms for participation, 204–5